D0928096

Cross-Cultural
Business Behavior

To Hopi

Richard R. Gesteland

Cross-Cultural Business Behavior

Marketing, Negotiating and Managing Across Cultures

HANDELSHØJSKOLENS FORLAG
Copenhagen Business School Press
Solbjergvej
DK 2000 Copenhagen

DISCARDED
UNIVERSITY OF TULSA - McFARLIN LIBRARY

HANDELSHØJSKOLENS FORLAG
Copenhagen Business School Press

UNIVERSITY OF TULSA - McFARLIN LIBRARY

Cross-Cultural Business Behavior
© Handelshøjskolens Forlag, *Copenhagen Business School Press*, 1999
2. edition, 3. impression 2000
Set in Plantin by ABK-Sats, Denmark
Printed by Reproset, Copenhagen
Cover designed by Kontrapunkt
Book designed by Jørn Ekstrøm

ISBN 87-16-13428-1

Distribution

Scandinavia:
Munksgaard/DBK, Siljangade 2-8, P.O. Box 1731,
DK-2300 Copenhagen S, Denmark,
phone: +45 3269 7788, fax: +45 3269 7789

North America:
Copenhagen Business School Press
Books International Inc.
P.O. Box 605
Hendon, VA 20172-0605, USA
phone: +1 703 661 1500, fax: +1 703 661 1 1501
E-mail: intpubmkt@aol.com

Rest of the World:
Marston Book Services, P.O. Box 269,
Abingdon, Oxfordshire, OX14 4YN, UK
phone: +44 (0) 1235 465500, fax: +44 (0) 1235 465555
E-mail Direct Customers: direct.order@marston.co.uk
E-mail Booksellers: trade.order@marston.co.uk

All rights reserved. No part of this publication may be reproduced or used in any form or by any means –
graphic, electronic or mechanical including photocopying, recording, taping or information storage and
retrieval systems – without permission in writing from Handelshøjskolens Forlag, *Copenhagen Business
School Press*.

HF 5389
.G47
1999

Table of Contents

Foreword to the Second Edition

I am grateful to Lauge Stetting and Mette Trier of the Copenhagen Business School Press for this opportunity to update and expand the original version of this book. The major addition is a group of Negotiator Profiles for the Baltic States, Czech Republic, Hungary, Poland, Romania and Russia.

A number of universities and institutes in these Central and Eastern European countries were kind enough to invite me to conduct seminars for both students and practicing managers in 1997 and 1998, allowing me to bring my knowledge of business customs and practices up to date.

The first edition proved to be popular with business people as well as universities and colleges around the world. Translated into German, Polish and Lithuanian, it has been adopted as a textbook by more than a dozen business schools in Denmark, Hungary, Lithuania and the U.S.

It is my hope that this second edition will help get international negotiators off to a good start when entering new markets.

Introduction

This is intended as a practical guide for the men and women in the front lines of world trade, those who face every day the frustrating differences in global business customs and practices.

Cultural differences frustrate us because they are confusing and unpredictable. This book aims to reduce that confusion and introduce some predictabilty by classifying international business customs and practices into logical patterns.

Scientists today believe the human brain is programmed to think in terms of patterns. Certainly I for one seem to learn and remember complex information more readily when it is organized according to some logical system.

With this in mind, over the last decade or so I have worked out a simple way to categorize those cultural variables which cause international deal makers the most problems. Thousands of managers and business school students who have attended our Global Management seminars tell me our "Patterns" approach makes sense. Time after time seminar participants come up after a presentation to say, "Now I understand what went wrong at that negotiating session last year!"

The Sources

The material for this book comes from three decades of observing myself and others spoiling promising deals because we were ignorant of how business is done. The cases are all based on incidents that actually took place during the author's 35 years in marketing, sourcing, managing and leading seminars around the world. Chapter 10 is a partial exception in that a number of examples were drawn from conversations with businesss travelers in international airport lounges and hotel bars.

My 26 years as an expatriate manager in Germany, Austria, Italy, Brazil, India and Singapore was an especially rich source of material. I owe an enduring debt to colleagues in the Florence, Frankfurt, Vienna, Sao Paulo, New Delhi and Singapore offices I managed for their personal support over so many years as well as for invaluable insights too numerous to mention.

For one to whom learning languages has never come easily, seeing co-workers in Florence and Frankfurt switch instantly and fluently from Italian, German or French into Spanish, English or whatever was a truly humbling experience. It was the same story in Singapore where some colleagues spoke English, Mandarin and Malay along with Cantonese, Hokkien and Teochew.

This linguistic virtuosity was inspiring because I believe bilingual or multilingual ability is an essential springboard to intercultural competence. And intercultural competence is or should be the goal of every effective expatriate manager and international negotiator.

The source for the Negotiator Profiles which make up Part Two were the more than one thousand business negotiations I have conducted in some 45 different countries. Organized loosely according to the *Patterns* expounded in Part One, the Profiles are intended as thumb-nail sketches of the negotiating behavior a visitor can expect to encounter in the markets covered.

The writings of anthropolgists, scholars of intercultural communication and researchers provided insights over the years which helped me formulate the Patterns. Among the works I have found especially useful are those by Edward T. and Mildred Reed Hall, Geert Hofstede, Robert Moran and William Gudykunst. Obviously none of these experts is responsible for the shortcomings which will inevitably show up in this book.

Three academic institutions have been instrumental in sharpening the focus of this book:

–   The *Export Institute of Singapore:* Site of the "Going Global!" seminars and other programs we have conducted since 1994. The participants in these programs – both Singaporean and expatriate managers – have constantly stimulated my thinking with their questions, comments, and criticisms. My special thanks to Executive Director Ng Wei Min and his outstanding staff.

–   The *Niels Brock Copenhagen Business College:* Where I have had the privilege of lecturing several times a year since 1993 to a wide range of bright young Danish students preparing for careers in international business. Mogens Gruelund, Elsebeth Riis-Petersen, Hanne Baumann, Flemming Steen, Jens Graff, John Knudsen, Ulla Regli and so many other Danish colleagues have provided ongoing support and creative ideas.

– The *Management Institute of the University of Wisconsin:* Organizer of the popular three day "Negotiating in the Pacific Rim" workshops attended by both novices and veterans of international marketing and sourcing from all over the United States. It has been a pleasure working with Professor Linda Gorchels and my genial colleague George Seyk in Madison twice a year since 1994.

Two truly great Danes played key roles in getting this book out of my head and onto paper. Jens Graff – friend, colleague, marketing professor and author – has had the patience to listen to my theories of international business behavior for years.

In 1995 Jens introduced me to Lauge Stetting, the thoughtful savant in charge of the Copenhagen Business School Press. For me Lauge's most outstanding virtue is his patience: an important attribute when working with dilatory writers such as myself.

Still and all, the primary impetus for writing the book came from just one person: My wife Hopi, who has shared the joys and frustrations of international living with me for 36 very eventful years.

One more major source remains to be acknowledged. Namely, the multiple culture shocks and cultural adjustments which Hopi and our six children – Richard, Lester, Reed, Thor, Kamala and Clio – helped me weather.

Moving from one country to another almost inevitably causes culture shock, and the severity of the shock is directly proportional to the cultural distance between the two countries concerned. In our case for example, moving from Europe to India was an especially severe culture shock.

Repeated shocks and adjustments tend to make you sensitive to cultural differences – initially of course mostly to the differences which divide cultures. But we have found that those repeated adjustments also made us aware of the myriad similarities that bind us all together.

Part One

1. Patterns of
Cross-Cultural Business Behavior

Here are a few of the questions you will find answered in the pages that follow:

- What cultural gaffe caused top executives of a major Saudi Arabian company to break off promising negotiations with a California firm?
- Where did a Danish export manager go wrong when he lost a lucrative contract by inadvertently insulting a Mexican customer?
- Why did a North American importer end up with 96,000 cotton shirts he couldn't sell because they were improperly labeled?
- What did a world-famous European brewery do to cause their Vietnamese partners to abruptly halt negotiations on a joint venture project?
- Which all-important rules of protocol did a Canadian executive violate when he deeply offended a potential Egyptian customer?
- How do successful global marketing companies such as McDonald's overcome troublesome cross-cultural variations in taste preferences?

Two Iron Rules of International Business

Why is a thorough knowledge of international business customs and practices especially important for export marketers? Because of *Iron Rule # 1:*

- In International Business, the Seller Is Expected to Adapt to the Buyer.

If you are the buyer in an international transaction, cultural differences are less important – unless of course you want to negotiate the best deal!

What if you are not involved in a buy-sell transaction. Suppose you are travelling abroad to negotiate a joint-venture agreement, an acquisition or a strategic alliance? Now who is expected to do the adapting? That is where *Iron Rule # 2* comes into play:

- In International Business, the Visitor Is Expected to Observe Local Customs.

Is this just another way of saying, "When in Rome, do as the Romans do?" No. Actually, I disagree with that old saw. My advice is not to mimic or copy local behavior. Instead, just be yourself.

But of course "being yourself" should include being aware of local sensitivities and generally honoring local customs, habits and traditions.

This book will have served its purpose if it helps prepare readers to follow the two Iron Rules. Let's start by previewing the Patterns of Cross-Cultural Business Behavior.

Deal-Focus vs Relationship-Focus

This is the "Great Divide" between business cultures. Deal-focused (DF) people are fundamentally task-oriented while relationship-focused folks are more people-oriented.

Conflicts arise when deal-focused export marketers try to do business with prospects from relationship-focused markets. Many RF people find DF types pushy, aggressive and offensively blunt. In return DF types often consider their RF counterparts dilatory, vague and inscrutable.

Informal vs Formal Cultures

Problems occur when informal business travelers from relatively egalitarian cultures cross paths with more formal counterparts from hierarchical societies. Breezy informality offends high-status people from hierarchical cultures just as the status-consciousness of formal people may offend the egalitarian sensibilites of informal folks.

Rigid-Time vs Fluid-Time Cultures

One group of the world's societies worships the clock and venerates their Filofaxes. The other group is more relaxed about time and scheduling, focusing instead on the people around them.

Conflict arises because some rigid-time visitors regard their fluid-time brothers and sisters as lazy, undisciplined and rude while the latter often regard the former as arrogant martinets enslaved by arbitrary deadlines.

Expressive vs Reserved Cultures

Expressive people communicate in radically different ways from their more reserved counterparts. This is true whether they are communicating verbally, paraverbally or nonverbally. The confusion that results from these differences can spoil our best efforts to market, sell, source, negotiate or manage people across cultures. The expressive/reserved divide creates a major communication gap.

Let us now move to Chapter Two where we explore The Great Divide.

2. The "Great Divide" Between Business Cultures

Relationship-Focus vs Deal-Focus

Whether marketing, sourcing or negotiating an international alliance, the fundamental differences between relationship-focused (RF) and deal-focused (DF) markets impact our business success throughout the global marketplace.

The vast majority of the world's markets are relationship-oriented: the Arab world and most of Africa, Latin America and the Asia/Pacific region. That is, they are markets where business people get things done through intricate networks of personal contacts.

RF people prefer to deal with family, friends and persons or groups well known to them – people who can be trusted. They are uncomfortable doing business with strangers, especially strangers who also happen to be foreigners.

Because of this key cultural value, relationship-oriented firms typically want to know their prospective business partners very well before talking business with them.

In contrast, the deal-focused approach is common in only a small part of the world. Strongly DF cultures are found in northern Europe, North America, Australia and New Zealand, where people are relatively open to doing business with strangers.

This "Great Divide" between the world's cultures affects the way we conduct business from the beginning to the end of any commercial relationship. For starters, even the way we should make the first approach to potential buyers or partners depends upon whether they are in DF or RF cultures.

Making Initial Contact

Because DF people are relatively open to dealing with strangers, export marketers can normally make direct contact with potential buyers in these

Fig. 2.1

DEAL-FOCUSED CULTURES:
Nordic and Germanic Europe
North America
Australia and New Zealand

MODERATELY DEAL-FOCUSED:
Great Britain
South Africa
Latin Europe
Central and Eastern Europe
Chile, southern Brazil, northern Mexico
Hong Kong, Singapore

RELATIONSHIP-FOCUSED:
The Arab World
Most of Africa, Latin America and Asia

---

markets. Let's take the United States as an example. Perhaps because they are raised in a highly mobile immmigrant society, most Americans are open to discussing business possibilities with people they don't know.

The success of telemarketing illustrates this openness. Each year Americans buy over $300 billion dollars worth of goods and services from total strangers, and half of it is business-to-business selling. No wonder the USA is called the home of the cold call.

Of course even in America, the larger and more complex the transaction, the more the buyer wants to know about the seller. But the point is, in DF cultures the marketer can make initial contact with the prospective buyer *without any previous relationship or connection.* Having an introduction or referral is helpful but not essential.

This is the first major difference between DF and RF markets. An example from the world of international marketing will show how this key variable works in practice.

As the export manager for a Danish manufacturer, DanMark Widgets, Lars Larsen's market research reveals that his company's product line has strong sales potential in two major markets, the USA and Japan.

Since DMW markets abroad through exclusive distributors, Lars next works up a shortlist of three potential importers in each of the two markets. These are firms which already distribute related products to the main end-users of widgets in the United States and Japan.

Now Lars needs to get in touch with these potential distributors. He has to meet each importer personally in order to evaluate them and select the firm which will do the best job for DMW. How does he go about getting in touch with the prospective importers in each of these two contrasting markets?

Fig. 2.2 Making Initial Contact: DF vs RF Cultures

Direct Contact	DF		RF *Indirect Contact*
	USA		Japan

Since the U.S. candidates are likely to be open to dealing with strangers, Lars contacts them directly. He puts together a set of English-language brochures about DMW and its product line, writes a brilliant cover letter requesting an appointment for a meeting, and mails the package to his three American prospects.

Then a week or so later he picks up the telephone. "Good morning, this is Lars Larsen of Danmark Widgets. How are you today? Thanks, I'm fine too.

"Have you received the information we sent you last week? Oh good. Well, I'm going to be in the U.S. in a few weeks and would like to meet you for a discussion. Yes. Well, would the 14th be convenient for you?

"Splendid! We'll see you at nine o'clock then. I will confirm everything by fax today. See you on the 14th!"

And that's all there is to it. Making appointments in the USA is quick and easy if you have the right product or service to offer, because America is the quintessential deal-focused market. So our friend Lars makes two more phone calls to set up meeting dates with the other candidates, and his USA itinerary is complete.

Now it's time to tackle his Japanese schedule. After meeting with the American prospects, Lars will fly from Los Angeles to Japan to meet the three short-listed Japanese distributors. Is he going to send each of them that packet of information and then follow it up with a phone call?

No. Because our friend Lars has done his cross-cultural homework, he is aware that cold calls rarely work in strongly RF cultures like Japan.

Since DanMark Widgets is not yet well known in Japan, Larsen's prospects will probably not agree to a meeting based on a direct approach.

Japan is located at the opposite end of the DF-RF spectrum from the USA. That means Lars will get far better results by making *indirect contact* with his distributor candidates in Tokyo, Osaka and Nagoya. How does he go about doing that?

Often the best way to contact RF business partners is at an international trade show. That is where buyers look for suppliers, exporters seek importers and investors search for joint-venture partners. Business behavior at such exhibitions tends to be deal-focused because most of the attendees have come there for the express purpose of making business contacts.

Another good way to meet potential partners in RF markets is to join an official trade mission. All over the world today governments and trade associations are promoting their country's exports by organizing guided visits to new markets. The organizer of the trade mission sets up appointments with interested parties and provides formal introductions to them. These official introductions help break the ice, smoothing the way to a business relationship.

But suppose no widget trade show is scheduled for the next few months, nor is an official trade mission planned in the near future. There is one other proven way for Lars to make initial contact with his distributor candidates in Japan: he can arrange to be introduced by a trusted intermediary.

The Indirect Approach

Remember, RF firms do not do business with strangers. The proper way to approach someone who doesn't yet know you is to arrange for the right person or organization to introduce you. A third-party introduction bridges the relationship gap between you and the person or company you want to talk to.

The ideal introducer is a high-status person or organization known to both parties. So if you happen to be good friends with a respected retired statesman who just happens to be well acquainted with one of your importer candidates, that's wonderful. Alas, such cases of serendipity are rare in the real world of international trade.

A good second best might be the commercial section of your country's embassy in the target market. Embassy officials tend to be accorded high status in relationship-oriented cultures, and of course it is part of their job to promote exports.

Chambers of commerce and trade associations are other potential introducers. And what about your bank? If you want to do business in Japan and your bank lacks strong representation there you had better look for an international bank which does.

Or perhaps one of your golf buddies works for a company which has an active office in Tokyo. Maybe they can put in a good word for you. Freight forwarders, ocean and airfreight carriers and international law and accounting firms are other good sources of effective introductions.

Recognizing the importance of third-party introductions in their RF culture, the Japanese External Trade Organization (JETRO) is also willing to provide that service to reputable foreign companies.

In fact, having a proper introduction in Japan is so critical that specialized consulting firms have come into existence there whose main function is to introduce *gaijin* to Japanese companies. Of course, using a consultant is likely to cost you more than other ways of obtaining an introduction.

Pulling "Guanxi"

In the RF world, people get things done through relatives, friends, contacts and connections – in other words, though relationships. It's who you know that counts. The Chinese call these useful connections *guanxi*, a word well-known throughout East and Southeast Asia.

Of course, knowing the right people, having the right contacts helps get things done in deal-focused cultures as well. It's all a matter of degree. Even in an extremely DF market such as the U.S., people use "pull" or "clout" to get things done. Knowing the right person can often be very helpful.

But there is still a key difference. In strongly RF markets, initiating a business relationship can *only* be done if you know the right people, or if you can arrange to be introduced to them. Just try setting up a joint venture in China for example without having *guanxi* or using someone else's guanxi!

The bottom line: In relationship-oriented markets, plan to approach your potential customer or partner indirectly, whether via a trade show, a trade mission or a third-party introduction.

Although in this chapter we often refer to Japan, the indirect approach is critical throughout the RF part of the world.

A case which took place in Singapore during the early 1990s illustrates how essential contacts and introductions are to success in relationship-oriented markets, where people do not do business with strangers.

Case 2.1: "Exporting To Taiwan: *Guanxi* In Action."

You are the newly-hired marketing manager of Glorious Paints, a Singapore manufacturer of marine paints. It is a fast-growing company headed by three young, Western-educated directors.

Last year the marketing director led Glorious Paints to its first overseas sale, selling a large quantity of paint to Australia and New Zealand. Director Tan achieved this success by first sending information to potential distributors along with cover letters requesting appointments, then meeting with each interested candidate firm at their offices. After that Mr. Tan negotiated a distribution agreement with the company he decided was best qualified to handle that market area. This entire process took about four months and sales volume is already exceeding expectations.

Following that success you were hired to expand exports to other Pacific Rim markets. The director called you into his office to discuss market research showing that Taiwan is a very promising market with high demand and little local competition. So you were instructed to set up distribution there using the approach that had worked in Australia/New Zealand.

By searching a number of data bases you came up with the names and contact information of some 55 Taiwanese importers, agents, representatives and wholesalers involved in the paint business. Next you sent off brochures and product information to these prospects, enclosing a cover letter requesting an appointment to discuss possible representation. You expected perhaps five or six of the companies to reply.

To everyone's surprise, six weeks went by without a single response. At a strategy session Mr. Tan pointed out that many Taiwanese are not comfortable corresponding in English, so you fired off a second mailing, this time in Chinese. But after another two months not a single prospective distributor has answered your letters.

Mr. Tan is upset with your lack of progress in this attractive market. He has called an urgent meeting for this afternoon and expects you to come up with a solution. As you sit stirring your tea the questions revolve in your head like the spoon in the teacup. "What have I done wrong? This strategy worked fine with the Aussies. Why not with the Taiwanese? What do we do now?"

Because exporters are responsible for actively seeking overseas customers, we might assume that contacts and connections are less important for international buyers. But buyers engaged in global sourcing quickly learn the limits to this assumption.

First of all, exporters have to have a certain level of trust in their prospective buyers. Even letters of credit are not absolute guarantees of payments, and insisting on cash in advance restricts one's market potential. For that reason contacts and introductions can be as much a necessity for would-be overseas purchasers as for sellers.

The other problem is that not all resource markets are well organized or transparent, so that even buyers need to understand the local culture to get started. A good part of my career was spent managing international sourcing for a large U.S. company. This involved developing reliable and competitive sources of supply in the RF resource markets of the Middle East, Africa, Latin America and the Asia/Pacific region.

Dealing in Dhaka

Around 1989 we decided it was time to open a sourcing and quality-control office in Bangladesh, a rapidly-growing exporter of garments. As regional director for South and Southeast Asia based in Singapore, this task fell to me.

The first step was to arrange for legal registration. This is complicated because setting up an office in Bangladesh requires the approval of several different ministries and government agencies.

To handle the registration we talked to several local law, accounting and consulting firms. They said the approval process would take up to a year and quoted fees of up $10,000, hinting at "special expenses" – bribes to the responsible officials. Unwilling to engage in bribery, we shelved the idea of a Dhaka office.

Then a few weeks later one of my Hong Kong contacts phoned to ask a favor. "An old friend of mine from Bangladesh is checking into the Mount

Elizabeth Hospital near your office tomorrow for a major operation. The poor guy will be all alone in Singapore. Would you please stop by and give him my best wishes for a swift recovery?"

The old friend turned out to be a charming, well-read gentleman who had headed two different ministries in a previous Bangladesh government and was now a consultant in Dhaka. Chatting with him about many things that day, I also mentioned our wish to develop long-term suppliers in his country. After the operation I dropped by again with a couple of novels to wish him well.

Two days later the ex-minister phoned to thank me and offer his help. "Your company's plans will obviously help promote Bangladesh exports. If you wish, I will arrange to get your office registered within a month. Can you pay me $900, the cost of my airfare?" I quickly agreed, and three weeks later our Dhaka office was a legal entity – the fastest liaison-office registration ever recorded in Bangladesh.

How did he do it? Since he was personally acquainted with all the officials involved, the ex-minister was able to hand-carry our registration documents from one agency to another, have a cup of tea and get them signed without delay. And also without any "special expense".

This incident shows that in RF cultures, having the right contact can be just as important for buyers as it is for sellers. In the next chapter we will look at how to build those all-important relationships in RF cultures.

3. Deal First – or Relationship First?

Now let's get back to DanMark Widgets. Lars Larsen was fortunate: DMW's bank provided a letter of introduction to one of the Japanese candidate distributors, while the Danish embassy in Tokyo performed the necessary introductions to the other two. As soon as the three Japan appointments are confirmed, Lars and his colleague Christina take off for the USA on the first leg of their round-the-world sales trip.

Their first meeting is with Chicago Widget Systems, where the two Danes are given a friendly greeting and seated in a conference room. "Oh, you're from Copenhagen. I guess that's in Sweden, right?" Not totally surprised by the American's ignorance of European geography, Lars and Christina sip their coffee while answering questions about Danish pastry, Danish blondes and Danish beer.

Getting down to Business

And then, about five minutes after they entered the CWS, office they hear "Okay, now we'd better get down to business. Time is money! Why don't you tell us about those Superwidgets of yours that are selling so well in Germany." To international marketers who have done business in deal-focused cultures, that way of starting a meeting will sound quite familiar.

After all, why not get right down to business? The Danes asked for this meeting in order to evaluate CWS as a possible distributor. And the Americans agreed to the meeting to find out whether they would be interested in handling the DMW line. So why should buyer and seller "waste time" with extraneous preliminaries?

Obviously exporter and importer will want to learn a lot more about each other before they are ready to sign a distribution agreement. But that comes later. Meanwhile the two sides are sizing each other up while they discuss price, payment terms, specifications, quality, quantity, delivery dates and all the other issues involved in an international distribution agreeement. They talk business right from the start and get to know each other as things proceed.

Deal-focused buyers and sellers socialize over drinks, meals and on the golf course. But they also build rapport right at the bargaining table in the course of hammering out an agreement.

Which is why after one or two meetings with each of the U.S. companies our two Danes feel they have learned enough to make a tentative ranking of the three candidates. References and credit reports remain to be checked, but Christina and Lars already have a pretty good idea of which of the three would make the best American partner for DanMark Widgets.

In deal-focused markets you can usually get down to business after just a few minutes of small talk. And you can learn most of what you need to know about your potential DF counterpart in a matter of days rather than the weeks or months it will take in strongly RF cultures such as Japan.

Figure 3.1 shows that the USA and Japan at opposite poles in terms of relationship-focus and deal-focus.

Fig. 3.1 Deal First or Rapport First?

Deal	DF		RF	*Rapport*
First	USA		Japan	*First*

Having done their cross-cultural homework our two Scandinavian marketers already know about this key difference. That's why they know they're in for quite a different meeting scenario in Tokyo.

Getting to Know Each Other

At Nihon World Widget their first meeting starts with the elaborate greeting ritual of the *meishi*, the formal exchange of business cards (more about that in Chapter 9). Lubricated with large quantities of tea the two sides then dialogue about everything on earth except the matter that brought them together: widgets.

The visitors answer polite questions about Copenhagen and Denmark and respond with a similar number of questions about Tokyo and Japan. The two sides discuss weather, sports, music, movies...all part of the RF "getting to know you" game.

Nor are Christina and Lars surprised when the meeting ends without a single mention of business. When Watanabe-san suggests another meeting on Wednesday they accept his offer of arranging transport back to their hotel.

The second meeting with NWW again ends without a discussion of widgets. But this time Watanabe-san invites his visitors to a Japanese dinner – a good omen. At the restaurant the four Japanese men are impressed with the elegant way Christina handles her chopsticks. Lars is somewhat less adept with the unfamiliar utensils but shows that he can sip his *sake* with aplomb.

It's when dinner is over that Christina really demonstrates her thorough grasp of Japanese social protocol. She suddenly puts a hand to her temple and excuses herself politely. "Watanabe-san, I'm so sorry. I seem to have developed a rather bad headache. Would you mind terribly if I go back to the hotel now?"

Of course Mr. Watanabe does not mind! This diplomatic headache frees the men to spend the next three or four hours in the way they should: building a relationship over beer, karaoke and whisky – probably a good deal of each!

So it's no great surprise when at next morning's meeting it is Christina who leads the Danish side of the business meeting while Lars gulps quantities of aspirin and black coffee. The Japanese now feel they know their foreign counterparts well enough to discuss business. They signal their readiness by asking a number of detailed questions about those famous Superwidgets.

It takes time, patience and sometimes a cast-iron liver to develop a strong relationship in RF markets such as Japan, South Korea and Taiwan. Getting inebriated together seems to speed up the rapport-building process in East Asia – but normally only for men. While there are exceptions these days, women usually don't fit in at these quasi-adolescent male bonding rituals.

The best way to get to know your local counterpart varies from one RF culture to another. In much of the Arab world, steaming platters of rice and lamb may take the place of booze. Brazilians and Mexicans love to talk about their art, music, literature and films. And then there is golf. In many parts of the world today a five iron closes the culture gap faster than a fifth of Scotch.

Yes, building trust and rapport with your customer is important everywhere in the world, not only in relationship-oriented markets. The big difference is that with Arabs, Africans, Latin Americans and most Asians you have to develop that climate of trust *before* you start talking business. In RF markets, you first make a friend, then you make a deal.

You Need to Develop a Personal Relationship

In RF markets the relationship you build with your counterpart will have a strong personal component in addition to the company-to-company aspect. Your customer or partner will want to know that you personally as well as your company are committed to the success of the venture.

For instance, Watanabe-san may want to be able to phone Lars Larsen at any hour of the day or night to solve problems and smooth out difficulties.

And because of this personal element it is important that continuity is maintained as far as possible throughout the relationship. Lars should personally handle the NWW account, should make the return trips to Tokyo and should be on hand when Watanabe-san and his colleagues visit Denmark.

If Lars is promoted or transferred to another assignment he must take care to personally introduce his replacement. Since the Japanese already know Christina she might be well placed to continue the relationship. However, the special challenges women face in doing business with Japanese and certain other RF cultures should be taken into account when making such a decision. The delicate issue of gender and international business will be addressed in Chapter 5.

Bureaucracy in RF Markets

Business negotiations last longer in RF than in DF cultures, for two reasons. First, it may take time to arrange an indirect approach. And then comes the lengthy process of building trust and developing a personal relationship.

When negotiating with government officials and public sector companies in relationship-focused markets, a third factor – bureaucratic inertia – often comes into play. Of course, officials everywhere tend to be cautious. They may find it safer to postpone a decision or to deny your request rather than to give their approval. Moreover, red tape often slows the process of getting things done. But in RF cultures suspicion of strangers, especially foreign strangers, often make officials even more hesitant to move things along.

That's why it took Volkswagen over nine years to negotiate the opening of an automobile factory with the government of China. And why McDonald's required more than 12 years to work out an agreement with the then Soviet government for raising the first Golden Arches in Russia.

Deal-focused executives should load their briefcase with an extra-large supply of patience when preparing to do business with bureaucrats in many RF markets.

The Importance of Face-to-Face Contact

The telecommunications revolution permits rapid correspondence with business partners around the world today. Telex, fax, e-mail, telephone and video-conferencing enable us to stay in constant touch with our international counterparts.

But none of the above has reduced the need for face-to-face contact with our relationship-focused customers and partners. RF business people are less comfortable discussing problems in writing or over the telephone. They expect to see their suppliers and partners in person more often than would be necessary in deal-focused markets.

The Role of the Contract

Deal-oriented business people rely on written agreements to prevent misunderstandings and solve problems. U.S. business people in particular tend to take a rather impersonal, legalistic, contract-based approach when disagreements and disputes arise. I have an American friend who says, "If you took all 860,000 lawyers in our country and laid them end to end... Hey! Come to think of it, that would be a great idea!"

Many U.S. companies bring a lengthy draft contract and a lawyer to the negotiating table with them. They then proceed to discuss the proposed agreement clause by clause, consulting the legal adviser every time a question arises.

This approach makes sense in America, the world's most litigious society. But it can be counter-productive in RF cultures where business people rely more on personal relationships rather than on lawyers and detailed contracts. In strongly RF markets a better approach is to keep the lawyers in the background until the late stages of the discussions, conferring with them during breaks.

Contrasting perceptions of the contract also cause misunderstandings between RF and DF cultures. For example, a Korean partner might expect to renegotiate the terms of a contract as conditions change, even if the agreement had just been signed in New York a month ago. The Koreans would expect their close relationship with their U.S. counterpart to facilitate such a renegotiation.

The New Yorkers on the other hand are likely to misinterpret an early request for changing the contract terms as a sign that their new Korean partners are tricky, fickle and unreliable. RF cultures depend primarily on relationships to prevent difficulties and solve problems, while deal-focused cultures depend on the written agreeement to fulfill the same functions.

As more companies from both sides of the Great Divide do business globally we can expect these misunderstandings to slowly diminish. In the meantime however executives need to be alert to cross-cultural differences that can wreck even the most promising international business deal.

4. Communicating Across The Great Divide
Direct vs Indirect Language

RF and DF business cultures also differ in the way they communicate. Deal-oriented negotiators tend to value direct, frank, straightforward language, while their relationship-focus counterparts often favor a more indirect, subtle, roundabout style.

In my experience this communication gap is perhaps the greatest cause of misunderstandings between RF and DF business people. Confusion arises because the two cultures expect quite different things from the communication process.

Harmony vs Clarity

It is all a question of priorities. When communicating with others, the priority for DF business people is to be clearly understood: they usually say what they mean and mean what they say. German and Dutch negotiators for example are known for their frank, even blunt language.

RF negotiators in contrast give top priority to maintaining harmony and promoting smooth interpersonal relations. Because preserving harmony within the group is so important, RF people carefully watch what they say and do to avoid embarrassing or offending other people.

Fig. 4.1. The Cross-Cultural Communication Gap

Direct Language DF_____RF *Indirect Language*

Over the last 35 years I have noticed that the nearer the RF end of the continuum a culture is located, the more careful and indirect people are with their language. On the other hand, the nearer they are to the DF end, the more frank and direct people tend to be.

Things can get quite interesting when the two parties in a negotiation come from opposite poles, as is the case for example when most Americans and Japanese interact. For example, I have had the pleasure of negotiating with Japanese companies since 1971 and cannot recall hearing the word "no" even one time.

Most Japanese, Chinese and Southeast Asian negotiators I have encountered seem to treat "no" as a four-letter word. To avoid insulting you they may instead murmur "That will be difficult" or "We will have to give that further study." Popular variations are "Maybe" and "That will be inconvenient."

Mind you, one of our sons speaks the language fluently and worked for a large Japanese company in Tokyo. While there he dated a number of Japanese young ladies and although he won't admit it, I think he may have heard "no" once or twice!

Case 4.1 illustrates the contrasting approaches to business communication in RF and DF cultures.

Case 4.1: Bilingual Labels

As one of North America's largest importers of cotton garments, Great Northern Apparel of Toronto decided it was high time to start sourcing mens dress shirts in China. From an industry contact in the United States vice president Pete Martin heard about Evergreen Garments, a large manufacturer in Guangzhou specialized in supplying the U.S. market.

After considerable correspondence Pete Martin flew to Guangzhou to finalize the purchase agreement for 8000 dozen shirts. Discussions with the Evergreen Garment people proceeded amiably. Pete and the Evergreen team needed a full week of meetings to agree on fabric construction, size and color breakdown, packing, delivery, price, payment terms and the other details of a large transaction.

Exhausted from these lengthy negotiations, Pete was really looking forward to the signing ceremony. At this point however Pete remembered that Evergreen had not yet exported garments to Canada and thus might not be familiar with Canadian labeling requirements. So he explained that all apparel sold in Canada must have labels with the fiber content and laundering instructions in both French and English.

This news caused the Chinese side some concern because they lacked

French-language expertise and strongly preferred to deal only with Chinese and English. Managing Director Wang replied with a smile, "Mr. Martin, I am afraid that supplying labels in French and English will be difficult. This question will require further study."

Pete Martin repeated that bilingual French/English labels were required by Canadian law. "Please understand that we really have no choice on this – it's the law."

After a short discussion with his team, Mr. Wang again spoke up with a smile: "Mr. Martin, we will give your request serious consideration. I'm afraid it will be very difficult, but of course we at Evergreen Garments will do our best to solve the problem." Relieved to have settled this final detail, Pete signed the contract of purchase and said his formal goodbyes to Mr. Wang and his Evergreen team.

Seven months later Pete got a call from the quality control chief at the Great Northern warehouse. "Mr. Martin, we have a problem. You know those 96,000 shirts that just came in from China? Well, they've got bilingual labels on them all right – but they're in English and Chinese!"

Pete Martin was stunned. He thought Evergreen had agreed to supply French/English labels. How would you explain to him why the shirts were delivered with the wrong labels?

Strongly RF people also have subtle ways of saying no with body language. Some Arabs lift their eyebrows to politely refuse a request – the nonverbal equivalent of the American slang expression, "No way, Jose'!"

In many cultures clicking the tongue with a "tsk-tsk" sound indicates a negative response.

Japanese and Thais often smile and change the subject or simply say nothing at all. I have found that silence during a meeting with East Asian negotiators often means, "Forget it, Charley!"

The Myth of the Inscrutable Oriental

Some suspicious deal-driven negotiators think all this indirectness is designed to confuse or mislead them. It was in fact the RF-DF communication gap which gave rise to the myth of the "inscrutable Oriental."

But verbal subtlety and indirectness is only part of the story. To DF types, East and Southeast Asians seem inscrutable also because they hide their emotions, especially negative emotions. In these cultures showing impatience, irritation, frustration or anger disrupts harmony. It is rude and offensive. So people there mask negative emotion by remaining expressionless or by putting a smile on their face.

Thais for example seem to smile all the time. They smile when they are happy, they smile when they are amused, they smile when they are nervous, they smile even when they are absolutely furious. Thai people smiile because to openly display anger would cause everyone concerned to lose face.

Communication and "Face"

In the highly relationship-focused cultures of East and Southeast Asia, both sides lose face when a negotiator on one side of the bargaining table loses his temper. The person who displays anger loses face because he has acted childishly. And by openly showing anger he has also caused the other party to lose face. It doesn't take much of that to bring a promising negotiation to a lose-lose impasse.

As an unfortunate example, let's look at what happened recently during a long drawn-out negotiation in Ho Chi Minh City. Executives from one of northern Europe's largest breweries had been haggling for months with a Vietnamese public sector company over the details of an agreement to build a joint-venture brewery in central Vietnam.

Towards the end of a particularly frustrating day the leader of the European team could simply no longer mask his irritation. First his face got bright red. Shaking with anger, he clenched his fist so hard the wooden pencil he was holding suddenly snapped in half.

At that sound the room instantly become silent. A moment later the entire Vietnamese team rose as one man and stalked out of the conference room. The next day a three-line fax arrived at the headquarters of the European brewery informing them that the Vietnamese would never again sit down at the same table with "such a rude, arrogant person" as the head of the European team.

What to do now? Months of painstaking discussions had already been invested in this complex project. To save the deal the Europeans decided to repatriate the offending manager and replace him with a stoic type famous for his poker face. Some months later the agreement was duly signed and visitors to central Vietnam can now imbibe lager and pilsner to their heart's content.

What could the deal-focused head of the northern European team have done to prevent that fiasco? When I asked participants in one of our recent Global Negotiator seminars that question, the best answer was "Take a walk!" Exactly. Call for a recess. Have a cold drink. Go for a brisk walk. Do whatever it takes to relax and cool down.

Your face turning red is an involuntary response you can't control. But you can take a break before something snaps.

While Westerners associate the concept of "face" primarily with East Asian and Southeast Asian societies, it is in fact a cultural universal. The Italians call it *honore*, the Spaniards *dignità*, the Anglo-Saxons self-respect. Nowhere in the world do human beings enjoy rude and offensive behavior. We tend to feel uncomfortable when others are angry with us or when we are embarassed, mocked or singled out for criticism.

It is true that people in relationship-focused culture are often especially sensitive to face, perhaps because RF cultures are group-oriented. One's self-image and self-respect depend very much on how one is viewed by others. That is why business visitors need to be especially conscious of how their verbal and nonverbal messages may be interpreted in RF cultures.

Miscommunication Across Cultures

The strong East Asian concern for covering negative emotion can be confusing to outsiders from deal-focused cultures. When we moved Germany to Singapore in 1988 my wife and I decided to try learning Mandarin on weekends. We hired Stefanie, a pleasant young woman who had recently immigrated from Taiwan to tutor us.

My lessons were interrupted late that year when my mother passed away and I had to fly to Wisconsin to attend the funeral. Unfortunately, I had barely returned to Singapore when my brother phoned again to break the sad news that our father had passed away. As you might imagine, this was a very difficult time for me.

It happened to be a Saturday when I got back from this second funeral, and Stefanie dropped by to enquire why I had missed over a month's worth of lessons. Suffering from grief compounded by jet lag and exhaustion, I blurted out that both of my parents had just died.

A stricken look flashed across the young woman's face for just a fraction of a second, and she gasped. Then Stefanie suddenly laughed out loud, right in my face. And proceeded to giggle for several seconds.

Now, intellectually I was quite aware that people from some Asian cultures hide their nervousness, embarrassment or severe stress with a laugh. I also knew I should have broken my sad news much more gently. After all, Stefanie was a Chinese person raised in the Confucian way: She revered her parents. For her the sudden realization that she could perhaps lose both of them almost at the same time must have come as a terrible shock.

Nevertheless my immediate reaction to her laugh was visceral. I felt as though I had just been hit very hard in the stomach. Even though I understood rationally what had happened I had difficulty relating to Stefanie as I had before the incident. A few weeks later she stopped coming and we had to find a new Mandarin tutor.

"Low-Context" and "High-Context" Communication

We have seen that RF negotiators tend to use indirect language in order to avoid conflict and confrontation. The polite communication of Asians, Arabs, Africans and Latins helps maintain harmony. The meaning of what they are saying at the bargaining table is often found more in the context surrounding the words rather than in the words themselves. The U.S. anthropologist Edward T. Hall, guru of cross-cultural communication, coined the useful term "high-context" for these cultures.

In contrast, when northern Europeans, North Americans, Australians and New Zealanders speak, more of the meaning is explicit – contained in the words themselves. A listener is able to understand what they are saying at a business meeting without referring much to the context. Hall termed these cultures "low-context".

For a Japanese executive trying to do business in Amsterdam this difference in communication styles quickly becomes obvious – as it does for a Swede or German trying to close a deal in Tokyo. That's because Japan lies at the high-context/RF end of the culture continuum while Sweden and Germany are perched at the low-context/DF end.

What is less obvious are differences between cultures which are located fairly close together on the continuum. For example, let's look at Greater China, the constellation of the PRC, Hong Kong (culturally somewhat distinct from the rest of China) and Taiwan. We will add Singapore as well because although the population of the Lion City is only about 77 percent Chinese, the business culture is strongly Chinese-oriented.

Figure 4.2 shows that while China – the mother culture – is still located at the RF and high-context end of the continuum, Taiwan, Hong Kong

Fig. 4.2

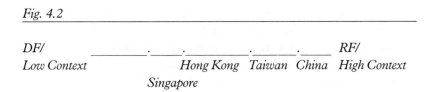

DF/ _____.____._____._____.____ *RF/*
Low Context   *Hong Kong Taiwan China High Context*
                      Singapore

and Singapore are spotted at varying distances away. People doing business in these three outposts of Chinese culture notice that while they are definitely more RF and indirect than say Australia, they are also more deal-focused and direct than most of their counterparts in the PRC.

Old Pacific Rim hands know that Hong Kongers and Singaporeans are somewhat more open to direct contact than PRC Chinese, require a shorter time for building rapport and tend to use more direct language.

Equally interesting, recent research by a Danish scholar reveals similar fine gradations of cross-cultural business behavior among markets at the deal-focused/low-context end of the spectrum. Professor Malene Djursaa of the Copenhagen School of Business studied the interaction of over 50 Danish, German and British businessmen and published her findings in the June 1994 issue of the *European Management Journal.*

Although all three of these European cultures are unmistakably low-context, they also display significant differences – differences that can cause problems for people doing business in the three markets. While the British are clearly more low-context and deal-focused than Arabs, Mexicans or Koreans, at the same time they are also more high-context and RF than their Danish and (especially) German counterparts.

Fig. 4.3

DF/ _____._____._____._____ *RF/*
Low Context   *Germany   Denmark   UK*   *High Context*

In lengthy interviews with the business people of these three related cultures, Professor Djursaa learned for example that Germans find personal relationships to be more important in the UK than back home. The interviews also reveal that the British employ more roundabout, indirect language than the Danes. Further, the Danes reported that they get down to business more quickly than the British but less quickly than the Germans.

The research of Hall, Djursaa and many other scholars confirms what many business people have learned from experience: Differences in cross-cultural business behavior create invisible barriers to international trade.

Variations in verbal and nonverbal behavior can cause culture clashes, but a skilled interpreter can often smooth over verbal problems. That's what is going on when an interpreter takes several minutes to render in Japanese or Chinese what a DF speaker just said in a couple of short sentences. Part of the translator's task is to cloak overly blunt statements with the proper amount of polite circumlocution.

Saying It Like It Is vs Saving Face

Even when indirect RF and direct DF people are both speaking the same language – English for example – they are really speaking different languages. A Dutch or German negotiator will choose his words carefully so that his counterparts will understand exactly what he is saying. He wants no ambiguity, no beating around the bush.

Meanwhile his Arab, Japanese or Indonesian counterparts are choosing their words even more carefully – but for a completely different reason. RF negotiators want to make sure that no one at the meeting will be offended. No rude directness, no crude bluntness, no loss of face.

I personally come from a deal-oriented background. When an Australian, a German or a Dane describes me as a direct, straightforward person I take it as a compliment. That's because in DF cultures directness and frankness are equated with honesty and sincerity.

But those same adjectives coming from a Japanese would more likely be meant as criticism. Why? Because in RF/high-context cultures, directness and frankness are equated with immaturity and naïveté – perhaps even arrogance. In strongly RF cultures only children and childish adults make a practice of saying exactly what they mean. They just don't know any better!

The Two Meanings of "Sincerity"

As a final illustration of the differences in DF and RF communication styles, let us look at the constrasting meanings of the word "sincerity." To English speakers from the deal-centered part of the world, sincerity connotes honesty and frankness. A sincere friend for instance is one who tells you the truth even when that truth happens to be unpleasant.

In contrast, for RF people a sincere friend is one who always shows his willingness to be helpful. For example, suppose a West Asian asks a deal-focused person for a favor which the latter knows he will not be able to do. The DF friend would probably show his sincerity by responding, "Very sorry, I won't be able to do that because..."

The West Asian however would regard such a person as a very fickle friend indeed. A sincere friend would reply, "Of course! I will do my best and let you know..." In relationship-oriented cultures you show sincerity by declaring your willingness to help out – even when you cannot or will not do the favor.

In the next chapter we move from the DF/RF divide to that between formal and informal business cultures.

5. Formal vs Informal Business Cultures
Status, Hierarchies, Power and Respect

Many promising international deal have fallen through when a negotiator from an informal culture confronts counterparts from more formal cultures. In this chapter we will look at several examples.

Formal cultures tend to be organized in steep hierarchies which reflect major differences in status and power. In contrast, informal cultures value more egalitarian organizations with smaller differences in status and power.

Why does this matter when we are doing business abroad? Because these contrasting values cause conflict at the conference table. Business people from formal, hierarchical cultures may be offended by the breezy familiarity of counterparts from informal, relatively egalitarian societies. On the other hand, those from informal cultures may see their formal counterparts as stuffy, distant, pompous or arrogant.

Such misunderstandings can be avoided if both sides are aware that differing business behaviors are the result of differing cultural values rather than individual idiosyncracies.

Culture Clash in Germany

I learned about the infomality/formality divide the hard way in the early 1960s when my employer, a Chicago export management company, transferred me to Germany to expand sales in Europe.

My first appointment was with our largest account, an importer/distributor of hand-tools located in Stuttgart. I spent that day in meetings with the boss of the company, Doctor Wilhelm Müller, and found myself saying "Herr Dr. Müller" and "Dr. Müller" the whole day. This formality was oppressive for a young man from the United States, one of the world's more informal cultures. So returning to Frankfurt that evening I phoned my German friend.

"Hans, I'm really tired of all this medieval formality. How many times do I have to meet with this guy before I can start calling him "Willi"?"

Fortunately, Hans straightened me out on the formality issue right then. "You are asking when you can start calling Dr. Müller by his first name? Well, the answer is *niemals, Dummkopf!* Never, you dummy!"

Of course Hans was right. I spent the next two years addressing this distinguished gentleman in the proper German way. And when I met his wife I called her "Frau Doktor." Why? Because that's the proper form of address in Germany, a relatively formal society.

I soon learned that most of Europe follows the same rules of formal address. Your French contact remains Monsieur Dupont, not René. And for years in Italy we addressed the head of a our largest supplier in Italy with the honorific "Commendatore" until we got to know him well enough to call him Gustavo.

By way of contrast, my most recent meeting in Sydney, Australia started with a hearty "G'day mate! Let's 'ave a beer!" Now that, dear reader, is an example of an informal culture!

Formality actually is about status, hierarchies, power and respect. Whereas informal cultures are supposed to value *status equality*, formal cultures value hierarchies and *status differences.* Ignorance of this distinction can cause serious problems across the bargaining table. A participant in one of our export marketing seminars in Europe related an incident which illustrates the point.

Case 5.1: How to Insult a Mexican Customer

José Garcia Lopez, a Mexican importer, had been negotiating with a Danish manufacturing company for several months when he decided to visit Copenhagen to finalize a purchase contract. The business meetings went smoothly, so on the last day of his visit Sr. Garcia confided that he looked forward to signing the contract after his return to Mexico.

That evening the Danes invited Sr. Garcia out for an evening on the town. Flemming, the 40 year-old export manager and his 21 year-old assistant Margrethe hosted an excellent dinner and then took their Mexican prospect on a tour of Copenhagen nightspots. Around midnight Flemming glanced at his watch.

"Sr. Garcia, I have a very early flight tomorrow to Tokyo. I hope you'll forgive me if I leave you now. Margrethe will make sure you get back to your hotel all right and then drive you to the airport tomorrow morning. I wish you a good flight!"

Next morning in the car on the way to the airport José Garcia was uncharacteristically silent. Then he turned to the the the young assistant: "Margrethe, would you please tell your boss I have decided not to sign that contract after all. It is not your fault of course. If you think about what happened last evening I believe you will understand why I no longer wish to do business with your company."

To repeat, formality has to with relative status, organizational hierarchies and how to show respect to persons of high status. That is why international marketers always should know whether they are dealing with formal or informal cultures. Figure 5.1 shows "who's who".

Fig. 5.1

INFORMAL CULTURES
Australia
USA
Canada
New Zealand
Denmark, Norway, Iceland
FORMAL CULTURES
Most of Europe and Asia
The Mediterranean Region and the Arab World
Latin America

In formal, hierarchical cultures status differences are larger and more important than in egalitarian, informal cultures. Formal ways of addressing people is one important way of showing respect to persons of high status.

Showing Respect in Europe

Let's take Dr. Wilhelm Müller as an example. I addressed this German gentleman formally because that is the German custom. But the cultural value behind that venerable custom really has to do with showing appropriate respect.

First of all, Wilhelm Müller was considerably older than I was. And in formal cultures age confers status.

Secondly, Herr Müller had earned a doctorate – an academic distinction of great importance in Germany. One acknowledges that distinction by including the title when addressing such a person. This bit of protocol is important because today some 60 percent of top managers in German manufacturing concerns hold a doctorate, usually in engineering.

Showing Respect to the Customer

But there is a third and supremely important reason for according great respect to Dr. Wilhelm Müller – a reason that is valid far beyond Germany and Europe. Namely, this guy was my *customer.*

International marketers must remember that all over the world these days the customer is king. (Except in Japan, that is. Because for Japanese businesses the customer is *GOD!* We can all learn something from the way our Japanese colleagues and competitors treat their customers.)

Hierarchies and Status in Asia

People from egalitarian societies are often unaware of the importance of status distinctions in hierarchical cultures. During the five years we lived in Singapore we were friends with an American couple who invited us for dinner several times. At the first party there were a number of Singaporean couples present, but none of the locals accepted subsequent invitations.

The American couple had no idea why their Singaporean friends no longer came to dinner, but my wife and I knew. You see, these particular Yanks happened to be strongly egalitarian. They liked to have their maid sit at the dinner table with them. Now, like most Asians Singaporeans respect authority, honor social hierarchies and value clear status differences. Feeling uncomfortable sitting at the same table with a Filipina maid, they said nothing but simply stayed away.

As the world's most egalitarian people, Scandinavians sometimes have a special problem doing business in strongly hierarchical cultures. Recently an associate of mine from a Nordic country visited good friends of ours in Bangkok. Svend politely shook hands with the host and hostess – and then with their young Thai maid as well. Much to Svend's surprise the maid immediately burst into tears, ran out and spent the whole evening sobbing in her room.

Our Bangkok friends are a Thai-American couple. They gently explained to Svend that as a *farang* – a Caucasian foreigner – he automatically enjoys high status, whereas a domestic worker is of lower status. In Thailand people so far apart in social status do not shake hands. So when Svend grabbed her hand she thought he was making fun of her and was absolutely mortified.

The sharp divide between egalitarian and hierarchical societies can act as an invisible barrier to exports. Marketers from informal cultures often do not know how to show respect to high-ranking persons from formal cultures, who may be easily offended by perceived slights.

The bottom line for export marketers and deal-makers in today's global marketplace is that ignorance of cultural differences is not an acceptable excuse for failure. Case 4.2 shows how you can lose business due to ignorance of cultural differences.

Case 5.2: How to Insult an Egyptian Customer

A major Canadian high-tech manufacturing firm was deep in negotiations with an Egyptian public sector company. Vice President Paul White was pleased to learn that the head of the Cairo-based company was leading a delegation to Toronto with a view to concluding negotiations.

White was even more pleased when upon his arrival Dr. Mahmud Ahmed hinted strongly that discussions were moving along nicely and that a favorable outcome was likely. After all, this contract represented the largest and most profitable deal White's company had worked on to date.

Quite aware of the importance of relationship-building, Paul invited the Egyptian delegation to an elegant reception and buffet dinner at the prestigious Grand Hotel, with Dr. Ahmed as the guest of honor.

Dr. Ahmed was his usual charming, affable self when he arrived at the party and warmly shook hands with Paul. After a few minutes of chit-chat the Canadian led his chief guest to the drinks table stocked with wine, liquor, fruit juices and soft drinks. "Well now, what can I offer you to drink, Dr. Ahmed?"

"Oh, nothing for me right now," replied the Egyptian with a smile. The two men conversed pleasantly about sports, music and other mutual interests for a while and then White guided his guest to the buffet table loaded with delicacies Dr. Ahmed was known to especially like. Paul was surprised when Dr. Ahmed once again declined politely, saying that he wasn't hungry.

Puzzled by his guest's lack of interest in food and drink, Paul wondered what the problem might be. Then the Canadian host was drawn into conversation with some of the other guests and did not notice when Dr. Ahmed left the party early.

At the negotiating session next day Dr. Ahmed was cool and distant. No progress at all was made towards an agreement. That afternoon Paul learned that the head of the Egyptian company was complaining vociferously to his colleagues about the "rude and offensive treatment" he had undergone at the dinner party. "I certainly do not intend to do business with such discourteous people," he was heard to say.

With the delegation due to leave Canada in three days, Paul White was desperate to know what was happening. Was this a negotiating ploy – a pressure tactic? Or had his team really offended Dr. Ahmed somehow? If so, what could he do now?

The two preceeding disaster cases were real-world examples of how not to do business in formal cultures. Now let's look at an example of how to do it right.

Showing Respect in Asia

An American consultant with a decade of business experience in South Asia arranged for his Chicago client to meet with the Minister of Textiles in Bangladesh. The Chicago company had asked for a favorable decision on a complex issue involving garment quota allocations but was not optimistic about the outcome. A U.S. competitor who had made a similar request the previous month had seen their application summarily rejected by mid-level bureaucrats in the ministry.

It was a sweltering day in Dhaka and the minister's air conditioner was not in operation. This caused the visitors considerable discomfort because at the consultant's insistence they were dressed in dark wool suits, starched shirts and ties. The two Westerners sat steaming and dripping sweat while the minister chatted away amiably, cool and comfortable in airy white muslin.

After about an hour and a quarter of what seemed to be aimless conversation, the minister stood up and with a broad smile informed the petitioners that he had decided to grant their request.

The consultant learned the next day from a government contact that the minister had deliberately not turned on his room air conditioner for the meeting. The contact hinted that His Excellency may have been "-testing" the Western visitors.

Nonverbal Ways of Showing Respect

The general lesson here is that when dealing with government officials in hierarchical countries it is important to show proper respect and deference. This advice is particularly important for Europeans, Americans and Australians negotiating with senior officials in countries with a history of Western colonial domination. Bureaucrats throughout South and Southeast Asia can be easily offended by overly casual behavior on the part of Westerners. Innocent informality may be misinterpreted as disrespect.

Wearing a suit and tie to meetings during the hot season sends a positive signal of respect, and keeping one's jacket on in a non-airconditioned office signals even greater respect.

Australian, Danish and American managers attending our seminars sometimes complain that they are at a competitive disadvantage globally because businessmen from hierarchical cultures already know all about formality, status differences and how to show respect, while those from egalitarian societies may not.

These managers have a valid point. A key rule of international business protocol is that when in an unfamiliar situation, always err on the side of formality at first. That may mean for instance addressing people by their surname and title rather than first name, dressing more formally and following local etiquette when shaking hands and exchanging business cards.

So when calling on prospects in a hierarchical culture, the Japanese or Germans in their dark suit, white shirt, polished shoes and polished manners may indeed have an initial advantage over some of their more informal Aussie or Yankee competitors.

Status Barriers

However, there are four classes of international business people who have to operate at an even greater disadvantage when trying to sell goods to strongly hierarchical buyers. These are:

– People on the lower rungs of the corporate ladder in their own company,
– Young people of either sex,
– Women,
– Men and women of any age involved in international sales and marketing.

The reason is that formal cultures tend to ascribe status according to one's age, gender, organizational rank and (especially in Asia) whether one is the buyer or the seller. Therefore a woman who is a young export sales specialist potentially suffers under a quadruple handicap when operating in formal, hierarchical cultures such as Japan, South Korea and Saudi Arabia.

Which makes our next case quite interesting. Case 5.3 is about a woman who succeeded as a very young export marketer in all three of these tough markets in spite of her four-fold handicaps. (As with all the other cases in this book, this incident actually took place.)

Case 5.3: Women in International Business

In certain hierarchically-organized cultures women rarely gain senior positions in commercial organizations. Especially in South Korea, Japan and Saudi Arabia, men are traditionally accorded higher status in the business world than females. The top positions in most companies are held by men who are not used to dealing with women in business on the basis of equality.

In direct contrast, many women in more egalitarian cultures around the world are successful entrepreneurs or executives in major corporations. The two opposing views of the role of women in business can lead to a culture clash when females try to do business in traditional, hierarchical societies.

Despite the potential problems however, some enterprising women refuse to be shut out of promising markets by what they regard as male chauvinist attitudes.

A bright young Danish woman we'll call Tonia is a case in point. Tonia was a tall, striking blonde of about 20 employed by a Singaporean jewelry manufacturer. She was also studying international marketing part-time at the Export Insitute of Singapore. Having heard about the gender barrier

Tonia, asked one of her EIS lecturers: "Which major markets in the world would you say are the most difficult for a woman to do business in?"

"Saudi Arabia, Japan and South Korea," replied the lecturer without hesitation.

The next day Tonia asked for a meeting with her boss, the marketing manager of the jewelry company. She volunteered to undertake a sales mission during the semester break to those very markets, and after some careful preparation left on a two-week trip to Tokyo, Seoul and Riyadh.

The next semester Tonia proudly reported to the class that she had been able to sell her company's fine jewelry successfully in not just one but all three of those particularly tough markets. Not only that, she had even been offered a job as marketing manager by one of her new customers!

The Gender Barrier

Although the gender barrier unquestionably exists in hierarchical cultures, being an obvious foreigner may lower that barrier significantly. For example, while there are millions of Japanese women working for companies in Japan, they are almost all "office ladies" performing clerical duties. Japanese women in a business setting are automatically asssumed to be secretaries and treated accordingly by the overwhelmingly male management. So Japanese women generally lack the status necessary to interact effectively with corporate decision-makers.

But those same male executives often see a foreign female as a *gaijin* first, and only second as a woman. Knowing that foreign women sometimes hold managerial positions, many Japanese executives are willing to give them a chance.

The Youth Barrier

The age barrier is quite a different matter. The most common question from young international marketers and managers of either sex attending our training seminars is, "Since being young is such a handicap to doing business abroad, what are we supposed to do?"

I usually start by reminding the questioner that youth is actually an advantage in some markets – the USA in particular. But without a doubt, a person of tender years will find it difficult to be taken seriously by older business people in formal, hierarchical cultures.

The ultimate solution of course is to grow older. But that's going to happen soon enough anyway. What to do in the meantime? I recommend this three-step procedure for young export marketers. (Because "the customer is king," youth is not such a major handicap for a buyer.)

How to Overcome the Youth Barrier with Hierarchical Buyers

Get introduced by an older man. Preferably by the oldest male you can find who is still able to walk. This ploy works because enough of his maleness (if you are a woman) and his seniority will rub off on you to get you started. But be nice: After the introduction let the old guy go back to sleep while you run the meeting!

Be a true expert in your field. This works because just about everywhere in the world today *expertise confers status.*Once they get over the shock of your youthfulness, customers in formal, hierarchical markets have the very same concerns as their egalitarian counterparts, and your quiet competence gives them confidence that you will provide them with good service.

A note of caution here. Remember to *show* them your expertise rather than tell them about it. The only thing worse than a show-off is a young show-off.

Learn the local business protocol. Since you will probably be making your sales presentation to an older male who is a buyer, you are of course heavily outranked. It's something like a private trying to sell to a general. So you must know how to show proper deference without actually grovelling. (Although here I am reminded of a certain Sears Roebuck buyer who posted a sign for the benefit of his suppliers, "GROVELLING IS GOOD!")

Other Status Factors

While age, gender, organizational rank and whether one is buying or selling are the key determinants of status and power in most hierarchical societies, other factors such as family background, level of education and knowledge of "high culture" also confer status in certain markets.

For example, in Latin America and much of Europe a deal-focused business person whose interests are limited to making money tends to be looked down upon. Higher status goes to the individual able to converse intelligently about art, music, literature, history, philosophy and the cinema. Business visitors who would like to be well-regarded in those markets should consider brushing up on such subjects.

How to conduct business in other cultures without offending customers and business partners is such an important issue we are devoting a separate chapter to International Buisiness Protocol. But first let's take a careful look at another Cultural Divide, the one between rigid-time and fluid-time cultures.

6. Time and Scheduling
Rigid-Time vs Fluid-Time Cultures

Globe-trotting business travelers quickly learn that people look at time and scheduling differently in different parts of the world. In rigid-time societies punctuality is critical, schedules are set in concrete, agendas are fixed and business meetings are rarely interrupted. Edward T. Hall invented the term "monochronic" for these clock-obsessed, schedule-worshipping cultures.

In direct contrast are "polychronic" cultures, where people place less emphasis on strict punctuality and are not obsessed with deadlines. Polychronic cultures value loose scheduling as well as business meetings where several meetings-within-meetings may be taking place simultaneously.

Fig. 6.1

MONOCHRONIC BUSINESS CULTURES
Nordic and Germanic Europe
North America
Japan

MODERATELY MONOCHRONIC
Australia/New Zealand
Russia and most of East-Central Europe
Southern Europe
Singapore, Hong Kong, Taiwan, China
South Korea, South Africa

POLYCHRONIC BUSINESS CULTURES
The Arab World
Most of Africa
Latin America
South and Southeast Asia

Alert readers will note a couple of particularly interesting entries in this chart. One is Japan, which was classified as polychronic by Edward T. Hall back in the 1960s. But today the Japanese are as schedule-obsessed and clock-conscious as the Swiss.

The other is Singapore, a polychronic Southeast Asian entrepot just 30 years ago and today a moderately monochronic business culture. Both countries are proof that culture does change, albeit slowly.

Of course, orientation to time varies not only among different countries but often within a given country as well. As we will see below with Italy, there can be regional variations. Another example is Brazil, where temperate Sao Paulo is relatively monochronic whereas Rio is strongly polychronic. Similarly people in the more industrialized southern coastal provinces of China are more clock-conscious than those in the less-developed interior. And your South Korean meeting is more likely to start on time if it takes place in Seoul than in a small town in the countryside.

Europe: The North/South Divide

For international business people the problem is that contrasting conceptions of time and scheduling cause conflicts. Let's look first at Europe, where the meaning of punctuality for instance varies according to whether you are in the northern or southern part of the Continent.

Suppose you are an export marketer scheduled to meet your Hamburg customer at 9 am tomorrow. Knowing how important *Pünklichkeit* is to Germans, what time should you arrive at his office in order to be considered punctual? Veterans of the German market agree that 8:55 am would be just about right.

Getting there at nine on the dot would of course be technically acceptable, but arriving five minutes ahead of time shows that you share your customer's obsession with being on time.

The worst thing would be to show up late. Tardiness signals lack of discipline. Some Germans feel if you are ten minutes late for a meeting you may well be ten weeks late with your delivery. *Pünklichkeit* and *Zuverläßigkeit* (reliability) are closely related concepts in this most monochronic of cultures.

Let's say your next sales meeting is in Munich. The laid-back Bavarians are more relaxed about time, so you could arrive right on time – possibly even two minutes late – without destroying your chances for a sale. And you can still be confident that your local counterpart will be punctual.

Where the Clock Slows Down

But when you hop across the Alps for your meeting in Milan, the rules change. There your customer or contact may well show up ten minutes or so late without feeling obliged to apologize. And as you travel south through Italy you find that schedules become even more fluid. In sunny Rome your local counterpart is likely to waltz in half an hour after the agreed time and greet you as though nothing at all is wrong.

At this point some of our seminar participants usually ask, "But what about that famous saying, "When in Rome, do as the Romans do." Doesn't that mean that in Italy for example we can be relaxed about punctuality as well?"

That's not the way things work in global business. If you are an export marketer the "When in Rome..." rule of thumb is trumped by a higher rule we have already invoked: "The seller has to show respect to the buyer." Being on time is a key way of showing respect – even in a polychronic culture.

The polychronic approach to time becomes more obvious as you move further south. By the time you reach Naples, 45 minutes' tardiness is considered no big deal. And then of course comes Sicily. According to my Florentine friends, if your Sicilian counterparts show up at all on the day of the meeting they are considered punctual!

This European example with its *soupçon* of exaggeration is meant to contrast the rigid-time business cultures found mostly in temperate latitudes with the more relaxed, fluid-time cultures located primarily in hotter climes. For whatever reason, the closer you get to the equator the slower the clock seems to run.

But now dear reader, here's a little quiz – just one question. In the example of the north/south divide in Europe did you feel I was putting down the Italians, criticizing their lack of punctuality? If that was your impression it shows you were probably raised in a monochronic culture where punctuality, tight scheduling, firm agendas, rigid deadlines and uninterrupted meetings are important virtues.

On the other hand, if you did not think I was criticizing southerners you more likely grew up in a polychronic culture. That is, in a society where people spend less time worshipping the clock and more time attending to strong interpersonal relationships.

In fluid-time cultures business people may be tardy for your meeting because they had to help a friend or family member solve a problem. Or perhaps an earlier meeting ended later than expected. In polychronic cultures it is inexcusably rude to end an ongoing meeting just because you happen to have another one scheduled.

The Indonesians have a delightful expression for polychronic time. They call it *jam karet* or "rubber time" – flexible, stretchable meeting times, schedules and agendas. Most Indonesians place a higher value on human relationships than on arbitrary schedules and deadlines.

The contrast between polychronic and monochronic cultures is magnified these days by the monumental traffic problems found in many developing countries.

One day last year I spent three and a half hours getting from one side of Bangkok to the other for a meeting. Traffic can be even worse in Cairo. Unless you anticipate that degree of traffic gridlock in certain cities and plan accordingly, even Germans and Swiss visitors might occasionally find themselves a minute or two late for a meeting.

Centuries ago when all societies on Earth were polychronic, a sun dial was accurate enough to keep track of time. Then some sadistic inventor had to go and ruin a good thing, developing that cruel torture instrument we know as the clock. Now when the bloody alarm goes off at 6 am, monochronic people wonder whether worshipping the clock is such a great idea after all.

Polychronic Culture Shock

Consider the case of a fluid-time person undergoing her first collision with a monochronic culture. Not long ago a Malaysian business woman flew to the USA for an important conference scheduled for 10 am on a Monday. She arrived in Boston late that Sunday evening, had trouble falling asleep because of jet lag and overslept a little the next morning.

On Monday the Malay lady had difficulty finding the meeting location in her rental car, got lost and finally arrived well after lunch – four hours late for her meeting. The Americans she was supposed to meet came out of the conference room to tell her, "Oh sorry, right now we're in the middle of our afternoon meeting. And our calendar seems to be kind of full this week... Well let's see, can you make it for Wednesday of next week?" But since she had to be back in Kuala Lumpur by that date our Malay lady never was able to reschedule that important meeting.

Not long after her return to Malaysia this charming polychronic woman attended one of our Global Negotiator seminars in Southeast Asia. During the lunch break she related that sad story as an example of how rude and schedule-obsessed Americans can be. "So there I was in Boston, having flown half-way around the world just for that meeting. And those people did not even have the common decency to rearrange their schedule for a foreign visitor who was a little late. Can you believe it?"

As we have learned, the meaning of "a little late" differs according to whether you are in a monochronic or polychronic culture.

Monochronic Culture Shock

Monochronic people are equally prone to culture shock when doing business in polychronic markets. I often hear northern Europeans and North Americans complain about the "rude behavior" of business contacts in the Middle East, Latin America as well as South and Southeast Asia. "They always keep me waiting and then continually interrupt the meeting to take phone calls and receive unscheduled visitors."

Many rigid-time visitors are convinced that their counterparts in Rio de Janeiro, Bangkok or Casablanca deliberately keep them waiting as a negotiating power play. Why do you suppose monochronic travelers think that way? Because in London, Stockholm or Amsterdam, if the person you are to meet keeps you cooling your heels without a damn good reason, it probably *is* a power play. All of us tend to interpret the behavior of foreigners in terms of our home culture.

The next incident concerns a young U.S. expatriate manager who has just taken up his first assignment outside North America and Europe. This case illustrates what happens when a monochronic manager encounters strongly polychronic business behavior for the first time.

Case 6.1: Waiting in New Delhi.

Richard was a 30 year-old American sent by his Chicago-based company to set up a buying office in India. The new office's main mission was to source large quantities of consumer goods in India: Cotton piecegoods, garments, accessories and shoes as well as industrial products such as tent fabrics and cast iron components.

India's Ministry of Foreign Trade had invited Richard's company to open this buying office because they knew it would promote exports, bring in badly-needed foreign exchange and provide manufacturing knowhow to Indian factories.

Richard's was in fact the first international sourcing office to be located anywhere in South Asia. The MFT wanted it to succeed so that other Western and Japanese companies could be persuaded to establish similar procurement offices.

The expatriate manager decided to set up the office in the capital, New Delhi, because he knew he would have to meet frequently with senior government officials. Since the Indian government closely regulated all trade and industry, Richard often found it necessary to help his suppliers obtain import licenses for the semi-manufactures and components they required to produce the finished goods his company had ordered.

Richard found these government meetings frustrating. Even though he always phoned to make firm appointments, the bureaucrats usually kept him waiting for half an hour or more. Not only that, his meetings would be continuously interrupted by phone calls and unannounced visitors as well as by clerks bringing in stacks of letters and documents to be signed. Because of all the waiting and the constant interruptions, it regularly took him half a day or more to accomplish something that could have been done back home in 20 minutes.

Three months into this assignment Richard began to think about requesting a transfer to a more congenial part of the world – "somewhere where things work." He just could not understand why the Indian officials were being so rude. Why did they keep him waiting? Why didn't the bureaucrats hold their incoming calls and sign those papers after the meeting so as to avoid the constant interruptions?

After all, the government of India had actually invited his company to open this buying office. So didn't he have the right to expect reasonably courteous treatment from the officials in the various ministries and agencies he had to deal with?

Three decades as a monochronic person doing business in polychronic markets has taught me how to avoid some of the frustration. Here are three practical tips for rigid-time business travelers:

– Find out in advance which of the markets you are going to visit are in fluid-time cultures. Forewarned is fore-armed.
– Come armed with a well-filled briefcase. Instead of wasting time in the reception area twiddling your thumbs, compulsively looking at your

watch and muttering curses, catch up on all that paperwork you never seem to have time for.
- Above all, BE PATIENT!

Punctuality

Punctuality may also vary according to the occasion. Take Singapore, where business meetings usually start within five or ten minutes of the scheduled time. In contrast, wedding dinners are guaranteed to begin at least two hours after the time given on the invitation – by which time some of the weaker guests have fainted from hunger. Many of my Lion City friends fortify themselves with an early dinner at home as a precautionary measure.

Or take Sao Paulo. I got used to business conferences starting 20 or 30 minutes late there, so when I received a dinner invitation for eight I decided to arrive about 8:30. But that proved to be quite a shock for the hostess: She was just getting out of the shower when I rang the doorbell. That's how I learned that an 8 pm dinner invitation in Brazil means you are supposed to arrive no earlier than nine and preferably closer to ten.

Not so with the Norwegians. My wife and I were invited along with several other expat couples to the home of Norwegian friends in Singapore. We all arrived at the house a few minutes before seven and stood around outside chatting with each other until exactly 7 pm, when one of the Scandinavian guests rang the doorbell. The monochronic Norwegians expect you to appear on time for any engagement, whether social or business.

Some rigid-time business people refer to Latin cultures as *mañana* societies. This kind of put-down doesn't seem to bother my Brazilian friends who tell me, "Brazil is the Land of Tomorrow. The only problem is, tomorrow never comes." But for polychronic folks in general the issue is really one of priorities. What's more important, they ask, people or an abstract concept like time?

Agendas: Fixed vs Flexible

Monochronic meetings tend to follow an agreed outline or agenda. At a typical negotiation in Germany, Switzerland or the Netherlands you can expect that to start off with a few minutes of small talk and then proceed in linear fashion from Item 1 to the last item on the agenda with no major digressions.

In France or Italy however the "warmup" chat is likely to last several times as long. And if there is an agenda at all you may start with Item 5, proceed to Item 2 and then wander off in several different directions at once. Polychronic meetings tend to follow their own inner logic rather than a fixed outline. The important thing is that everyone has his or her say.

What's more, in a decade of working with Italians, French, Spanish and Portuguese I found that in the end we usually accomplished what we came to do. The longer warmup time served to get us all on the same wave length. And some of those "senseless digressions" led us to creative solutions which helped us reach agreement.

As a monochronic person living for more than a decade in Latin Europe, Latin America and South Asia, I now find the polychronic way equally congenial. In international business one soon learns that there is usually more than one way to achieve your goal. So choose the approach that best fits the local circumstances.

Schedules and Deadlines

Some strongly polychronic cultures have an aversion to rigid deadlines. Many Arab businessmen for example believe it is impious and irreligious to try to see into the future. God, not man is in charge of what will happen. The Arabic term *Insh'allah* – "God willing" – expresses that belief.

With counterparts from polychronic cultures it can be a mistake to set rigid deadlines and try to enforce them. Instead I recommend the following approach:

- If you need something delivered or some action taken by say March 1, get your polychronic counterpart to agree on February 1 or even January 15.
- During the whole time leading up to the deadline stay in frequent touch with your counterpart. Face-to-face contact is the best way to expedite matters.

In other words, put a comfortable margin in your scheduling and then maintain a close relationship with your counterparts.

Let's remember that while it is rude to be tardy in a monochronic culture, it is equally rude to patronize polychronic cultures who refuse to bow down in worship of Chronus, the god of time.

Let's now consider another important division between business cultures.

7. Nonverbal Business Behavior
Expressive vs Reserved Cultures

In Chapter Three we looked at the verbal communication problems faced by people doing business across cultures. In this chapter we consider the difficulties problems caused by differences in nonverbal communication.

People of other cultures misunderstand our body language just as they may misinterpret the words we speak or write. Fortunately however, we can learn the highlights of another culture's nonverbal language much quicker than we can its verbal language. There are three types of interpersonal communication:

- *Verbal* communication has to do with words and the meaning of words.
- *Paraverbal* language refers to how loudly we speak those words, the meaning of silence and the significance of conversational overlap.
- With *Nonverbal* communication (also called body language) we communicate without using any words at all.

Expressive vs Reserved Cultures

Varying degrees of expressiveness in paraverbal and nonverbal behavior cause unexpected problems for international managers and negotiators. Let us look at a relevant incident.

In 1989 and 1990 I made numerous trips from Singapore to Thailand in connection with setting up a Bangkok office for the U.S. company I was working for. As regional director for South and Southeast Asia, one of my responsibilities was to help our local manager recruit Thai staff.

With the help of a Thai human resource consultant we placed recruitment ads in Bangkok newspapers, screened the applicants and selected about 10 young Thais for employment interviews. While the interviews with the men went smoothly enough, the female candidates were not responding well at all. That was a serious problem because qualified English-speaking office workers and management trainees are not easy to find in Bangkok. And now my interviewing approach seemed to be turning off a number of promising candidates.

I asked our human resources consultant what the problem was. She thought for a moment and then began talking around the issue politely, obviously trying hard to spare my feelings. (Remember, Thais tend to be relationship-focused, high-context, hierarchical people. She did not want to offend a *farang* client – especially not a white-haired one.)

Finally though our advisor managed to gently convey the message that I was talking too loud, using too much facial expression and too many hand gestures. She explained that the soft-spoken Thai women tend to interpret a loud voice as a sign of anger and my animated facial expressions and gestures warned the women that I might not be quite right in the head.

So here was an angry, insane "farang" trying to interview potential employees. Small wonder those Thai women were not particularly interested!

This was a problem of undue expressiveness. During the eight years I lived in Italy as a manager responsible for southern Europe and the Mediterranean region I had gradually become more expressive in order to be understood there. But now in Thailand, a very restrained culture, the exuberant Latin communication style was causing a problem.

So for the rest of the interviews that week I tried hard to modulate my

Fig. 7.1

VERY EXPRESSIVE CULTURES
The Mediterranean Region
Latin Europe
Latin America
VARIABLY EXPRESSIVE
USA and Canada
Australia and New Zealand
Eastern Europe
South Asia, Africa
RESERVED CULTURES
East and Southeast Asia
Nordic and Germanic Europe

voice, maintain an expressionless face – except for a smile of course – and keep both hands folded in front of me. It worked, and we were able to hire several bright young Thai men and women who were a credit to the company.

Figure 7.1 reveals which markets are expressive and which are reticent. Note that Latin Europe and the Mediterranean area are among the world's most expressive cultures while Thailand is the opposite – one of the most reserved. So the culture clash related above is understandable. But as we will see in the next case, problems can arise even when cultures involved are somewhat closer together.

Case 7.1: Baffled in Bangkok

Jane Reynolds was the executive director of an important trade association in Singapore. An outgoing, enthusiastic American who was successful in gaining the cooperation of the association's members, she had lived in Singapore for over ten years and got along with people there very well.

Jane was pleased when she was asked to chair the annual meeting of a Thai women's organization in Bangkok. Although Mrs. Reynolds was an experienced speaker and discussion leader, this was the first time for her to chair a conference in Thailand. When Jane asked friends and colleagues for advice, they warned her that Thai women tended to be somewhat shy in public. They would probably be hesitant to offer their views and opinions in front of a large group.

So Jane was delighted when during the morning session first one and then two other Thai participants quietly offered useful comments and suggestions. She showed her delight in characteristic fashion: Getting up from the table with eyebrows raised and arms waving, Mrs. Reynolds exuberantly thanked the three women and praised them for their contributions, making sure to speak loudly enough that all the attendees would be able to hear.

The meeting then continued, but for some reason there was no more input from the floor. In fact the Thai women stopped responding to the chairperson's questions as well, remaining silent for the remainder of the conference.

After the meeting two of the Thai members who had spoken up approached Jane and tearfully asked, "Why were you so angry with us this morning? We don't know what we did to upset you so." Jane hastily replied that she wasn't angry or upset at all, but the two women just mumbled their goodbyes and walked sadly away.

Jane Reynolds returned to her hotel that afternoon completely baffled by the reaction of the Thai participants. She wondered why things had suddenly gone wrong at the conference after such a promising beginning...

Paraverbal Negotiating Behavior:
Vocal Volume and Inflection

Reserved, soft-spoken business people also run into problems when negotiating with more expressive counterparts. A few years ago in Alexandria, Egypt two American buyers were negotiating a contract with a large public sector manufacturing company.

Raymond was an expressive, somewhat loud-mouthed Yank while Clem was unusually restrained and soft-spoken for an American. Clem led off the discussion of contract terms in a low monotone. After about ten minutes first one, then another and finally all three Egyptian negotiators fell sound asleep at the conference table despite having swallowed toxic-level doses of high-octane Turkish coffee.

Raymond had spent enough time in that area to know that Egyptians tended to be very expressive communicators. They liked to speak loudly enough to be heard clearly, often raised their voices to emphasize important points and were known to literally pound the table when still further emphasis was called for. So after just a few minutes of Clem's low monotone the three executives apparently concluded that this guy had nothing really important to say and proceeded to drift off.

The Americans of course saw this as a problem. A negotiation with one side fast asleep is unlikely to be extremely fruitful. So the buyers called for a short break during which the officials gulped more coffee and Clem decided to leave the meeting for a tour of the city.

When the four men reconvened Raymond continued the discussion in a voice that was loud, clear and spiced with vocal inflection. By the time Clem rejoined the meeting that afternoon the two sides had reached agreement on the major points. It is amazing what negotiators can achieve when they are wide awake and paying attention!

"But wait a minute! Aren't the sellers supposed to adapt to the buyers?" Yes – unless of course that buyer really wants the deal and happens to know how to close the communication gap.

Paraverbal Negotiating Behavior: The Meaning of Silence

Expressive people tend to be uncomfortable with more than a second or two of silence during a conversation. In contrast, people from reserved cultures feel at ease with much longer silences. Japanese negotiators for example often sit without speaking for what seems like an eternity to voluble Mexicans, Greeks or Americans. After three or four seconds the latter feel compelled to say something – anything – to fill the awful silence.

If nature abhors a vacuum, expressive cultures abhor a lull in the conversation.

Unfortunately the loquacity of expressive people tends to irritate the reticent Japanese, who seem to value the space between the spoken words just as much as the words themselves. Negotiators from reserved cultures do not feel the need to engage in constant, stream-of-consciousness blabbing the way many of their expressive counterparts do.

Paraverbal Behavior: Conversational Turntaking vs Conversational Overlap

"Conversational overlap" is a twenty-dollar term for interrupting another speaker. While expressive people regard interruptions as a normal part of conversation, overlap is considered extremely rude by people from reserved societies. For instance, northern European and North American negotiators are often frustrated by the constant interrruptions they experience while conducting meetings in Italy, Spain or the former Yugoslavia.

Scandinavian researchers have studied conversational patterns during business negotiations between restrained Swedes and their more expressive Spanish counterparts. They found that Spanish negotiators interrupt Swedes about five times as often as Swedes interrupt Spaniards. Since Scandinavians find interruptions disruptive and rude, it is easy to see how conflict can arise during meetings with expressive southerners.

Fig. 7.2

EXPRESSIVE NEGOTIATORS: Overlapping each other.
1st Speaker: _____   _____   _____
2nd Speaker: – – – – – – – – –   – – – – – – – –

RESERVED NEGOTIATORS: Taking turns to avoid overlap.
1st Speaker: _____   _____   _____
2nd Speaker: – – – –   – – – – – –

JAPANESE NEGOTIATORS: Intervals of silence between speakers.
1st Speaker: _____   _____   _____
2nd Speaker: – – –   – – –   – – – – –

Figure 7.2 diagrams the differences in conversational behavior across the international bargaining table.

This diagram shows that expressive negotiators typically overlap each other whereas more reticent ones take turns in a sort of verbal table-tennis match. But the super-polite Japanese not only take turns to avoid overlap, they go a step further, often pausing five or ten seconds before taking their conversational turn.

My experience is that problems occur with overlap unless both sides know about this cultural difference. Otherwise Latins and Arabs tend to think the Japanese are at loss for words or indecisive and the Japanese may find their voluble counterparts rude and insulting.

We know that at a sales meeting it is primarily the seller's responsibility to adapt his or her conversational behavior. During joint venture or strategic alliance talks however each side should strive to meet the other half way. The problem is, cross-cultural negotiators can make those adjustments only when they are aware that the potential for a communication conflict does exist.

The Four Key Elements of Nonverbal Negotiating Behavior

Veterans of cross-cultural business meetings find that differences in these four facets of body language are potentially the most disruptive in international negotiating sessions:

– PROXEMICS: Spatial Behavior, Interpersonal Distance.
– HAPTICS: Touch Behavior.
– OCULESICS: Gaze Behavior, Eye Contact.
– KINESICS: Body Movement, Gestures.

Distance Behavior: The "Space Bubble"

Every human being is surrounded by an invisible envelope of air called a "space bubble" which varies in size according to (a) where in the world we grew up and (b) the particular situation.

For example, two anglophone Canadians who have just met at a social event are likely to stand about an arm's length away from each other. But the space bubbles of the same two Canadians making love shrink to zero – they are meeting skin to skin.

No spatial problem exists as long as the people involved share similar-sized comfort zones. The difficulties begin in cross-cultural situations when different-sized space bubbles collide.

Figure 7.3 shows the approximate range of same-gender space-bubble sizes across cultures in a business situation.

Fig. 7.3 Distance Behavior: The Use of Space

CLOSE: 20 to 35 cms (8 to 14 inches)
The Arab World
The Mediterranean Region
Latin Europe
Latin America

DISTANT: 40 to 60 cms (16 to 24 inches)
Most Asians
Northern, Central and Eastern Europeans
North Americans

Space: When Worlds Collide

Some Arab men show their friendliness to other males by moving in so close you soon know what they had for lunch. If you are a large-bubble person you will probably instinctively step back, which of course signals the Arab you don't like him. Not at all a good way to start a productive business relationship!

On the other hand, a small-bubble business visitor meeting his East Asian or northern European counterpart risks being taken for an aggressive, even hostile person intent on intimidation.

The first few weeks in Italy I subconsciously tried to avoid those friendly Latin "space invaders" by keeping a conference table or desk between us. But our gregarious visitors from various parts of Italy and the Mediterranean basin would either walk right around to my side of the desk or lean towards me way across the table. Which made me feel they were constantly "getting in my face" – a revealing American phrase which connotes aggressive, threatening behavior.

However, once I understood why Latins and other Mediterranean peoples like to get so close I felt more comfortable during business meetings there.

Expressive people engage in more physical contact in public than men and women from more reserved cultures. Figure 7.4 classifies cultures by the degree to which touch behavior is accepted.

Fig. 7.4

HIGH CONTACT CULTURES
The Arab World and Mediterranean Region
Latin Europe and Latin America

VARIABLE CONTACT
Eastern Europe
North America
Australia

LOW CONTACT CULTURES
Most of Asia
UK and Northern Europe

How Touching!

Differences in touch behavior are serious enough for problems to arise even between cultures located fairly close together on the chart. For example, the "moderate" Americans do far too much shoulder-patting, elbow-grabbing and back-slapping to please most British people. But on the other hand, Latin Americans often accuse Yanks of being snobbish and stand-offish because they do not engage in enough physical touching.

Similarly, the variation between the British and the French is surprisingly large considering that these two European countries are separated only by a narrow channel of water. Some years ago researchers studied comparative touch behavior in Paris and London cafés by counting the number of times couples touched each other on the hand, arm, shoulder etc. They counted about 100 touches in Paris and...you probably guessed it...exactly zero times in London.

Even though the French are known to be a tactile people compared to the Brits, so large a variation between people of neighboring cultures warns us of what to expect when we venture abroad.

Touching: How?

Touch behavior regarded as proper in one culture may be quite inappropriate in another. Shortly after we relocated to New Delhi I was surprised by an incident which occurred during a trip to Bombay.

After a pleasant morning business meeting my Indian counterpart casually took my hand while we were walking to a restaurant for lunch. Now, at that point I had to make a quick decision. If a man wants to hold hands with me in Chicago, London or Frankfurt, I know exactly what is going on: In those cultures men who hold hands with other men are seing a clear nonverbal message of sexual interest. But here I was in India. Does same-gender hand-holding mean the same thing in South Asia?

For the next few seconds I was in a bit of a sweat. Then I remembered having seen a couple of our male friends in New Delhi holding hands with other men from time to time. I was glad to realize it was nothing more than a gesture of friendship. And even gladder that I had not hastily pulled my hand away – that would have been a very rude move indeed in India.

Touch Behavior: Shaking Hands Across Cultures

Among business people the world over the handshake is the most common form of physical contact. Figure 7.5 lists a few of the variations.
Most Europeans shake hands each time they meet and again when they

Fig. 7.5 The Handshake

Germans	Firm, Brisk and Frequent	*Arabs*	Gentle, Repeated and Lingering
French	Light, Quick and Frequent	*South Asians*	Gentle, Often Lingering
British	Moderate	*Koreans*	Moderately Firm
Latin Americans	Firm and Frequent	*Most Asians*	Very Gentle and Infrequent
North Americans	Firm and Infrequent		

take leave. North Americans shake hands less often than Europeans but more firmly than most Asians.

The Eyes Have It

Perhaps the subtlest form of body language is gaze behavior. We are easily confused when people use either stronger or weaker eye contact than we do. Figure 7.6 displays the variations.

I regularly conduct business with negotiators at both ends of the gaze-behavior spectrum. When meeting with Arabs, Turks and Latin Europeans I try to look them firmly in the eye whenever we are conversing. Very expressive cultures seem to value strong, direct eye contact.

Eye Contact in Expressive Cultures

Living in Florence taught me the importance of appropriate gaze behavior. One day I was walking to the train station accompanied by my friend Paolo. It was a only a ten-minute stroll and I thought we had plenty of time. However, every time Paolo had something to say he would touch me on the shoulder and turn me towards him so that we could look directly into each other's eyes. Since Paolo spoke every few steps, I ended up miss-

Figure 7.6

INTENSE EYE CONTACT
The Arab World and the Mediterranean Region
Latin Europeans and Latin Americans

FIRM
Northern Europe and North America

MODERATE
Korea and Thailand
Most Africans

INDIRECT EYE CONTACT
Most of Asia

---

ing my train. From that day on I mentally doubled my estimated walking time when in the company of a Latin European.

Where I grew up you chat with your companions as you walk side by side, automatically scanning the surface in front of you so as to sidestep the dog droppings. But in the truly expressive societies of this world, that kind of walking and talking would be considered cold and impersonal. Expressive people like to read your eyes and your face as they talk to you. Direct eye contact is a critical element of correct body language.

Italian gaze protocol in an automobile is especially interesting. Our first month in Florence found me on the *autostrada* headed for Milan at 140 kilometers an hour (over 85 mph) with my colleague Giorgio driving. Giorgio was briefing me on the complex negotiation scheduled for that afternoon and wanted to be sure I understood every single detail. So he kept studying my face intently to see if I was getting it while waving his free arm to emphasize the importance of what he was telling me.

I couldn't believe it. Here we were, hurtling around curves and roaring through dimly-lit tunnels at high speed in a car driven one-handed by a guy whose eyes were focused more on the passenger next to him than on the road ahead.

Half way to Milan I broke my long silence to croak, "Okay Giorgio, it's my turn to drive now!" And for the next eight years I did most of the driving – I never was able to get used to that particular facet of Italian gaze behavior.

Eye Contact in the Pacific Rim

Business visitors to East and Southeast Asia should prepare themselves to encounter exactly the opposite style of gaze behavior. There, a direct gaze may be interpreted as a hostile act. For instance, I try not to stare the Japanese in the eye across the conference table.

Many Japanese and other Asians feel uncomfortable with strong eye contact. Singaporean Chinese have asked me, "Why are you looking so fierce?" Intense eye contact makes many Asians think you are trying to intimidate them, to "stare them down." In Malaysia and Singapore – both countries with little violent crime – a man staring at another male is assumed to be provoking a fight. And a woman who makes more than fleeting eye contact with a man is assumed to want sex with him right then and there.

Some visitors think to avoid such problems by donning sunglasses. Unfortunately that solution creates another problem: In Southeast Asia it is rude to have dark glasses on when conversing with someone who isn't wearing sunglasses.

One more aspect of gaze behavior is of interest to globe-trotting negotiators. In the highly expressive, intense-gaze cultures of the Mediterranean region, two men talking to each other will stand directly facing each other. This stance allows plenty of opportunity for eye-reading and face-reading.

By way of contrast, in the more moderate-gaze cultures of the UK and North America two business people usually converse at right angles to each other. Anglo-Saxons feel less need for reading each other's expressions and may feel uncomfortable with too much face-to-face contact.

Nonverbal Negotiating Behavior: Kinesics

Two aspects of kinesics are of special importance for international negotiators: Facial expressions and hand and arm gestures. Expressive people employ plenty of both while their brothers and sisters from the more reserved cultures are famous for "poker faces" and little bodily movement.

Expressive negotiators gesticulate to add emphasis to what they are saying as well as to send nonverbal messages. Those from reserved cultures value restrained nonverbal behavior and discourage open display of emotion.

Expressive Latins seem to wear their hearts on their sleeves. They trust people who show their feelings openly and distrust those who mask their emotions. In contrast, the taciturn Japanese and Germans may regard such displays as childish and immature.

Facial Expression: Raised Eyebrows

Negotiators are likely to encounter raised eyebrows in many parts of the world. But flashing one's eyebrows sends different signals in different cultures.

Fig. 7.7

North Americans	Interest, Surprise
British	Skepticism
Germans	"You are clever!"
Filipinos	"Hello!"
Arabs	"No!"
Chinese	Disagreement

What this list shows is that the same expression can have a different meaning – sometimes even the opposite meaning – in another culture. The same applies to hand and arm gestures.

Ambiguous Gestures

Use of Left Hand. The left hand is considered unclean in Muslim, Hindu and Buddhist cultures. Avoid touching people or handing them objects such as your business card with the left hand. An American expatriate manager in Indonesia, the most populous Muslim country, learned that it was all right to sign documents with his left hand but he had to hand them to people with his right.

A participant in one of our "Negotiating in the Pacific Rim" seminars at the University of Wisconsin's Management Institute asked what to do in Thailand. He had traveled to Bangkok enough to know that the left hand is considered unclean there. But he also knew that to show respect to high-status persons you have to hand them a gift or a business card with both hands.

We explained that Thais and some other Asians have found a neat way
to dodge the horns of the two-hand dilemma. The approved procedure is
to offer the object in your right hand, cupping your right forearm with the
left hand. Thus both arms are involved, showing respect, while only the
(clean) right hand actually touches the object being passed.

Showing the Sole of Your Shoe. The bottom of your shoe or your foot are also
regarded as unclean in the same cultures. Foreign visitors should avoid crossing their legs in such a way that the sole of their shoe is visible to anyone.

Fist in Palm. Giving my first presentation in Southeast Asia, I emphasized
the key point by pounding the palm of my left hand with my right fist.
When several people in the audience gasped or tittered I knew I had com-
mited a *faux pas.* After the talk, two local people kindly told me that bit of
body language is similar to an obscene sexual gesture.

Index Finger: Pointing. Throughout East and Southeast Asia it is rude to
point at anyone with your forefinger. Instead, use your whole hand – flat
with the palm down in Japan, clenched with the thumb on top in most of
the ASEAN countries. You may also jerk your chin in the direction you
wish to indicate. The subtlest way is to simply glance in the direction you
wish to indicate.

Index Finger: Beckoning. During one of my seminars at the Niels Brock
Business College in Copenhagen a professor opened the lecture room
door and signalled to a colleague by crooking her index finger in the familiar Euro-American beckoning motion. Which provided me with a perfect
opportunity to explain that all over Asia, that particular gesture is reserved
for calling dogs and prostitutes. A repeated scooping motion of the right
hand is the polite way to beckon those who happen to be neither canines
nor ladies of the night.

Tapping Your Head. Non-Europeans are constantly amazed that body language can vary so widely within this tiny appendage of the Eurasian land
mass.

A good example is the head tap.

– In France, Italy and Germany if you tap your forehead or temple with
your finger while looking at someone you are saying nonverbally, "Hey,

you are stupid!" Be careful using that sign in Germany, where it is called *Vogelzeigen* and will cost you a DM 150 fine if the *Polizei* catch you doing it.

– In Spain or Great Britain that same gesture is self-referential and means, "I am so clever!"
– In the Netherlands, watch carefully. If a Dutchman taps the right side of his head with the index finger vertical it translates "You are a very smart person." But if he taps his forehead with the finger horizontal he is saying "You are an idiot!"

The "Thumbs Up" Sign. Be careful with this one too. While the raised thumb is slowly becoming a universal sign for "Great!" it isn't quite there yet. In Germany and other parts of Europe for example it signifies the numeral one. But to many Europeans and in the Middle East it is a very rude sexual sign.

The "Peace" Sign. The two-fingered gesture – forefinger and second finger extended with palm facing outwards – meant V for victory during World War II. But if you accidentally reverse your hand and flash the sign with your palm facing inwards, you have really done it. Should that happen you had better be bigger than the person you just insulted, because the peace sign reversed means roughly the same thing as "flipping the bird" – raising your middle finger with the palm in.

The "A-OK" Sign. The thumb-and-forefinger circle is easily the most dangerous and ambiguous of gestures. Of course most of its multiple meanings are harmless enough:

– American astronauts: "Everything OK. All systems go!"
– For the Japanese the circular shape looks like a coin, so it means "Now we are talking about money."
– In the south of France that shape symbolizes the zero, so it indicates quite the opposite – "nothing" or "worthless."

But in the Iberian peninsula, much of Latin America, parts of Europe and Russia, LOOK OUT! In those cultures it is used as a vulgar sexual suggestion – extremely insulting. The risk of giving offense is so great that I have stopped using the A-OK sign entirely for fear of using it in the wrong place.

The Cultural Relativity of Business Behavior

The susceptibility of gestures to misinterpretation reminds us of a universal truth: Behavior which is polite and proper in our culture may be rude and offensive in another. To help international business travelers avoid damaging blunders, our next chapter focuses on global business protocol.

8. Global Business Protocol and Etiquette

This is a good place to review Iron Law #1 of international business, which states that it is the the visitor's responsibility to understand local business customs and practices. That responsibility is twice as great if the visitor is on the sales and marketing side, because Iron Law #2 dictates that the Seller is expected to adapt to the Buyer's customs and practices.

Which brings us to the issue of business protocol, that is, the rules and norms of proper business behavior in a particular culture. International marketers and negotiators who flagrantly violate these rules risk alienating their local counterparts.

It's true that to err is human, but aren't we supposed to aim for zero defects these days? Maybe a reasonable goal would be to commit fewer blunders than any of our competitors. To achieve that goal we have to know a good deal about international business protocol. A good starting point is to learn as much as possible about local sensitivities before visiting a particular market. The following case shows what can happen when we do not.

A Slip of the Tongue

TransOceanic is a worldwide logistics services company involved in freight forwarding and container consolidation, based in the United States. For almost six months they had been working hard to expand their network of local representatives throughout the Middle East. TO's number one regional priority was to conclude a representation agreement with Arabco, one of Saudi Arabia's largest and most established logistics companies.

To achieve this goal, Regional Manager Ted Goodfellow of Trans-Oceanic had been meeting once or twice a month with Arabco. By now the two companies had agreed on all the financial, legal and technical issues. Ted was now back in Riyadh to wrap up the final details and sign the contract. This visit was largely a formality – both sides clearly wanted this agreement.

During the pleasant meeting with the top Arabco executives Goodfellow casually mentioned, "We at TransOceanic are really looking forward to working with you here in the Persian Gulf!" At that there was a moment of shocked silence on the Arabco side of the conference table. Then the three senior executives arose and strode angrily out of the room, breaking off negotiations.

Bewildered, Ted looked at the two junior Saudis who had remained behind. He hated to see six months of hard work going up in smoke. "What happened here?" he asked the young Arabs across the table. "Did I say something wrong?"

After some hesitation one of the Arabco employees explained that in Saudi Arabia, the body of water in question is called the *Arabian* Gulf. By misnaming it Ted had unintentionally implied that the Gulf belonged to Iran – a country which Saudi Arabia at that time considered hostile and threatening.

The bosses of Arabco were now too upset with Ted to listen to an apology from him. "Well, what should we do then to get these talks back on track?" asked Ted. At this the young Arabs shrugged, smiled faintly and ushered the American to the door. On the way back to his hotel Ted Goodfellow focused his mind on finding a way to repair the damaged relationship.

This regrettable incident happened in the early 90's to a friend of mine. We use this and similar cases in our negotiation seminars to demonstrate to sometimes skeptical managers the importance of knowing local sensivities.

Fortunately, these days a wide variety of books, newsletters, magazine articles, workshops, audio cassettes and video tapes is available to help the globe-trotting negotiator. For example, I like to consult Roger Axtell's *Do's and Taboos* books, published by John Wiley & Sons in the USA. They help you prepare for visits to new markets or to refresh your memory on markets you haven't been to for a while.

Those who prefer to learn while driving will benefit from the audio guides produced by International Cultural Enterprises Inc. of Deerfield, Illinois (USA). This company also publishes the *Worldwide Business Practices Report*, a useful monthly newsletter.

Patterns of International Business Protocol

Another way to learn the business protocol and etiquette of unfamiliar cultures is to apply the concept of cultural patterns outlined in the preceding chapters. Because the human brain seems to be programmed to think in patterns, this approach seems to work for the busy executives who attend our Global Management seminars.

As an example, let's recall the rules for making initial contact with a potential customer or partner abroad. When dealing with relationship-focused markets such as Japan, South Korea, China, Saudi Arabia and Brazil, you will recall that protocol demands an indirect approach: We need to be introduced by a credible third party. On the other hand, with deal-focused cultures such as the U.S., Canada and Australia a direct approach may work just as well. International business protocol can be that simple.

Things get more complex however when we start planning for the first meeting with our new contact. We will see that our "patterns of culture " approach explains some but not all protocol behaviors.

Meeting Protocol: Dress Code

Climate and culture both play a role in sartorial behavior. In the tropics and hot desert climes businessmen often wear an open-necked shirt and cotton trousers. But even in those markets it may be safer to wear a suit coat or blazer to the first meeting just in case. For meetings with government officials this formality takes on greater importance.

In most parts of the world business women can choose between a good dress, suit or blazer and skirt. For men a dark suit, conservative tie and dark socks will cover most meetings with high-status individuals. Here are a few culture-specific hints:

– Visits to Latin Europe and Latin America require special attention to the style and quality of both men's and women's apparel and accessories. Paying close attention to *la bella figura* is a key Italian value, for instance.
– In the Middle East your business contacts often judge you partly by the quality and price of your briefcase, watch, pen and jewelry. Wear and carry the best you have.
– Germans feel more comfortable doing business with men whose shoes are brightly polished.

- Throughout Asia it is a good idea to wear slip-on shoes such as high quality loafers because custom requires you to remove your footwear when entering temples, peoples' homes and some offices as well.
- Americans pay special attention to the condition of your teeth, so some Europeans include a visit to their dentist for a cleaning as part of their preparation.
- In Muslim countries female visitors should dress so as to show as little bare skin as possible.
- That is true of India as well. My wife Hopi and I have both had the experience of traveling there with women who against our advice started out wearing sleeveless blouses or tank tops, pleading the extreme heat. These visitors inevitably received so much unwelcome attention that by the second day they donned more seemly attire.
- Hopi's advice is to observe how the Indian women dress to beat the heat. That is, while you needn't necessarily don a sari, do wear only 100 percent cotton during the hot seasons and silks in the cooler seasons.

Meeting Protocol: Punctuality

In Germany, Switzerland, the Netherlands and other rigid-time cultures, it is imperative to be on time for the scheduled meeting. But remember, even in polychronic cultures the *visitor* is expected to be punctual in order to show respect. It is equally important to recall that if our counterparts keep us waiting in a fluid-time culture, they are not being rude. They are just being themselves – polychronic!

Nonverbal Greetings: Handshake, Bow, Salaam, Namaste or Wai?

For men being introduced to female counterparts, one of the few rules of etiquette that is almost universally valid is to wait for the woman to offer her hand. In most deal-focused cultures today business women expect to shake hands with men.

In some RF cultures however women may not want to shake a man's hand. For example in India male travelers should be prepared to exchange the elegant *namaste* gesture (called *namaskar* in the south), pressing the palms of both hands together at about chin level with perhaps a slight dip of the head. With Thai women the similar *wai* gesture is usually appropriate, although a few Bangkok women I do business with feel comfortable shaking hands.

Regarding Japan, we are frequently asked by Europeans, Americans and Singaporeans about bowing. In my experience non-Japanese often look awkward when attempting to bow. I recommend nodding your head respectfully while shaking hands, making sure to maintain gentle eye contact while doing so.

Nonverbal Greetings: Kissing: Hand, Cheek, Lips... Or None of the Above?

Non-European visitors tend to be perplexed by the variety of kissing rituals in the multiculturtal mosaic that is Europe. Here are some guidelines:

– Don't worry about kissing or being kissed the first time you meet.
– At subsequent meetings foreigners are excused from all that promiscuous kissing if they do not wish to participate. This will be a relief to many Asians who feel ill at ease with the strange and embarrassing custom of kissing people you barely know.
– For men who do decide to join in, when kissing a woman's hand or cheek you don't actually touch the skin. Just kiss the air a few millimeters (a small fraction of an inch) from her hand or cheek. For kissing purposes the space bubble shrinks considerably.
– Cheek-kissing: The proper Brits usually kiss just once (on the right cheek), the French twice (left, right) and the passionate Belgians three times: left, right, left.
– Hand-kissing: The reticent Germans seem to do very little cheek-kissing. Like the Italians and Spanish, a German is more likely to kiss her hand.
– In Vienna, though you may still occasionally hear an Austrian gentleman murmur, *"Küß die Hand, gnädige Frau!"* a foreigner need not feel obligated to actually kiss the lady's hand.
– For non-European women: When a man raises your hand to his lips, the appropriate response is to react as though this is about the fifth time it has happened to you today. Just acknowledge the galant gesture with a slight smile.
– Some male visitors to Russia are not quite comfortable with being

kissed on the lips by Russian men while enfolded in a great bear hug. My advice: Have another vodka.

Meeting Protocol: Forms of Address

The more formal the culture the more likely you will confine yourself to using the person's family name plus any applicable title or honorific. This is sometimes a problem for Yanks and Aussies doing business in East Asia.

For example, you really do not need to know the full name of a senior Korean, especially if he is your customer or potential customer. "Manager Kim" or "Chairman Park" shows the appropriate degree of respect in this very hierarchical society. Visitors to Japan who interact with women should remember that the polite prefix *san* can mean "Miss", "Ms" or "Mrs" as well as "Mister."

The Chinese normally have three names of one syllable each, of which the first is the family name. So your counterpart Yi Er Man should be addressed as "Mr. Yi" rather than "Mr. Man."

But be careful. To accommodate foreigners Chinese often reverse the names when they have their business cards printed. Those ever-polite Japanese sometimes do this too. When in doubt, just ask.

Indonesia's largest ethnic group, the Javanese, commonly have only one name. But middle class Javanese may have two and those of the upper class three names. In neighboring Malaysia be conscious of the fact that there is a complex hierarchy of nobility reminiscent of medieval Europe. If your counterpart qualifies as a "Tan Sri" for instance, be sure to use that title both in correspondence and in person.

In Spain and the Hispanic countries of Latin America, look for two family names. The Mexican Pablo García Mendoza for example would be "Señor García" to you. Unless of course he is a university graduate in which case he becomes *Licenciado* ("Licenciada" for a woman) García.

What about the more informal cultures? In the USA the saying goes, "I don't care what you call me just as long as you call me for dinner." Nevertheless, physicians and surgeons are normally addressed as "Dr." on all occasions. Ph.D's on the other hand are usually called "Dr." only when he or she is "on duty."

Of course even in the informal USA there are hierarchies. Whereas at a Silicon Valley startup company everyone may be on a first-name basis, in larger, more traditional corporations executives are often addressed as Mr., Miss, Ms. or Mrs. – at least in the office.

Verbal Greetings

Many cultures employ standard expressions as verbal greetings. For instance Americans often say, "Hi, how are you?" Some Asians and Europeans seem to be confused by this rhetorical question, thinking the Yank is actually asking after their health. In fact it's a meaningless expression calling for the automatic response, "Fine! How are you?" whereupon everyone gets right down to business.

I remember a meeting in Amsterdam at which two friendly, low-context Dutchmen complained that Americans are superficial people because "When you ask how we are, you really don't give a damn, do you?" Some Germans agree with that statement. Unlike Americans, a German is likely to ask "*Wie geht es Ihnen?*" only if you have been ill and she wants to know if you have recovered.

But the fact is, Europeans also employ various meaningless mantras when being introduced to someone for the first time. Germans for example will say "*Sehr angenehm,*" meaning it is a great pleasure to meet you. Now, excuse me. How do they know whether it is going to be such a great pleasure when they don't even know you yet? My German friends blame it on borrowings from the British "Pleased to meet you" or from the French "*Enchanté!*" (literally "I'm enchanted to meet you!")

My favorite verbal greeting is one I heard almost every day for several years in Singapore. The lift operator in our office building on Orchard Road used to ask me, "Have you had your lunch?" whenever I entered the elevator. Passengers in the lift who were new to Southeast Asia often wondered why the old gentleman would ask me that at 7:30 in the morning. The polite answer to this one is of course, "Yes, thank you. Have you had yours?" regardless of the time of day.

Meeting Protocol:
Exchanging Business Cards

Many visitors to the United States are struck by how casually Americans treat that little bit of cardboard. An American is likely to stuff the card in his back pocket, toss it onto the desk, scribble on it or pick even pick his teeth with it at the lunch table.

More formal cultures tend to treat the name card with more respect. I always enjoy observing the ritual of the *meishi* in Japan, for instance. There the "meishi" or business card is exchanged with great ceremony. It is always presented and received with both hands, scanned carefully for four or five seconds, placed respectfully on the conference and then later put reverently into a leather – not plastic! – card wallet.

Business vistors to the Pacific Rim will note that the ceremony of the meishi has spread to most parts of East and Southeast Asia – a very hierarchical part of the global marketplace. There we are expected to treat the name card with the same respect we show the person who gave us the card.

Giving and Receiving Gifts

In contrast to most DF cultures, RF people tend to value exchanging gifts because it is an accepted way to build and cement strong personal relationships. On these questions the wise business traveler relies on local contacts or consults some of the guides mentioned above. The following tips are intended to give the reader an idea as to the complexity of exchanging gifts across cultures.

Business Gifts

WHAT to Give: Watch out for culture-specific taboos. Avoid sharp objects such as knives – in some cultures they symbolize the ending of a relationship. In China avoid clocks and watches, which bring bad luck because the word for clock sounds like another Chinese word which refers to death.

– Good choices are quality writing instruments, branded whisky or cognac (in non-Muslim cultures), picture books about your city, region or country and products your home country is famous for.

– WHEN to give: In Europe, after the agreement is signed. In Japan and most other Asian countries, at the end of the meeting. Note that North America is not a gift-giving culture. Many companies have strict policies concerning gifts, especially for people with purchasing responsibilities.

– HOW to Give: In Japan the wrapping of the gift is at least as important as the gift itself. In Japan and the rest of Asia, present and receive any gift with both hands – except in Thailand where you hand over the present with your right hand supported by your left. In Asia your gift will probably be unwrapped after you leave. In Europe and North and South America it will more likely be opened in front of you.

While the nuances of gift-giving are important, not every blunder is fatal. For example, a few years ago a Chinese delegation came to Copenhagen to sign a contract for a large purchase of railway equipment. On the last evening the Danes presented the each of the senior Chinese with an expensive and tasteful gold desk clock.

The next morning on the way to the airport the junior member of the visiting delegation whispered to his young Danish counterpart, "You know, you really should not give clocks to Chinese people. Clocks remind us of death, bring bad luck." Then as the Dane was groaning inwardly with dismay the Chinese smiled and added: "But that's all right. No one in this group is superstitious."

Hostess Gifts: Europe

Gifts are not always for business contacts of course. Let's say you are invited to dinner at the home of your potential joint venture partner. Should you bring flowers for the hostess? Well, consider just a few of the taboos:

- Red roses are out because they imply that you are romancing the hostess.
- Red carnations are bad unless you know your hosts are good Socialists.
- Mums, calla lilies, white asters and dahlias are no good because they are for funerals.
- Remember to always bring an uneven number – except that bouquets of six and 12 are OK.
- In Germany and some other countries don't forget to unwrap the bouquet before presenting it to the hostess.
- If it is to be fairly large dinner party, remind yourself to have the flowers delivered earlier in the day because your hostess will be too busy attending to guests to find a vase and water for your silly blooms.

So how about a bottle of wine instead? That's also a bit tricky in Europe because your host might get the impression you think his wine cellar is inadequate. If you absolutely must bring wine, select a very fine bottle from a renowned winemaker – preferably one from your home country if you come from a wine country.

"Well then, what IS the best choice for a hostess gift?" Candy or cakes. A box of fine chocolates, for example. Or a tin of the very best biscuits (cookies). And something for the children would also be a good idea.

Meeting Protocol: Refreshments

In Asia and the Middle East, visitors will be offered hot tea or coffee. Savvy travelers wait for their host to take a sip before putting cup to lip. They always accept the offered beverage, a symbol of hospitality, and avoid asking for anything that has not been explicitly offered. To request a Coca-Cola for example could cause your hosts loss of face if it does not happen to be available.

Wining and Dining

Here again the "no-nos" are many and varied, so the smart visitor relies on local advisers or culture-specific guides. Just think about food and drink taboos:

- Observant Muslims do not drink alcohol or eat any pork product. Many avoid shellfish as well. Jews share some of these food taboos.
- Hindus avoid both beef and pork; most are strict vegetarians.
- Buddhists are often strict vegetarians, but many Thai Buddhists enjoy beef as long as someone else has done the slaughtering for them.
- Timid travelers may have trouble with spicy, strong-smelling or unfamiliar foods. For example, some of our friends in Singapore, Malaysia and Thailand love to torment first-time visitors by ordering durian – the "King of Fruits" – for dessert.
- This Southeast Asian fruit has a mild, somewhat custardy flavor but exudes a most unusual fragrance. To put it delicately, it stinks like a stopped-up sink – or worse. I did learn to savor durian in pudding form, but can't eat it raw without holding my nose.

Some food and drink taboos are really serious, such as offering your Musilm guest a pork chop or your Hindu friend a T-bone steak. Other taboos are simply amusing. Italians for example only drink cappucino in the morning, before about 10 am. So I like to go into a coffee bar around 3 pm and order *"Un cappuccio, per favore!"* just to enjoy the startled expression on the *barista's* face. Unless he catches on quickly to my foreign accent, that barista thinks he has just met one very weird Italian indeed!

Amusement aside, knowing the rudiments of local business protocol shows your counterpart that you are a serious and committed potential supplier or partner. And making fewer blunders gives you an edge over your less conscientious competitor.

In the next chapter we examine an especially touchy issue: corruption and bribery.

9. Culture, Corruption and Bribery

This guide to negotiating across cultures would be incomplete without a look at how to do business successfully in difficult markets, where corruption is rife and bribing government officials is accepted practice.

The international bribery issue is repeatedly mentioned by Global Management clients and seminar participants around the world as an issue of concern. They ask, "How can I do business around the world without having to pay bribes?" This chapter is an attempt to answer that question.

Official corruption prompts business people in certain major markets to make under-the-table payments in order to get things done. In some countries these payments are sanctioned by custom even though formally illegal under local law. Regardless of how bribes are regarded locally, however, most of the business executives who attend our negotiating seminars want to know how to avoid them.

The Downside of Bribing Officials

Today the U.S. government is the only one in the world which legislates heavy penalties – fines and prison sentences – for any of its citizens caught bribing overseas officials. In contrast, many European countries not only condone such payments, they permit their companies to claim foreign bribes as a tax deduction.

Nevertheless, business people of any nationality have good reasons for avoiding the bribery trap:

- *Ethics.* This is a cultural variable. Some societies regard bribery as an unethical practice which corrupts both the giver and the recipient of the bribe.
- *Corporate Ethics.* The regulations of many companies prohibit bribery.
- *Expense.* Illegal payments can become a major business expense. Hong Kong companies report that bribes account for about five percent of the cost of doing business in China. In Russia the cost is said to range up to 30 percent, in Indonesia perhaps still higher.

– *Local Law.* Even countries where official corruption is widespread have laws on the books prohibiting the bribing of their government employees. While such laws may be only sporadically enforced, the foreigner unlucky enough to get caught is likely to face a capricious legal system as well as unpleasant prison conditions.

Now let's look at why official corruption and bribery are greater problems in some countries than in others.

Reputable organizations study the bribery issue. One of them is Transparency International, a Berlin-based group. TI publishes an annual Corruption Index of over 50 countries based on surveys of international business travelers.

Similarly, Hong Kong-based Political and Economic Consultancy (PERC) has surveyed expatriate managers to come up with a corruption rating for 11 Asian countries.

Poverty and Corruption

The lists compiled by TI, PERC and other organizations show that poverty is a common trait of "corrupt" countries. For example, TI lists Nigeria, Pakistan, Kenya, Bangladesh and China among the most corrupt countries. All of these are low-income developing economies with per capita GNP of less than $600 a year. India and Indonesia also belong to the "Top Ten."

By way of contrast, TI's five least corrupt countries are among the world's richest: New Zealand, Denmark, Sweden, Finland and Canada.

PERC's Asian survey results point to the same conclusion: the poorer countries such as India, China and Indonesia rank highest in official corruption while the richer economies – Japan, Hong Kong and Singapore – are the least corrupt.

The poverty-corruption link seems to stem from the fact that in low-income countries government officials are poorly paid. Low salaries tempt some (not all) government employees to supplement their income with "dash" or *la mordida*. Apparently, need tends to breed greed.

Bureaucratic Red Tape Breeds Corruption

Besides being poor, economies perceived as relatively corrupt also tend to be over-regulated – tangled in red tape. Commercial regulations are typically written in such a way as to give bureaucrats discretionary authority to arbitrarily decide an issue for or against a company. This authority provides venal officials with powerful leverage for extracting bribes.

Low government salaries combined with bureaucratic red tape probably account for most illegal payments demanded by officials in so-called corrupt markets.

Unfortunately however, this means little to executives trying to conduct honest business in poor, over-regulated economies. While international trade plus deregulation will eventually bring wealth to developing countries, negotiators want to know what to do NOW – before "corrupt" countries manage to move up the income ladder.

Our experience reveals five rules for avoiding bribes even in markets where illegal payments are commonplace.

Rule #1 is the simplest: Never assume you have to give a bribe, even in supposedly highly corrupt societies. Look for another way. He who expects to pay a bribe will end up doing exactly that.

Rule #2 is also simple: "Just say no." Tell the bribee your corporate policy forbids such payments. Of course, this ploy seems to work best for companies with sought-after products or a very big pencil. In other words, those with clout.

Just Say No

For example, during the 1960s and 1970s IBM had little trouble introducing its products anywhere. Foreign markets were anxious to have state-of the-art IBM equipment and knowhow.

Case 9.1 is another example.

Case 9.1: Using Your Clout.

The giant U.S. discount retailer Wal-Mart is also in a position to say no. According to apparel industry sources in Jakarta, when company founder Sam Walton visited Jakarta in the mid-1980s top officials Indonesian officials asked him why Wal-Mart was not sourcing any garments or other products in his country. The legendary "Mr. Sam" replied that he refused to buy goods in any market where it was necessary to bribe officials for the privilege of doing business.

Sam Walton was referring to the fact that Indonesian customs officials routinely demanded large bribes for clearing imports of materials and components which local manufacturers needed in order to produce finished goods for export. The government reacted swiftly. Within weeks the responsibility for determining the value of imports was removed from Customs and given to SGS, a private Swiss firm renowned for its probity.

The reorganization worked. By 1986 Sears Roebuck and other big retailers were able to source shoes, apparel and other consumer goods without the added cost and delays of official corruption.

Offer Legal Travel Perks and Favors

Rule #3: When a government employee asks for or hints about a bribe, look hard for legal and ethical way to meet his or her needs instead. Foreign negotiators often follow this rule in today's China, for example. Here are three practical ways:

- Offer an expense-paid visit to your plant, to a training course in your home country or to attend a business-related meeting, course or conference in a third country. All travel expenses are paid and often a daily cash allowance is added to the package. Such perks are well received in countries where shortage of foreign exchange makes overseas travel a rare privilege. At the same time, a legitimate business purpose is served.
- Make an appropriate donation. According to the business press, an American multinational found that a high official was blocking a proposed telecommunications deal in Southeast Asia. After the U.S. firm donated funds to build an ultra-modern hospital in the official's home district, that deal was immediately approved.
- Do a personal favor, something you would do for a friend or relative. For instance, help the official get his son, daughter, nephew or niece into a university in your homeland or in a third country.

Be Creative

Rule #4: Look for creative ways to accomplish your goals without giving in to graft. The next case illustrates this point.

Case 9.2: Using Your Head.

A foreign company headquartered in Singapore had to send technicians to Indonesian factories on a regular basis. About half of the company's techs had to slip a fifty dollar bill to the Jakarta airport immigration official on duty in order to get an entry visa stamped in their passports. It was always the same techs who were asked for the bribe.

Trying to figure out why only some of his travelers had to pay, the managing director one day examined his employees' travel documents. In the passports of the techs who were paying the bribes he soon noticed tiny pencil tickmarks in the lower right-hand corner of their visa stamps. But the visa stamps of those who weren't paying showed no such marks.

Discussing the matter with his technicians the boss soon figured out that immigration officials were routinely demanding 50 dollars from travelers new to Indonesia. They then marked the visa stamps of those who complied to show fellow officials that "this guy pays." On the other hand, if you refused they just shrugged and stamped your passport anyway, because of course no such payment is required.

That day the director erased all the pencil marks from his techs' passports and briefed them on the scam. Since then his company's travelers have paid no more bribes to immigration officials.

Rule #5 is the last one: Learn the culture of the country. Culture gives us invaluable clues to evading the bribery trap.

Culture and Corruption

Studies show that societies in which illegal payments are common happen to share a number of cultural values. Three of these values are of particular interest to us here:

- They are relationship-focused; personal connections are crucial.
- They are strongly hierarchical, valuing wide status differences.
- They are polychronic, with a relaxed attitude toward time and scheduling.

In the rest of this chapter we will discuss how these three characteristics provide clues to help business visitors avoid the bribery trap.

But first a word of caution. Obviously, these three common cultural values *per se* have nothing to do with official corruption. Cultures which are relationship-focused, hierarchical and polychronic need not be corrupt. The point here is that the societies identified by international business people as the most corrupt happen to share these particular cultural traits.

Anthropologists and sociologists may find such cultural correlations interesting. But for business people what counts is that these shared values suggest effective ways to avoid making illegal payments.

Relationship-Focused Cultures: The Importance of Contacts

While contacts are useful to business people everywhere, in RF cultures personal connections are absolutely essential. You have to know the right people – it really is "who you know" that counts.

Guanxi, meaning relationships or connections, is not the only word used to express this concept. The Egyptians have a similar expression, *wastah* – an intermediary or personal contact. The Russian word *blat* carries many of the same connotations.

While the term varies from country to country, the concept is the same: In RF cultures you need good contacts to do business. That's because RF-culture people tend to be uncomfortable dealing with strangers. Strangers are outsiders – not to be trusted. So to do business or solve a problem in these countries a foreigner simply must have the right connections.

The RF value leads unwary business visitors into the bribery trap. For example, on their first visit to a relationship-focused market foreigners often lack the right local contacts. They may think that spreading "baksheesh" around is the best way to expedite the lengthy process of developing good relationships.

After all, they may say, the exchange of gifts and favors is part and parcel of building guanxi. And expensive gifts are a form of bribery. However, the good news is that even in corrupt cultures it is possible to develop relationships without giving in to bribery.

Case 9.3: Using Your Contacts.

An expatriate manager in New Delhi got a rude shock one morning when he opened a letter from the municipal authorities. The letter informed Richard that under new city zoning regulations he had exactly 30 days to vacate the building in which his office was located. If he did not move out on time he would be jailed.

Richard quickly phoned several Indian friends and business acquaintances who confirmed that the officials were serious. For example, the manager of the Central Bank of India branch nearby had just been arrested for not relocating the branch in time.

Since the zoning change affected a large number of businesses in New Delhi, hundreds of people were racing around desperately looking for new locations, which were in short supply. Richard knew he needed to obtain an extension giving him more time to find office space, and the only official authorized to grant extensions was the director of the Delhi Housing Authority.

Next morning the anxious expat arrived at the DHA building at 6 am. When he finally pushed his way into the director's inner sanctum, Richard observed the harried bureaucrat brusquely rejecting one application for extension after another. But when the director saw Richard his face lit up. "Ah, how nice to see you again! That dinner party last month was truly delightful. My regards to your wife. Now, what can I do for you?" Five minutes later a much relieved expat manager left the DHA with a 90-day extension.

Analysis: In a RF culture, when you have developed a pleasant social relationship with someone that person will try his or her best to help you in time of need. This relationship may enable you to get the job done without bribery.

Case 9.4: Building Relationships.

A international sourcing team working for a U.S. department store group was in Cairo trying to bring a local flannel shirt manufacturer up to speed. As they were leaving their hotel for the airport, a senior Egyptian government official they knew rushed up out of breath to ask a favor.

He explained that the wife of Egypt's president was the sponsor of a charitable enterprise, a garment factory set up to provide jobs for orphan girls. The first lady wanted to know what it would take to upgrade the factory to international quality standards.

The two apparel specialists, an American and an Italian, hesitated at first because they had an important meeting the next day in Florence. In the end however they agreed and undertook a thorough evaluation of the factory. They followed up with a report recommending ways to improve quality and arranged for a production engineer from their company to make a more detailed analysis a month later.

While this special effort caused the team to miss their meeting in Italy, it paid off handsomely in terms of improved government relations. From that day forward the U.S. retailer enjoyed excellent government support for its business activities in Egypt.

Analysis: By doing a small, quite legal favor, the Italo-American team established relationships which smoothed the road for others from their company to do business successfully in Egypt.

Case 9.5: Building Relationships II.

When Richard's New Delhi office was upgraded to a regional office for South Asia, he had to begin making frequent trips abroad. This became a major hassle because as a foreign resident he was required to obtain two separate clearances each time he wanted to leave the country.

Richard's lawyer was able to obtain the tax clearance, but for the police clearance he had to apply at the Foreigners' Regional Registration Office in person. These visits normally took the better part of a day.

That all changed however when Richard was introduced to the chief of the FRRO at a New Delhi cocktail party. It turned out the two men shared an interest in Indian military history. After an hour or so of pleasant conversation Colonel Singh said goodbye, adding "Now don't forget. Any time you need a clearance just have the desk sergeant bring you straight to my office."

For the remainder of his stay in India Richard was able to have his paperwork taken care of in an hour or so while enjoying a fascinating conversation. In RF cultures it's who you know that counts. The right personal contacts save you time, money and frustration.

Polychronic Cultures: The Meaning of Time

Another value which happens to be characteristic of "corrupt" societies is a relaxed approach to punctuality, schedules and deadlines. Frustrated by inexplicable delays, executives from clock-worshiping monochronic cultures are often willing to make under-the-table payments in order to expedite a government decision.

In this connection it's a good idea to remember that the English word "tip" is probably derived from the phrase "To Insure Promptness."

Case 9.6: "Hands Up! Your Money or Your Time."

A multinational firm we'll call WMN, with a regional head office in Singapore, decided to open representative offices in Thailand, the Philippines and Indonesia. WMN's regional director in Singapore engaged a reputable international law firm in each country to handle the registration formalities.

While the rep offices in Bangkok and Manila were up and running within three months, it took two long years for the Jakarta operation to be approved and registered. In contrast XYZ, a major competitor of WMN, was able to set up its Jakarta office within just 90 days.

Analysis: WMN's post mortem revealed that the law firms they used both in Thailand and the Philippines enjoyed long-standing close relationships with the responsible government officials. In contrast, the law firm WMN retained in Indonesia turned out to lack these valuable connections.

Shortly after WMN's Jakarta office was finally registered, the Singapore regional director met an executive from XYZ company at a social function there. The latter readily admitted to having expedited the office registration process by handing out large "facilitation payments."

Lesson A: Except in Singapore, bureaucrats in Southeast Asia tend to move rather slowly. To speed things up you often have to either know the right people or bribe the right people.

Afterword: XYZ company closed its Jakarta office less than three years after it opened because its "operating expenses" had become too high. Certain government officials kept coming back to the well for more. In contrast, WMN's Jakarta office is still there.

Lesson B: While an illegal payment may promise you a shortcut, it often leads to a dead-end. The bribe that buys you time today may cost you dearly tomorrow.

Case 9.6 mentions Singapore as a market where government works. The Lion City is a living example of the fact that effective government removes a major cause of bribery.

Hierarchical Cultures: Status, Power and Respect

The third relevant value of "corrupt" countries is the existence of steep organizational hierarchies with wide status differences. In hierarchical societies, lower-ranking officials are often reluctant to make decisions, preferring to pass the buck to their superiors.

Business visitors aware of this trait know the importance of negotiating with the highest-ranking official they can reach. Unfortunately, once they are in touch with the high-level official some foreigners assume they still have to pay a bribe in order to get a favorable decision.

Case 9.7: To Solve Your Problem, Go to the Top of the Hierarchy.

A young Western manager responsible for the Middle East was guiding a delegation of three businessmen on their first visit to pre-revolutionary Iran. When he stepped up to the check-in counter at Isfahan Airport the clerk smiled and said cheerfully, "Sorry sir, the flight to Kerman is fully booked. No seats available today. Next flight in three days."

"But we booked this flight weeks ago! And our reservations were reconfirmed just last week. See, it's marked here on the tickets..." The clerk shrugged and looked at the foreigner expectantly.

Experience told the visitor that fifty dollars was the going rate to make the four seats suddenly available, but he had no intention of playing the game. "Well then, I guess I'll just have to talk to General Manager Zahid."

At this the clerk's smile suddenly vanished. "Oh, that will not be necessary. You're in luck: I have just found four seats for you."

Analysis: A huge plaque in the departure hall advertised the name of the boss of the airport in letters so large a visitor could hardly avoid noting the man's name. However, the clerk became cooperative because he thought the traveler might know his boss personally. In Iran subordinates often live in fear of their superior's disapproval.

After word: As expected, the plane to Kerman was in fact empty except for the four foreigners.

Of course, getting to the top of the hierarchy is not always so easy. But remember Rule #4? While using your brain is always a good idea, sometimes a bit of brawn comes in handy as well.

Case 9.8: When It Is Not Easy to Get to the Boss.

The week Richard arrived in New Delhi to begin his expatriate assignment he found out that the waiting time for a telephone was a little over three years. Since it would be impossible to run his business without a phone, Richard made inquiries. Old Delhi Hands told him that $5000 under the table would get him a phone within a month.

Richard's employer had strict rules against bribery, so he wrote a letter to the director general of the local telephone company explaining in detail why he needed the phone. Then he made an appointment for a meeting.

Arriving at the telephone company for the meeting, Richard at first thought there was a riot in progress. He saw a mob of about 500 people screaming, waving pieces of paper and trying to push past uniformed guards to enter the building.

The expat's assistant enlightened him: "Oh, it's like this every day here. These people have been waiting years for a telephone and want to see the director general to plead their case. As I told you, you will have a very difficult time getting to see him."

Since he had a confirmed appointment Richard decided to fight his way through the crowd. It took half an hour to bull his way into the director-general's office and stand in front of his desk. The big boss stood up wearily and shook Richard's hand. "Well, I can see you really want that telephone you wrote me about. Sorry about your ear – my secretary will apply some iodine. You can be sure you will have a phone in your Jor Bagh office this week."

Analysis: Telephone instruments and connections are in short supply in developing countries around the world. Those who cannot or will not pay a bribe try to get to someone who can help them. Richard had a very strong case for needing the phone, but he got it because he stood out from the crowd of other deserving supplicants.

First, he was the only foreigner in the mob   other expatriates sent their subordinates to try and fight their way through. Equally important however, Richard's shirt was in shreds, his shirt was torn and his left ear bleeding. While his willingness to endure abuse showed he really wanted that telephone, more importantly it demonstrated respect for the director general's position.

After word: As promised, the phone was installed 48 hours later.

After word II: However, the next week Richard found out he had another problem: It would take over 18 months to get a telex – also an absolute must for his office. When he phoned the director general about the telex, the latter listened for a moment and then interrupted Richard's plea with a chuckle: "Don't worry, you won't have to spoil another shirt coming to see me. I will see to it that you have your telex installed within three days."

In Case 9.8, getting to the boss obviously did pay off. However, there are times when even going to the boss is not enough to get the job done – you may have to go to the boss's boss.

Case 9.9: Going All the Way to the Top.

Though the Ministry of Foreign Trade had invited Richard's company to open a office in India, other government agencies such as the Ministry of Finance were obstructing his efforts. One day in September while the expat was trying to figure out how to gain the cooperation of these officials, a call came in from the office of Prime Minister Indira Gandhi.

The PM's social secretary phoned to say that Mrs.Gandhi wanted to buy Christmas presents for her grand kids, the children of her son Rajiv and his Italian wife Sonia. "Since you represent Sears Roebuck in India, can you get us a Wish Book quickly?"

After thinking a moment Richard replied, "Yes of course. It will be our pleasure. But you will understand that we wish to present it to the Prime Minister in person." Later that day an official invitation to the PM's office was delivered by messenger.

Richard found Mrs. Gandhi in a conference with several of her key ministers. The PM glanced meaningfully at the officials gathered in the room, including the Minister of Finance, and asked the Sears manager: "I trust you are getting good cooperation from the various ministries?"

"Yes Prime Minister, your government's support is excellent" was Richard's reply. And as if by magic, from that day forward government officials in fact became very supportive indeed.

Analysis: The Ministry of Foreign Trade wanted Richard's company to succeed. The expat had notified MFT officials of his forthcoming meeting, and these people in turn had briefed the PM on the importance of Sears Roebuck's efforts in India. Mrs Gandhi obviously scheduled the meeting so that her ministers would be on hand to get the message.

Richard's diplomatic reply allowed the obstructionists to save face. For the next few years Sears found it much easier to do business in India, where government plays a very large role in the economy.

"But in a REAL Crisis
You Would Still Make a Payoff, Right?"

We get that question from time to time at our seminars and on consulting assignments. While international executives tend to agree that bribes are avoidable in many situations, what happens when it really comes to the crunch? What about a life-threatening crisis, for example?

Case 9.10: Life and Death in Delhi.

Like many other developing countries, India tried to conserve hard currency by promoting local production of expensive pharmaceuticals. New Delhi did this by licensing a domestic producer to develop a certain drug while banning all imports to guarantee the licensee a monopoly.

This import-substitution policy almost killed Richard's son years ago. When four-year old Lester took a bad fall in Delhi, his parents took him to the local hospital with a fractured skull and massive brain concussion. Doctors told Richard and Hopi the little boy was dying of severe brain damage.

A few hours later the doctors reported there was still a faint hope, but Lester would need several specific medications within the next 48 hours. The pharmacy however had bad news for the distraught parents. Three of the required drugs were unavailable because imports had been banned for the last two years, even though the domestic licensees were still not yet in production.

Since Lester had to be kept totally immobile he could not be evacuated. Hopi and Richard were stymied: They could neither get the life-saving drugs into the country nor get their dying son out of it.

Luckily however a desperate phone call and telex to friends in Europe put the three drugs on the next Lufthansa flight to Delhi. When the German captain landed at Palam Airport at 6 am he phoned Richard to report, "Yes, I do have the drugs with me. But Customs won't let me bring them in. Better bring a thick wallet with you – you know what I mean."

Hopi stood vigil at Lester's bedside while Richard left for the airport armed with two thick wallets, one stuffed with rupees and the other with dollars. But when the Chief of Airport Customs insisted it was impossible to bring banned medicines into the country, the expat didn't reach for either of those wallets. Instead Richard blurted out, "But Sir! While you and I are standing here arguing, my son is dying in the hospital."

At this news the Chief looked stricken. "What? Your SON? Why didn't you tell me it was your son? Well, never mind now – just follow me!"

With tears in his eyes the Chief personally stamped the sheaf of documents "APPROVED" and showed Richard where to pay the 200 percent import duty. (That's where all those rupees came in handy – no checks or credit cards accepted.) He then personally escorted Richard all the way to the parking lot to make sure he got past airport security without delay.

Twenty minutes later Richard arrived at the hospital with the medications, just under the wire.

Analysis: Some strongly hierarchical cultures tend to value sons over daughters. This is the case for example in India, where poor families give up many daughters for adoption, but few sons.

Afterword: A hard-headed young man, Lester defied the dismal prognosis by making a total recovery from the concussion. He went on to learn several languages including Chinese, earned his BA from the University of Wisconsin, his MA from the University of California and is now a successful software consultant.

Afterword II: When Richard and Hopi's daughter Clio heard this story a few years ago, she asked, "Dad, if it had been me instead of Les, what would you have told that Customs officer?"

Richard didn't need to stop and think. He replied, "Clio, I would have told him exactly the same thing. I would have said, "But Sir! My son is dying in the hospital!""

In this chapter we cited a number of examples from the real world of global business to illustrate the Five Rules for accomplishing your international business goals without paying bribes. We warmly welcome input from readers who would like to share their own experiences with a view to helping others avoid the bribery trap.

10. Marketing Across Cultures

Customer Focus in the Global Marketplace

So far we have dealt with the cross-cultural challenges faced by business people engaged in face-to-face selling, buying and negotiating in the global marketplace. In this concluding chapter of Part One we look at how cultural differences affect the people responsible for designing the products and planning the international marketing campaigns.

Industrial products are less impacted by culture than consumer goods. True, the people giving the sales presentations and negotiating the contract details have to be concerned with cultural variation regardless of product type. But whereas industrial goods normally require little or no product adaptation, that is not the case with consumer goods.

Consumer Goods: Food and Beverages

Let's start with food and drink. As an example, Americans have been eating what they call "sweet corn" since pioneer days, lightly boiled and brushed with butter and salt. But when U.S. producer Green Giant tried to market canned corn in Europe during the 1960s they failed utterly, finally having to close down the factory they had built in Italy.

The problem was simple. When it comes to food and beverages, tradition and taste preferences are key elements in the purchasing decision. And except for northern Italians (who love *polenta*) Europeans regarded "maize" or "Indian corn" as animal fodder, not fit for human consumption. The market was not ready.

My family and I witnessed this cultural difference in the late 1960s when we lived outside of Vienna and raised sweet corn in our garden. It was a great hit with our American friends but we could not even give it away to our Austrian neighbors.

Twenty years later things we found that things had changed. Well-traveled Europeans brought back a taste for exotic foods sampled on holiday around the world. So by the mid-1980s sweet corn could be found all over Europe. In Germany for example it was an essential part of the popular *amerikanischer Salat*. Food preferences may change slowly, but they do change.

Disaster at Euro Disney

Differences between European and U.S. dining habits played a supporting role in bringing the Disney theme park near Paris to the verge of bankruptcy. Disney, one of the world's most successful global marketers, initially refused to adapt its food and beverage service formula to the European customer.

When it opened in 1993, Euro Disney's restaurants offered insufficient seating capacity. Whereas Americans visiting Disneyland and Disney World in the USA eat lunch anytime the spirit moves them, the French and other European visitors wanted lunch at the same time, around 1 pm. Nor did European visitors accept standing in queue for an hour or so.

What made matters worse was that Euro Disney restaurants offered no wine or beer. That was because Disney's U.S. eateries are "family restaurants" where alcoholic beverages are out of place. What did it matter that European traditions and expectations are totally different?

By late 1993 Euro Disney had run up losses approaching one billion dollars – a large sum even for a large company. Disney management responded by putting a European in charge of the operation to make changes. Among the modifications made was an important addition to the menu: Visitors can now quaff beer or sip wine at what is now called Disneyland Paris, which has now moved into the black.

For the folks at Disney, the European fiasco was a temporary blip in a brilliant record of success in marketing across cultures. But even this glitch could have been avoided had Disney execs studied the European history of McDonald's, another superstar of global marketing.

Marketing the Big Mac

The Golden Arches have successfully spanned cultural gaps for decades. McDonald's formula seems to work all over the world with only minor modifications. I happened to witness one such modification when the first Indonesian "McD" opened in the early 1990s in Jakarta. Scanning the new restaurant's offerings, I was at first puzzled and then impressed when the word "hamburger" appeared nowhere on the extensive. Big Mac, yes. Burgers, sure. But no hamburger.

Then it hit me. In the world's most populous Muslim country, any reference to "ham" might well offend some customers. Few Jakartans would be likely to know that the word "hamburger" is actually derived from the German city of Hamburg and that it is supposed to contain only beef – no pork products.

As the Golden Arches rise over India the word hamburger will also be absent, but this time for two different reasons. First, because both Muslims and Hindus eschew pork. Second, because Hindus venerate the cow and would never tolerate beef on the menu. So look for chicken and lamb-burgers there instead.

McDonald's is an icon of global marketing because they provide their customers with a basically identical eating experience wherever the Golden Arches appear. But they also pay close attention to local tastes and expectations. Some examples:

- In Singapore the Sausage McMuffin served at breakfast time is made from spicy ground chicken rather than pork. Some 15 percent of the Lion City's population is Musilm.
- Also in Singapore they came out with the "Kiasuburger," an oversized sandwich whose name derives from the Hokkien word meaning "afraid to lose out." The Kiasuburger was designed to assure Singaporean gourmands that they would not leave the place hungry.
- In Japan the Golden Arches rise not in suburban shopping malls as in the USA but in small satellite restaurants close to train and subway stations, and serve mostly take-out customers.
- Responding to a recent trend back to more traditional Japanese tastes, teriyaki burgers often appear on the menu alongside the Big Mac. Mild curries, rice dishes and rice balls have been added from time to time in an attempt to beat tough local competitors such as Mosburger.
- In Moscow, restaurant employees had to be specially trained to smile in the friendly McDonald's way. That's because Russians do not feel comfortable smiling at strangers.
- McDonald's recently opened its first kosher restaurant in Israel, near Tel Aviv. And its Mecca site in Saudi Arabia serves only halal beef, slaughtered according to Islamic law.
- European customers can order black currant milk shakes in Poland, veggie burgers in the Netherlands and salmon burgers in Norway.

These local variations on a global theme have helped McDonald's become the number one fast food provider just about everywhere. The Philippines is a rare exception. There the local Jollibee chain has relegated the Big Mac to second place. Jollibee caters to Filipino palates with burgers, fried chicken and spaghetti, all offered with sweet, spicy flavors. The U.S. giant is now fighting back with additional localized menu items such as spicy burgers, rice and *longganisa* sausage.

Euro Disney could have learned two things from McDonald's. First, how to take a global strategy and localize it with appropriate tactical variations. Second and more specifically, how to handle an important cultural difference between European and U.S. dining habits. Americans tend to regard alcohol as a sinful indulgence to be kept out of "family" restaurants.

When we lived in Europe during the 1970s and early 1980s, the Golden Arches were 100 percent alcohol-free, just like they were in the good old US of A. But during the latter half of the eighties European customers began to drift away to local restaurants where they could enjoy a mug of beer or a glass of wine with their meal.

After some internal debate McDonald's management decided to tweak their global strategy and allow European franchisees to offer wine or beer according to their local customers' tastes and traditions. The lost customers soon returned.

While McDonald's reacted to local market requirements quickly in the 1980s, Euro Disney apparently needed the pressure of a near-billion dollar loss to make a similar menu adjustment in the 1990s. However, we should not forget that the Disney theme park in Japan has been a roaring success without any local modification at all. Perhaps the Asian success delayed Disney's response to the threat of a European failure.

International airlines have learned to modify menus to suit cultural preferences. American Airlines offers pizza on some flights, Kiwi serves Muslim dinners, El Al kosher hamburgers for childen, Japan Air Lines pepper-free meals and Lufthansa a raw vegetarian dish.

Besides McDonald's, other U.S. global food marketers are also adapting their menus to cater to local tastes. Some examples:

- *Burger King* modified their Singapore menu by adding curried chicken and the Rendang Burger: slices of beef simmered in a hot and spicy sauce.
- *Wendy's* has offered their Japanese customers sandwiches filled with deep-fried pork cutlets served with a bowl of rice.

- In Japan *Kentucky Fried Chicken (KFC)* dropped mashed potatoes and gravy, adding french fries and chicken curry with rice while cutting the sugar content of its cole slaw in half.
- *Dunkin' Donuts* sells some interesting local variations in Southeast Asia, including mango, durian and pandan flavors.
- In Singapore *Pizza Hut* offers several special toppings. The Singapura has beef with onion and chili flakes, the Kelong features sardines, onions and fresh chili while the Merlion is loaded with mutton and chilis. Meanwhile for Thai customers they add pineapple to the toppings and place little bowls of hot sauce on the tables.
- *Shakey's* offers the Temasek Special pizza in Singapore: marinated beef with cucumbers, satay sauce and chilis. Patrons can also create their own toppings with such ingredients as green peas and whole kernel corn.
- *Campbell Soups* is busy creating a whole range of Asian offerings in its research and development laboratory in Hong Kong. Its first success there is watercress and duck gizzard soup. Campbell actually learned about localization in its home market, making blander soups for the U.S. Midwest and spicier versions for the Southwest. This domestic experience helped them in the Mexican market, where they created a cream of chile poblano soup.
- *Blue Diamond Growers,* a world power in marketing almonds, flavors the nuts it sells in Mexico with chili peppers, cheese and lemon.

The Knorr Dry Soup Story

Fast-food companies are not the only ones with failures and successes in adapting products to local markets. Dehydrated soups were popular in Europe where we discovered them as American expatriates, but they were practically unknown on the other side of the Atlantic.

CPC International had the U.S. distribution rights for Knorr, a leading European brand of dry soups. Planning to introduce the Knorr line to the American market, CPC conducted some basic market research. When consumer test panels reacted favorably to the taste of the product, CPC proceeded to bring Knorr soups to market.

However, despite positive test results, sales turned out to be so disappointing that the company considered withdrawing the dry soups from the U.S. market. Such a move of course would have entailed writing off large market research and development expenses.

Analysis showed that although American consumers did like the taste of the dry soups, they were not willing to spend 15 to 20 minutes cooking and stirring the soup. U.S. consumers were used to "instant" canned soups which require only four or five minutes of heating before serving.

Thus, while CPC marketers took U.S. taste preferences into account, they overlooked a countervailing cultural value: the American drive to save time in food preparation.

At this point the CPC people got creative. They decided to market the tasty dry soups as a base for sauces and chip dips. So they added to the Knorr packages directions for mixing the soup powder for sour cream and other liquids. This approach brought immediate success, with Knorr quickly gaining a major share of the U.S. sauce and dip markets.

Chocolate

One would expect chocolate to be a major exception to the need for cultural adaptation. After all, chocolate surely is the universal flavor. It is popular all over the globe, right?

Ah yes, but not necessarily the *same* chocolate! Americans prefer bland milk chocolate, as do many Germans. The Dutch tend to like white chocolate and the French the dark, bitter variety. Russians haven't taken to Mars "M&Ms" because they are not as filling as other chocolate confections. Asians love the combination of chocolate with ginger.

Coffee

What about coffee, which seems to go so well with a bit of chocolate after dinner? People everywhere drink coffee. Well, it's the same story:

- *Nescafe*, the largest food company in the world, makes over 200 varieties of coffee to suit local tastes.
- The Japanese love canned coffee, which is sold both hot and cold in vending machines all over the country.
- As you move from south to north in Europe, the preference moves from very dark to light coffee.
- Greeks prefer it sweet and gritty, mixed with the grounds. Ditto the Egyptians.
- The Italians prefer a caramelized roast yielding a darker black color, a strong taste and a distinctive aftertaste.

- The "French roast" popular in France and other markets produces a medium to medium-dark color and flavor.
- The Viennese love a full cup of medium-dark blended coffee topped off with sweetened whipped cream: the famous *Kaffee mit Schlagobers.*
- Most Germans and Scandinavians prefer lightly-roasted coffee with a slightly acidic taste.
- In the USA, be careful when you order "regular" coffee. Regular means "black" in Chicago, "with milk" in Boston and "with milk and sugar" in Rhode Island. "Regular" can also mean non-decaffeinated coffee.

Milk

With coffee goes milk. The Italian company Parmalat encountered strong consumer resistance in the U.S. to its brand of heat-treated milk. Despite the convenience – it does not require refrigeration – Americans prefer their milk fresh and cold. So whereas over 70 percent of the milk sold in Europe is heat-treated, in the U.S. the market share is under one percent.

This is no surprise to me. During our eight years in Italy none of our children was able to develop a taste for room-temperature milk.

Coca-Cola

After all those varieties of coffee, it is refeshing to find one beverage that actually is standard: Coca-Cola, the best-known of all global brands. Although some cola connoisseurs report variations in sweetness from country to country, the company insists the formula is the same every-where in the world. Unlike many other mass-consumption items, the core product itself does not have to be modified to suit local tastes.

Nevertheless, other elements of the marketing mix do vary from market to market. At a party in Singapore recently, Coca-Cola's manager for Southeast Asia told me how he was able to overcome a distribution bottle-neck in Bangkok. Instead of the big trucks Coke uses elsewhere to deliver to retailers, they employ dozens of little *tuk-tuks* which wriggle their way through tiny holes in the permanent gridlock that afflicts Thailand's capi-tal. Creative adaptation again!

On the other hand, in China Coke has invested large sums in delivery trucks because of inadequate distribution. They also employ platoons of sales reps who travel around on motorcycles calling on retailers.

Coca-Cola is also modifying the assortment offered in China. Under government pressure they are developing other soft drinks for the local market. So far they have come up with Tian Yu Di, a soft drink in three flavors: lychee, mango and guava. In Hong Kong Coke's beverage assortment includes soy milk and flavored tea drinks.

To compete in the lucrative Japanese market – where the ad slogan is "I feel Coke" – Coca-Cola has to bring out new sodas, fruit-based drinks and cold canned coffees every month. Oolong tea seems to be one of the local favorites.

One more cultural difference: Coke finds that its sugar-free sodas sell much better in the diet-conscious U.S. than anywhere abroad.

Beer

Marketers of beer encounter a number of significant market variations. The Dutch brewer Heineken for example tailors its advertising pitch to each market. In France and Italy, traditionally wine-drinking cultures, they market Heineken as a drink for all occasions. It seems to be working because beer consumption is rising rapidly in both markets.

Farther East the Dutch brewer targets young professionals, promoting Heineken as a taste of refined European culture. In the U.S., Heineken is also promoted as a status symbol, an upscale European import.

In perhaps the ultimate bow to cultural preferences, Heineken recently developed a special alcohol-free version of its low-alcohol Buckler brand for the Saudi Arabian market.

There's no Accounting for Taste

The significance of cultural preferences becomes clearer when we take a look at the wide range of foods which are regarded as delicacies in one country and disgusting in another. For instance, in the heart of Florence you can get a steaming platter of boiled cow's stomach. If you are lucky you can also find a Tuscan trattoria there serving cock's combs and thistle blossoms.

The French do not regard offal as awful. Cow's stomach is also served there, as are curried lamb's brains, pig's trotters and blanched pig's intestines. Another favorite is grilled sweetbreads (the thymus gland) skewered on licorice sticks.

People who find those menu selections a bit strange might prefer some of the goodies available in Thailand. These include crocodile filets fried with mustard sauce and choice cuts of cobra and python served with steamed bamboo worms. Other taste treats are mountain frog, ground lizard and curried soft-shell turtle stewed in lemon-grass broth.

More familiar to some business travelers are such Chinese and Southeast Asian favorites as sea slugs, drunken prawns, soups made from bird's nests cemented together with avian saliva, crocodile steaks and goat penis soup. The Vietnamese on the other hand seem to prefer armadillo meat washed down with coffee brewed from beans vomited by weasels.

And then we have the Japanese obsession with *fugu* or blowfish. The blood, liver, gut and genitals of this delightful sea creature contain the lethal poison tetrodoxin. Chefs must pass a rigorous exam before being certified to serve fugu. Just as well, because when something goes wrong death is swift and painful.

A Chacun Son Gout (To Each His Own)

All these widely-diverging taste preferences present opportunities for alert international marketers. Americans export the dark meat parts of chicken to Russia, Latin America and Asia because Yanks prize the bland white breast meat while other consumers prefer the juicy thighs and other cuts.

Australians commercial fishermen used to discard the fins of the sharks they caught as inedible. Now they export the fins to China, Hong Kong and Taiwan where they are converted into the very expensive shark's fin soup.

American poultry processors have always thrown away certain parts such as chicken feet and turkey testicles as they prepare the meat for market. But in the late 1980s clever enterpreneurs realized that these "inedible" poultry parts were regarded as expensive delicacies in Hong Kong and Taiwan. So they got rich by cleaning, packaging and exporting these treasures to Taiwan and Hong Kong. In Greater China, boiled chicken feet are a popular snack food, and turkey testicles are regarded as potent aphrodisiacs – nature's own Viagra.

And finally, consider the lowly sea urchin. At least it used to be considered lowly along the coast of Maine in the U.S., where lobstermen threw them away. But in 1987 the Japanese learned of the availability of Maine urchins and began to import them. Japanese gourmets feast on the roe as well as on the undeveloped sex organs of immature sea urchins as an aid to sexual potency. As a result, Maine exports of these delicacies have jumped from zero in 1987 to over $75 million currently.

The Name Game

Focusing on the local customer also means being aware of how your brand name translates in different languages. A bartender in Frankfurt told me the after-dinner liqueur Irish Mist was a hard sell for a quite a while because *Mist* in German means dung or manure.

The marketing people at an Italian toilet tissue manufacturer located near Florence once asked us whether their product would sell well in the UK. They couldn't understand why we recommended changing their brand name for English-speaking markets. After all, SOFFASS had always served them well in the home market.

Globalize...or Localize?

"Customer focus" has been a popular buzz phrase for the 1990s. But we sometimes forget that customers' values, attitudes and beliefs differ around the world. The savvy international marketer knows how to focus on the local customer while still thinking globally.

We have seen that cultural differences create invisible barriers to trade. But at the same time – as we saw with chicken parts, shark fins, sea urchins and turkey testicles – those same cultural differences also create new market opportunities.

Problems and opportunities: Two good reasons for learning what makes international customers tick.

Part Two

International Negotiator Profiles

Summary

Patterns of Cross-Cultural Business Behavior

Characterisitics of relationship-focused business cultures
– People are usually reluctant to do business with strangers.
– Make initial contact indirectly: at trade shows, on official trade missions or via intermediaries, introductions and referrals.
– At meetings, take plenty of time to build trust and rapport before getting down to business.
– It is important to maintain harmony, avoid conflict and confrontation during discussions.
– Negotiators tend to be sensitive to issues of "face", dignity, self-respect.
– A preference for indirect, high-context communication to avoid offending others.
– Effective communication and problem-solving require frequent face-to-face contacts.
– Lawyers are usually kept in the backround during negotiations.
– A reliance on close relationships rather than contracts to resolve disagreements.

Deal-focused business cultures
– An openness to talking business with strangers.
– Though introductions and referrals are always helpful, it is generally possible to contact potential customers or business partners directly.
– At meetings, people get down to business after just a few minutes of general conversation.
– When communicating, the priority is clarity of understanding. Little thought is given to maintaining harmony with counterparts during negotiations.
– Little attention paid to issues of face.
– Expect direct, frank, low-context communication most of the time.
– Much communication and problem-solving handled via telephone, fax and e-mail rather than in face-to-face meetings.
– Lawyers are often seated at the negotiating table.

– A reliance on written agreements rather than personal relationships to resolve disagreements.

Formal, hierarchical business cultures

– Formality in interpersonal communication is an important way of showing respect.
– Status differences are valued and tend to be larger than in egalitarian societies.
– Expect to address counterparts by family name and title rather than by given name.
– Protocol rituals are often numerous and elaborate.

Informal, egalitarian business cultures

– Informal behavior is not regarded as disrespectful.
– People are uncomfortable with obvious status differences, which are smaller than in hierarchical societies.
– Expect to address most counterparts by given name rather than surname and title shortly after meeting them.
– Protocol rituals are relatively few and simple.

Polychronic business cultures

– People and relationships are more important than punctuality and precise scheduling.
– Schedules and deadlines tend to be quite flexible.
– Meetings are frequently interrupted.

Monochronic business cultures

– Punctuality and schedules are very important to business people.
– Schedules and deadlines tend to be rigid.
– Meetings are seldom interrupted.

Reserved business cultures

– People speak more softly, interrupt each less other and are more comfortable with silence than is the case in expressive cultures.
– Expect interpersonal distance of about an arm's length and little physical contact aside from the handshake.
– Avoid intense, continuous eye contact across the negotiating table.
– Expect very few hand and arm gestures and restrained facial expression.

Expressive business cultures
- People often speak quite loudly, engage in conversational overlap and are uncomfortable with silence.
- Expect interpersonal distance of half an arm's length or less and considerable physical touching.
- Direct, even intense eye contact across the negotiating table signals interest and sincerity.
- Expect lively facial expressions along with vigorous hand and arm gesturing.

Group 1

Relationship-Focused, Formal, Polychronic and Reserved

India – Bangladesh – Indonesia – Malaysia
Thailand – Philippines – Vietnam

The Indian Negotiator

The present-day culture of India is a veritable palimpsest, with layer upon layer of formative influences: Ancient Hindu traditions, Islamic customs brought in by Muslim conquerors from Central Asia and carryovers from the days of the British Raj. With close to a billion inhabitants, India is the second most populous country in the world. It is also an extremely complex culture – multilingual, multi-ethnic and multi-religious.

Indians speak over 300 different languages, not including dialects. Fourteen are official languages, enumerated in the constitution. While Hindi is the dominant tongue, some of the other official languages are also of major importance. For example, there are more Bengali speakers in the world than native Russian-speakers.

In terms of religion, the majority of Indians are Hindus, but over 100 million are Muslims. Other religions include Sikhism, Buddhism and Christianity.

The Language of Business. While Hindi is the most important indigenous language, it is spoken fluently by only about a third of the population. The mind-boggling linguistic diversity serves to promote English as a lingua franca within the country; most Indian business people speak it fluently.

But do watch out: The delightful Indian variety of English is sprinkled with local terms which sometimes confuse foreign visitors. If you hear your partner referring to a lack of rupees he may be talking about a *lakh* of rupees...meaning 100,000 of them. And if your customer shocks you by saying she has just "fired" her assistant, relax. That just means she reprimanded him.

Whereas English-speaking suffices for business visitors, many expatriates learn the language of the region they are based in. For example, this writer found written Hindi useful for reading road signs and the spoken version handy for asking directions and communicating with taxi drivers.

A basic knowledge of Hindi was also helpful when checking production at factories. Management always said, "Oh, no problem! Delivery will be right on time, quality is perfect." But when the boss was out of earshot and I asked the foreman in Hindi how things were going, the whispered reply often enough was, *Sahib, muskil hai!* – meaning there was a big problem after all.

Hierarchy, Status and Caste. Indians generally respect age, rank and social position. Younger people are expected to defer to elders, so white hair confers status. Hindus belong to whatever caste they are born into. They cannot move up the caste ladder by getting a PhD, by getting elected to high office or by becoming a millionaire. Some 14 percent of Hindus fail to qualify for even the bottom rung of the caste ladder – these are the untouchables, or "harijans".

Polychronic Time. In Hindi the word *kal* can mean both yesterday and tomorrow, and *kal-kal* translates as either the day before yesterday or the day after tomorrow. Which makes kal (pronounced "cull") an apt symbol for India – a land of the future hamstrung by the red tape of its bureaucratic past. You need patience in this market, most especially when dealing with officials.

In a government office, expect to be kept waiting half an hour or more without the courtesy of an apology. Your meeting is likely to be interrupted every few minutes while the harried official across the desk takes phone calls, signs piles of documents and receives drop-in visitors.

It's a mistake to interpret this behavior as rude or reflective of sloppy work habits. Indian officials enjoy higher status than business people. And time has a different meaning in India. Clocks seem to tick to a slower beat – it's a question of culture and climate. My response is to always carry a large briefcase stuffed with reading material and overdue expense reports. India taught me to regard waiting time as an opportunity rather than a problem.

Business Protocol

Dress Code. Men wear a dark suit when meeting government officials. For most private sector meetings, a suit in the cooler months, shirt and tie or bush shirt (worn outside the trousers) without a tie in the summer. Women wear a conservative dress or blouse and skirt (below-the-knee length). Avoid revealing garb such as thin T-shirts, sleeveless blouses and tank tops.

Meeting and Greeting. Men usually shake hands, using moderate pressure. With female counterparts the graceful "namaste" or "namaskar" gesture may be used: palms together with fingertips just below chin level while bowing the head slightly.

Forms of Address. Usage varies widely across the subcontinent, especially between northern and southern India. Two useful rules: ask your counterparts how they wish you to address them, and always use a person's professional or academic title, e.g Doctor Gupta, Professor Aggarwal.

Exchanging Cards. Offer and receive cards with the right hand only.

Garlanding. This elegant custom is the South Asian way of greeting honored guests. But what do you do with the garland after it has been draped around your neck? The appropriate response is to smile in thanks, remove it gently as soon as the flash bulbs stop popping, and carry it in your hand until your hosts relieve you of the fragrant burden.

Wining and Dining. When entertaining Indian guests, remember that most Hindus are serious vegetarians: Some may eat chicken and lamb but certainly not beef. And neither Muslims nor Hindus eat pork. If you are a guest in a traditional Indian home, politely decline food or refreshments the first time they are offered. To accept immediately signifies greediness and poor breeding. Expect your Indian guests to similarly refuse. The gracious host or hostess responds by repeating the offer at least twice. It would be rude indeed to accept your guest's initial refusal at face value!

Negotiating Behavior

Once you have built a comfortable relationship with your local counterpart, the formal negotiation process can begin. Be prepared for tough, drawn-out bargaining sessions. Indians are often experts at bazaar haggling, so remember to build a safety margin into your opening position.

At some point in the bargaining process your counterpart may play the poverty card. The fact is, decades of protectionism and over-regulation have made India a high-cost economy despite its low labor costs. To this day, despite ongoing reforms India remains a high-cost producer of most goods compared to China and some other Asian supply markets.

The Bangladeshi Negotiator

Western business people have tended to dismiss the market potential of this populous South Asian nation ever since Henry Kissinger called it an economic basket case in the mid-1970s. But despite its poverty – the 120 million mostly Muslim inhabitants average under $300 in per capita GDP – profitable opportunities still exist for foreign exporters, importers and investors.

Most market potential is concentrated in textiles, by far the country's most successful industry. Over one million people work in the 2000 or so garment factories which account for 60% of total Bangladeshi exports. U.S. apparel retailers and wholesalers buy half of those apparel exports, over $1 billion worth. So manufacturers of textile machinery and supplies should be looking for export and joint-venture investment opportunities.

But poverty is not the only deterrent to commercial interest in Bangladesh. Bureaucratic red tape as well as differences in business customs and practices are also barriers to trading with this developing country.

The Right Local Contact. The right contact is a well-connected person or organization able to cut through the jungles of red tape without having to pay *bakhsheesh,* the local term for a bribe. The problem is, someone with good connections today may be in out in the cold when a new party comes to power. Visiting business people should plan to work together with their local representation to develop the requisite connections.

Building Relationships. This includes relationships with government officials. The state controls most of the Bangladesh economy with a heavy hand, which can cause endless frustration for business people. But the good news is that South Asian officials tend to be more open to dealing with foreign businessmen than is the case in East Asia.

Unfortunately, many foreigners bungle the chance to establish effective relationships with the public sector. They unthinkingly adopt a patronizing tone with Bangladeshi officials because of the country's poor socio-economic condition. This is a major faux pas. It is important to show appropriate respect when meeting with government officials, who enjoy high status in the Bengali culture.

In most Bangladesh businesses all important decisions are made by the managing director, who is typically unwilling to delegate any of his authority. When this person is overburdened or "out of station" your urgent fax is likely to go unanswered.

Business Protocol

Dress Code. One way to show respect to officials in Bangladesh is to dress more formally than you might think appropriate in a hot, humid climate. The dress code for men is a dark suit, starched white shirt and conservative tie. Women can wear a lightweight suit or a dress of cotton or silk. Visitors should wear clothing of natural fibers – synthetics quickly become very uncomfortable in Dhaka or Chittagong.

Women in Business. Female business visitors are still fairly rare in Bangladesh. However, women who dress modestly and avoid behavior which could be construed as flirtatious experience few problems.

Meeting Behavior. During meetings with senior government officials and private sector executives, be ready for anything. Meetings often start half an hour or more late. Then assistants and secretaries rush in with papers to be signed, incoming phone calls punctuate your carefully rehearsed presentation, friends and relatives drop in for a gabfest.

Bengalis are delightful conversationalists. They are famous within the South Asian subcontinent for being talkative, which is another reason meetings tend to run on...and on. The proper response to all this is to stay calm, avoid showing impatience. While such meeting behavior would be considered very rude in monochronic cultures, it is normal procedure in South Asia.

Gift Giving. Your local counterparts will appreciate small, quality gifts from abroad. Since the majority of Bangldeshis are Muslims, be careful offering liquor as a gift. If invited to a private home, an ideal gift is a box of good imported candies or cookies (biscuits).

Entertaining. Eating with the fingers is acceptable in Bangladeshi restaurants. Outside of Western restaurants men and women often dine separately. Avoid visiting the washroom during the meal. Be aware that as Muslims, many locals do not drink alcohol and avoid all pork products.

Unlike in Pakistan and many other Muslim countries, in Bangladesh homes the female members of the household often join male guests at the dinner table.

Gestures. Observe the left-hand taboo. The "thumbs-up" gesture is regarded as obscene. Remove your shoes before entering a mosque.

Negotiating Style

Bazaar Haggling. Bangldeshis are a friendly, hospitable people who enjoy the give and take of a lively bargaining session. Expect your negotiations to take more time than they would in deal-focused cultures. It is important to keep a smile on your face even when discussions become a bit heated.

Bargaining Range. Your local counterparts expect your opening bid to include a wide margin. They will expect you to grant concessions on price and terms. Therefore the wise negotiator will build a healthy margin into his or her initial position. You can limit the constant haggling by inisiting on a quid pro quo of equal value for each concession granted.

The Indonesian Negotiator

Indonesia's business culture is complex due to the diversity of its demographic makeup. Its population of 200 million includes Javanese, Bataks, ethnic Chinese and 300 other groups. It is the world's fourth most populous country and by far the largest Muslim nation. Business visitors find the culture relationship-focused, hierarchical and relaxed about punctuality and deadlines. Indonesian negotiators tend to be softspoken, friendly and polite.

The Language of Business. The national language is Bahasa Indonesia, similar to Malay. Perhaps because the country was colonized by the Dutch rather the British, English is not as widely spoken as it is in Singapore or Malaysia. So if you are meeting your local counterpart for the first time it would be wise to inquire whether an interpreter will be necessary.

If you plan to set up an office or subsidiary, keep in mind that English-speaking middle managers are often hard to find in Indonesia. To solve this problem many foreign companies recruit management in the Philippines where experienced managers fluent in English are easier to find.

"Face" and Communication. This is a traditional, hierarchical, face-conscious society. Which means that more egalitarian, informal negotiators may have trouble communicating with Indonesians. Four tips regarding face:

- Avoid open confrontation at all costs.
- Avoid words or actions which might embarrass or shame someone. For example, never correct or criticize your Indonesian counterpart in front of other people.
- Higher status people never apologize directly to people of low status. Domestic servants or manual workers are likely to feel acutely embarrassed by a formal apology from a superior. A smile and perhaps a small gift accomplishes the same result without the embarrassment.
- No one wants to tell you bad news. If your local business partner delays telling you about a problem until it is too late to do anything about it, do not get upset. Remember that Indonesians are showing you respect

by shielding you from bad news. You can solve this communication problem by developing a climate of trust with your local counterparts.

As a matter of fact, you will find that a close personal relationship is the basis for solving most business problems in Indonesia.

Communication

Indonesians are embarrassed by elaborate expressions of gratitude, responding best to a simple "thank you." They tend to speak rather softly, rarely interrupt another speaker, may be startled by loud talk and are easily offended if interrupted in mid-sentence. Your Indonesian counterpart may laugh or giggle when nervous or embarrassed. Be careful not to join in the merriment until you know exactly what the laughter is all about.

Gaze Behavior. Intense eye contact such as would be appropriate in southern Europe or the Middle East is considered "staring" in Southeast Asia and may make Indonesians uncomfortable. Also, if you wear sunglasses in Indonesia do remember to remove them when meeting a local person. Talking to someone from behind dark glasses is very rude in this society.

Taboo Gestures. Because Indonesia is a Muslim culture, the left hand is regarded as unclean. Avoid touching people, passing food or offering your business card with your left hand. It's okay to sign a document with your left hand if you are a southpaw but remember to give it to someone with your right hand. Pointing at people or objects with your index finger is impolite. If you need to point, close your (right) fist and aim it thumb-first in the direction indicated. To call a waiter, simply raise your hand the way you did in school. Or you can extend your right arm and make a scooping motion with your hand.

Business Protocol

Dress Code. The way you dress can show either respect or disrespect to your counterpart. Because of the tropical climate men may find it uncomfortable to wear a suit. Nevertheless, do don a dark suit when meeting a high level governemnt official. For meetings in the private sector, a long-sleeved white shirt and tie with neat trousers is appropriate. Women should wear a modest dress, lightweight suit or skirt and blouse.

Meeting and Greeting. Expect a gentle handshake accompanied by moderate eye contact when meeting someone for the first time. While Europeans for example shake hands each time they meet and depart, this is not necessary at subsequent meetings in Indonesia. When in doubt just do as your counterpart does. Except for the handshake Indonesians avoid physical contact with people they do not know well.

Names and Titles. While many Javanese have only one name, people of the middle and upper classes often choose a family name. These surnames typically end in "o" as in Sukarno, Suharto and Subroto. If you are introduced to a male with the single name Budi, for example, you should address him as Mr. Budi. If he has a second name he becomes Mr. _____. Do not be surprised if your local counterparts call you by your given name preceded by Mr., Miss or Mrs. That's why Mr. Bob and Mrs. Mary are frequently heard appellations in Jakarta.

Refreshments. At any business meeting you can expect to be served tea or a cold drink. No matter how thirsty you may be, wait until your host has taken a sip before drinking. To do otherwise would be a sign of disrespect or poor manners.

Gift Giving. Unlike many other Asian societies, Indonesia is not a gift-giving culture. If you do give someone a gift, do not expect it to be unwrapped in your presence.

Negotiating Behavior

Sales Presentation. Take time to gauge the English-language capability of your audience before launching into your pitch. Use plenty of visuals and handouts, especially with materials having to do with numbers. Avoid anything smacking of "hard sell." Think in terms of *offering* your product or service rather than *selling* it.

Bargaining Range. Indonesians love to bargain. Since you are likely to run into unanticipated cost factors, remember to build some extra margin into your opening bid or quotation. With negotiations often dragging on for months, your counterparts have a lot of time to keep chipping away at your initial position. Smart negotiators anticipate this and keep a good supply of bargaining chips in their back pocket.

Decision-Making. The decision-making process takes four to six times as long as in most of Europe, North America and Singapore. Remember to pack a large supply of patience when you come to do business in this part of the world.

Written Agreements. Indonesians tend to regard their relationship with you as more important than the agreement they they signed. They usually prefer to sort out problems in face-to-face meetings rather than by calling a lawyer or by referring to the fine print in the written agreement. Of course you should get everything in writing to avoid later misunderstandings, but try to be sympathetic to your Indonesian partner's request to renegotiate some of the contract terms later.

The Malaysian Negotiator

Malaysia is a diverse, multi-cultural, multi-ethnic society. Malays account for around 50 percent of the population, ethnic Chinese about 30 percent and ethnic Indians (mostly of South Indian origin) 8 percent. Non-Malay "bumiputeras" and a small Eurasian element round out the mix.

Business visitors interacting with the public sector will deal mostly with Malays, while in the private sector both Chinese and Malays are active. Ethnic Indians are more often found in the professions: Law, medicine and education. It is important to remember that all Malays are Muslim, but not all Muslims are Malays.

Language of Business. The national language is Bahasa Melayu, but English is widely spoken, especially in the private sector. Visitors can usually conduct business without an interpreter.

"Face" Issues. Malaysians are sensitive to perceived slights. The easiest way to lose face and cause others loss of face is to display impatience, irritation or anger. Showing negative emotion disrupts the harmony of the meeting and may be interpreted as arrogance. Business visitors from more informal, direct cultures such as the U.S. sometimes unintentionally offend Malaysians.

Communication

Some Malaysians giggle or burst out laughing when they observe a mishap, for example when someone slips and falls down. While in some cultures laughter under such circumstances would be considered inappropriate, in Southeast Asian societies it is simply a spontaneous reaction to an awkward or embarrassing situation. No offense is intended.

Malaysians use few gestures. They are likely to be startled or confused by sudden hand and arm movements. Using your index finger to point or beckon is impolite. If you need to point, close your (right) fist and aim it thumb-first in the direction indicated. To beckon a waiter, raise your hand or extend your right arm and make a scooping motion with the fingers of the right hand.

The left hand and the feet are regarded as unclean by both Muslims and Hindus. Avoid touching people or passing objects with your left hand. Likewise, avoid touching or moving any object with your foot and do not cross your legs in such a way that the sole of your shoe faces someone.

Striking the open palm of one hand with the fist of the other is an obscene gesture, and standing with hands on hips signals anger or hostility.

Business Protocol

Dress Code. How we dress shows either respect or disrespect to our counterparts. Because of the tropical climate, men may find it uncomfortable to wear a suit. Nevertheless, males should don a dark suit, white shirt and tie when meeting a high level government official. For meetings in the private sector a long-sleeved white shirt and tie with neat trousers is appropriate. Women wear a modest dress, lightweight suit or skirt and blouse, being sure to cover the upper arms. Skirts should be at least of knee length.

Meeting and Greeting. Customs vary within this very diverse society. One common greeting is a gentle handshake accompanied by moderate eye contact.

Other practices:

– Malays may offer a graceful *salaam*: with a slight bow, extending one or both hands to lightly touch the other person's hands, then bringing the hand(s) back to touch the greeter's heart.
– Indians may use the equally graceful *namaste* or *namaskar* gesture, placing palms together with fingertips just below chin level, accompanied by a slight bow or nod of the head.
– Male visitors should wait for women to offer their hand. If no hand is offered, the polite male just smiles and exchanges verbal greetings.

Exchanging Business Cards. With ethnic Chinese, exchange cards using both hands. With Malays and Indians, offer your card using your right hand with the arm supported at the wrist by the left. It is polite to study your counterpart's card before putting it away.

Refreshments. At business meetings you can expect to be served tea or a cold drink. If asked what you would like to drink, the polite response is, "Whatever you are having". Wait until your host has taken a sip before drinking.

Names. The name game is as complex as the culture. Customs vary among Malays, Chinese and Indians. In general, address each person you are introduced to with his or her title and name. If the person does not have a professional, academic or noble title, use Mr. or Miss/ Mrs./Madam.

Here are some culture-specific tips:

– With a Malay name such as Abdul Hisham Hajji Rahman, Rahman is his father's name and Hajji indicates the father visited Mecca. He is addressed formally as Encik ("Mr.") Hisham, less formally as Abdul Hisham. If Encik has made the pilgrimage he may be addressed as Hajji Hisham. A Malay woman is addressed with *Puan* plus her name. Remember that if her name is Noor binti Ahmad, she is addressed as Puan Noor – Ahmad is her father's name.
– Chinese family names precede the two given names. For example, Li Er San is addressed as Mr. Li. If he gives his name as James Li, he may suggest you call him James, but wait for him to do so. Since most Chinese wives do not take their husband's name, they should be addressed with Madam plus their maiden name rather than Mrs. plus the husband's name.
– Indian names vary by religion and also by region: That is, by the Indian region the person's ancestors came from. Indian Muslim names are similar to Malay names; a South Indian Hindu named S. Nagarajan is addressed as Mr. Nagarajan since "S" is the first initial of his father's name; an Indian Hindu from the north named Vijay Kumar would be Mr. Kumar, while his Sikh neighbor Suresh Singh is Mr. Suresh because the name Singh is common to all male Sikhs.
– Westerners are often addressed by their given name preceded by Mr., Miss or Mrs. So your Malaysian contacts may call you Mr. William, Mrs. Mary or Dr. Robert.

Titles. Titles are important in this rather formal, hierarchical society. Three common ones are Tun, Datuk (or Dato) and Tan Sri. Address Dato

Abdul Hisham Rahman as Dato. The king and the nobility are treated with great respect in Malaysia.

Gift Giving. Gifts are normally exchanged only between friends. If you or your company already has a relationship with your Malaysian counterparts, here are some suggestions:

– A gift is normally not unwrapped in the presence of the giver.
– Gifts of food are good, but avoid alcohol for Muslims and pork products for both Muslims and Hindus. If invited to a dinner or party, fruit, candy and cakes are acceptable gifts.
– Avoid giving knives, letter openers or clocks to a Chinese: Sharp objects suggest the cutting off of a relationship, while the Chinese word for timepiece sounds like the word for death.

Negotiating Behavior

Bargaining Range. Many Malaysians love to bargain. Since you may run into unanticipated cost factors, remember to build some margin into your opening bid or quotation. Smart negotiators keep a few bargaining chips for the all-important end game.

Lawyers, Contracts and Disputes. Malaysians prefer to resolve disputes in face-to-face meetings rather than via fax and e-mail, relying more on relationships than on contract clauses to resolve business disagreements. During the early stages of contract negotiations, it is wise to keep your lawyers somewhat in the background rather than at the bargaining table. To Malaysians, the presence of lawyers may signal lack of trust.

The Vietnamese Negotiator

A growing number of Vietnamese negotiators speak some English, especially in the South. You are less likely to encounter French or Russian speakers than was the case in the 1980s.

Vietnamese welcome business visitors without much regard to their nationality. For example, Americans encounter no particular bias despite the recent bitter war.

Causing loss of face can completely disrupt a promising business negotiation. On the other hand, saving your counterpart's face can contribute to the success of your negotiation. For instance, if you need to correct a Vietnamese negotiator's mistake, call for a break and diplomatically point out the error over a cup of tea. Your sensitivity to face will go a long way towards building a strong relationship with Vietnamese.

Business visitors should avoid raising their voice at the bargaining table: A loud voice indicates anger or childishness in Southeast Asia. Always wait until the Vietnamese negotiator has finished speaking before chiming in.

Business Protocol

Dress Code. When meeting with senior government officials men should wear a dark suit and a conservative tie in order to show proper respect. For other business meetings a long-sleeved shirt and tie for men and a conservative dress or skirt and blouse for women are appropriate attire.

Exchanging Business Cards. Receive your counterpart's business card with both hands, scan it carefully and then put the card away in a leather card case or place it on the table in front of you. Present your own card with your right hand or with both hands.

Names and Titles. Vietnamese names follow the Chinese pattern. If you are introduced to Nguyen Van Tuan for example, Nguyen is the family name and the others are given names. Visitors should address Vietnamese by their family name – and title, if any.

Gift Giving. Vietnam is a gift-giving culture. A good choice would be an expensive branded cognac or whisky. Other ideas are items typical of your region or tasteful logo gifts. Present the neatly wrapped gift with both hands. The recipient will probably put it aside and not open it until after you have left. When you are given a gift, accept it with both hands and open it later.

Wining and Dining. Entertaining and being entertained are important parts of building an effective relationship with your local counterpart. The major hotel restaurants in Saigon and Hanoi offer a good selection of Chinese, French and local cuisines. Finding a good restaurant is more of a challenge outside the major cities – rely on local advice.

Negotiating Behavior

Sales Presentation. North Americans, Australians and some other foreigners like to start every presentation with a joke or humorous anecdote. In Vietnam this approach would be inappropriate. Be careful not to over-praise your own product or company – let your brochures and testimonials speak for you. By the same token, avoid badmouthing your competitors. Instead, pass along to the Vietnamese clips of any critical articles that have been published about the competition. Remember to hand out copies or outlines of your presentation in advance. Use visual aids wherever possible.

Bargaining Range. Vietnamese negotiators tend to bargain vigorously and expect their counterparts to grant major concessions on price and terms. It sometimes appears that they measure their success at the bargaining table by how far they are able to move you away from your opening offer. Counter this tactic by building sufficient margin into your initial bid. Always leave yourself room for maneuver, and squirrel away some bargaining chips for the endgame.

Concession Behavior. Be prepared for some spirited horse-trading and bazaar haggling. Take great care to make any concession conditional – demand something of equal value in return. Give in to any demand with extreme reluctance...and then only after lengthy hesitation. This is the only occasion during the negotiation process in Vietnam when you should let your face show negative emotion: It's okay to signal how painful that last price concession was.

Expect the Vietnamese side to withhold any major concession until the endgame while at the same time they continuously push you to concede point after point. Just keep smiling and ignore any outrageous demand. Alternatively, keep smiling while you make an equally outrageous demand of the other side. Be patient, stay cool...and keep smiling.

Decision-Making Behavior. In public sector companies decisions are made by the top of the hierarchy. These high officials are very busy, so decisions usually take time. Larger private-sector firms are often headed by "retired" military officers; here again decision-making is slow. Smaller entrepreneurial firms may act more quickly.

Role of the Contract. Don't be surprised if your Vietnamese partner contacts you a few weeks after the signing ceremony with a request to renegotiate key parts of the agreement (such as price, for example.). Vietnamese expect that because of their close relationship you will agree to discuss changes in the contract any time conditions change.

The Thai Negotiator

Language is usually the first problem business visitors encounter. Thailand means Land of the Free, reflecting the country's unique status as the only Southeast Asian country which was never colonized. One result of this unique history is that relatively few Thais speak European languages. So while English-speaking negotiators rarely need an interpreter in former British colonies such as India, Sri Lanka, Singapore or Malaysia, it's a different story in Thailand.

Which is why it's a good idea to ask whether you need to arrange an interpreter for the first meeting with your local counterpart. If you plan to set up an office or subsidiary, keep in mind that qualified English-speaking middle managers are hard to find in Bangkok.

Thais value *kreng jai* – showing consideration for the needs and feelings of others. Deal-focused visitors sometimes unintentionally offend by being too direct and using hard sell tactics.

A related value is *jai yen* literally "cool heart". When the discussion gets lively, avoid raising your voice, displaying anger or openly criticizing your local partner.

That's one reason Thais smile so much. They smile when they are happy, they smile when they are sad, they even smile when they are hopping mad. Smiles and gentle words promote harmony; scowls and loud voices disrupt harmony.

Avoid words or actions which might embarrass or shame someone, even unintentionally. For instance, never correct or criticize your Thai counterpart in front of other people. Some Thais even feel uncomfortable if they are singled out for praise.

In this vertical culture, higher status people do not apologize directly to people of low status. Domestic servants or manual workers are likely to feel embarrassed by a formal apology from a superior. A friendly smile and perhaps a small gift of sweets accomplishes the same result without the embarrassment.

No one wants to tell you bad news. If your local business partner delays telling you about a problem until it is too late, do not get upset. Thais feel they are showing you respect by shielding you from bad news. The way to bridge this communication gap is to develop a climate of trust with your local counterparts.

Business Protocol

Dress Code. Men wear a dark suit and tie when meeting a senior government official, while a long-sleeved white shirt and tie with neat trousers is appropriate in the private sector. Women may wear a modest dress, lightweight suit or skirt and blouse.

Meeting Behavior. Visitors encounter a relaxed attitude to time and scheduling. The tropical climate and relatively low level of industrialization plus (in Bangkok) the traffic gridlock all conspire to frustrate business people from rigid-time cultures. Some visitors change hotels in Bangkok to be closer to the next day's meeting site, switching late at night to avoid the gridlock.

Like most of their neighbors in South and Southeast Asia, Thais consider people and relationships more important than schedules and deadlines. Your Thai contact may keep you waiting because he was caught in a traffic jam, or perhaps because the meeting before yours took an hour longer than expected. In the Thai business culture it would be unthinkable to break off an ongoing meeting in order to be on time for the next one.

The Name Game. Thai surnames tend to be long, multi-syllabic and difficult for foreign visitors to pronounce. Fortunately however, Thais are normally addressed by their first name preceded by *Khun,* as in Khun Somchai. Visitors are usually adressed as Mr. Jim or Mrs. Linda.

Meeting and Greeting. While a gentle handshake is appropriate when greeting Thai men, local women may employ the *wai* gesture: Both palms together at approximately chin level with the head slightly inclined. Raising the hands higher while bowing the head slightly more is appropriate when greeting a Buddhist monk. Thais avoid physical contact with people they do not know well.

Because the left hand is considered unclean, exchange business cards with your right hand only. To show special respect you may also present your card with the right hand, cupping your right elbow with the left hand.

It is polite to present gifts the same way, but be aware that Thais really do not expect business gifts.

Communication

Very reserved, Thais tend to speak softly and use almost no gestures. While Thais employ somewhat more eye contact than most Japanese, for example, intense eye contact such as would be appropriate in the Middle East or Latin America is considered "staring" and would make many Thais uncomfortable.

The foot is even more unclean than the left hand. Visitors should never sit in such a way as to show the sole of their foot or shoe. Nor should we point to or touch an object with our foot or shoe.

To be polite, a tall *farang* (European-type foreigner) should try to avoid towering over his or her local counterparts. Consider bending over just a little to reduce any natural difference in altitude.

Pointing at people with your index finger is impolite. Instead, aim your right fist thumb-first in the direction indicated or jerk your chin in that direction. Beckoning someone by crooking one's forefinger is rude, so raise your hand the way you did in school and make eye contact, or extend your right arm horizontally, plam down, and make a rapid scooping motion with your hand.

Negotiating Behavior

Adapting Your Presentation. Avoid overly long meetings. Plan to break up lengthy discussions with some social activities. Thais tend to be put off by all work and no play. *Sanuk* or "fun" makes hard work easier to take.

Bargaining Style. Be prepared for a certain amount of bazaar haggling. It's a good idea to add a comfort factor to your opening offer in order to make room for some tactical concessions later on price or terms. The decision-making process takes much longer than it does in more deal-focused cultures. Remember to bring plenty of patience with you to the negotiating table.

The Filipino Negotiator

The business culture of the Philippines is unique in Southeast Asia. True, Filipinos share the basic values, attitudes and beliefs of their ASEAN neighbors. But 400 years of Spanish colonialism followed by nearly a century of strong U.S. influence added other important features to the culture.

Business visitors from abroad will find the Filipinos deeply concerned about maintaining harmony and what Filipinos call "smooth interpersonal relations."

While there are over 70 languages and dialects in the Philippines, the national language is Pilipino, based on Tagalog. One legacy of the long U.S. presence is that most Filipinos engaged in international business speak fluent English. Visiting negotiators who use that language will have no more difficulty than they would in Singapore.

Those planning to set up an office or subsidiary should note however that it is now becoming more difficult to find competent English-speaking middle managers and technicians. That is because so many of them have been recruited to work as expatriates abroad.

Be conscious of the positive connotation of *pakikisma,* the Filipino term for togetherness and camaraderie. As in other Asian societies, the group is more important than the individual.

Like other Southeast Asians, Filipinos are sensitive to slights and issues of face. The traditional Filipino concern for face and self-esteem was reinforced by the Spanish obsession with honor and *amor-proprio,* meaning self-respect or self-esteem. Visiting business people should be sensitive to this concern when dealing with Filipinos of any rank or condition.

Filipinos strive to avoid *hiya,* meaning shame or embarrassment. They often phrase statements in a roundabout way to reduce this risk.

Taboo Gestures

Pointing at people or objects with your index finger is impolite. If you ask directions on the street, rather than pointing local people may respond by shifting their eyes or pointing the chin in the direction indicated.

Avoid standing with your hands on hips; this indicates anger, arrogance or a challenge.

Filipinos often greet each other by quickly raising and lowering their eyebrows. Accompanied by a smile, this gesure signifies a friendly "hello."

Two people of the same gender often hold hands in public; this usually indicates friendship.

Indicate the number "two" by raising your little finger and ring finger rather than the index finger and middle finger as in some other cultures.

Business Protocol

Dress Code. For men, a business suit, white shirt with tie or the *barong tagalog* – the formal Filipino shirt worn outside the trousers – are all appropriate. Women should wear a dress, lightweight suit or skirt and blouse.

Meeting and Greeting. Expect a gentle handshake accompanied by moderate eye contact when meeting someone for the first time.

Names and Titles. Many Filipinos have Spanish-sounding given names such as Maria and family names like Cruz. These names were adopted during Spanish colonial rule and do not indicate Hispanic ancestry. Many upper-class Filipinos follow the Spanish custom of having two surnames, their father's followed by their mother's. If your Filipino counterpart invites you to use her or his nickname, do so and invite them to use yours in return. If you don't have a nickname, think about inventing one.

Titles are important in the Philippines. As in Latin America, professionals are often addressed by their family name preceded by their title, e.g. "Attorney de la Cruz" or "Engineer Martin." People without professional titles are addressed with Mr., Mrs. or Miss followed by the surname. If the person has two family names, you need use only the first (father's).

Topics of Conversation. Good topics are family, food, culture, sports and Filipino history. Avoid discussing local politics, religion or corruption.

Gift Giving. Exchanging gifts plays an important role in relationship-building. *Utang na loob,* meaning debt of gratitude for favors or gifts, is an important component of the glue that holds this relationship-focused culture together. Filipinos do not usually open a gift in front of others.

Social Etiquette. If invited to a Filipino home, bring flowers or chocolates rather than alcohol as a hostess gift. A gift of wine or spirits would imply that your hosts may not have enough drinks for their guests. Note that when eating Filipinos often hold the fork in the left hand, using it to push food into the spoon which is held in the right hand.

When dining at someone's home, leave a bit of food on your plate. This assures your hosts they have fed you well. A clean plate signifies you haven't had enough to eat. In the Philippines, over-indulgence in alcohol is considered ill-mannered behavior.

Local Specialties. Filipinos enjoy *bago'ong*, a salty, pungent paste made from fermented shrimp and used as a sauce and condiment. Visitors can impress their local hosts by partaking of this Southeast Asian specialty. Your hosts may try to shock you with *balut*, an egg containing a fully-formed duck embryo. If you are not tempted by this purely Filipino delicacy, you can demonstrate your appreciation of local culture by declining with a smile rather than with an expression of disgust.

Negotiating Style

Making Your Presentation. Use plenty of visuals and handouts, especially with materials having to do with numbers. Avoid anything smacking of "hard sell." Think of *offering* your product or service rather than *selling* it.

Bargaining Range. Many Filipinos enjoy bargaining, so remember to build some extra margin into your opening bid or quotation. Smart negotiators keep a supply of bargaining chips for use in the end game.

Decision-Making. Coming to a business decision is likely to take longer than in more deal-focused cultures. Patience is a key asset for negotiators in this part of the world.

Group 2

Relationship-Focused, Formal, Monochronic and Reserved

Japan – China – South Korea – Singapore

The Japanese Negotiator

Many Japanese negotiators speak foreign languages, especially English. Nevertheless, you should ask your counterparts whether an interpreter will be needed.

Hierarchy, Status, and Respect. Younger, subordinate individuals are expected to defer to older, higher-ranking persons. Since few women have reached positions of authority in this traditional, hierarchical society, most men are not used to dealing with females on the basis of equality in a business context.

In Japan the buyer automatically enjoys higher status than the seller in a commerical transaction. To reflect that status difference, buyers expect to be treated with great respect. Hence young foreigners face significant cultural obstacles when trying to sell to Japanese customers. Here are four ways to overcome age and gender barriers with the Japanese:

– Be introduced by the eldest, most senior male colleague available. Status is a transferrable asset.
– Learn the verbal, paraverbal and nonverbal ways of showing proper respect. Showing respect gains you respect.
– Gradually establish your professional or technical credentials, taking care not to appear cocky or boastful. Expertise confers status.
– Women are often more skilled than males in reading body language. This ability is particularly valuable when dealing with Japanese, who rely heavily on nonverbal communication.

Formality and Rituals. To maintain surface harmony and prevent loss of face, Japanese rely on codes of behavior such as the ritual of the *meishi* – business cards. Japanese negotiators dress and behave formally and are more comfortable with visitors who do likewise.

Business Protocol

Dress Code. Dark suit, white shirt, conservative tie for men. Conservative suit or dress for women.

Meeting and Greeting. Expect a bow and a soft handshake. Avoid an excessively firm handshake or overly direct eye contact.

Exchanging Business Cards. It is polite to master the ritual of the *meishi*, or business card. Offer your card using both hands, holding it between thumb and forefinger with the side showing the Japanese printing facing up. Shake hands with a slight bow and state your name and your company's name. Receive your counterpart's card with both hands, study it for several seconds and then place it respectfully on the conference table in front of you or in your leather (not plastic) card holder.

Forms of Address. Address your counterpart with his or her family name plus the suffix *san*, as in Watanabe-san. In Japan the family name comes first, followed by given names. But on business cards meant for foreigners they may reverse the order, so when in doubt ask which is the family name.

Gift Giving and Receiving. Exchanging gifts is an important part of the business culture, contributing to relationship building. Be prepared with appropriate gifts for your Japanese counterparts. A good choice is an expensive cognac, a good single malt whisky or a tasteful item which is typical of your city, region or country.

Note that the wrapping and presentation of the gift are more important than the contents. Have your gifts wrapped in Japan or by someone knowledgeable of Japanese customs. Present the gift to your partner with both hands. The recipient will probably put it aside and open it later. You should also receive a gift with both hands and open it later.

Wining and Dining. Entertaining and being entertained are essential parts of building a close relationship with your counterpart. In Japan you may wish to reciprocate with an invitation to a Western style restaurant serving for example French or Italian cuisine. In your homeland or in a third country, a restaurant offering local specialties is usually a good choice.

To show your commitment to Japanese customs, master the art of eating with chopsticks and toasting appropriately. For males, ritual drinking is a traditional way to get to know your counterpart. It is sometimes appropriate to drink heavily, even to get drunk. For some Japanese businessmen, drinking alcohol seems to dissolve the stiffness and formality you may encounter during business meetings.

Japanese tend to rely heavily on *tatemae* or surface communication, telling you what they think you want to hear. After a few drinks they may let their hair down and indulge in *honne* communication, telling you what they really think. So alcohol can be a good lubricant to a sticky negotiation.

Women are generally not expected to drink, and certainly not expected to get drunk. Not being able to join in the male drinking ritual could represent a handicap for women trying to do business with the Japanese.

Males who prefer not to drink alcohol can legitimately excuse themselves on grounds of illness or religious rules. They may however thereby miss out on some opportunities to deepen the relationship and to learn more about their Japanese partners.

Negotiating Behavior

Making Your Presentation. Avoid opening with a joke or humorous anecdote. This would show lack of respect for the topic and for the audience. Speak clearly and simply. Avoid using double negatives and convoluted sentences, jargon, slang or unusual words.

Take care not to over-praise your product or company. Instead use testimonials or articles written about your firm. Use visual aids, especially for numbers, and provide copies of the presentation.

Bargaining Range. In some business cultures, starting off with a high price so as to leave room for bargaining is an effective strategy. This approach may backfire with the Japanese. You should have a cogent reason for any major concession on price or terms.

Concession Behavior. Japanese often find it difficult to grant concessions during a negotiation. This is because their bargaining position was usually arrived at via a long, drawnout discussion process within their company. Any change in this "package" may require further lengthy internal discussions. So bring plenty of patience to the table. And save any major concession until the endgame.

Decision-Making Behavior. Many Japanese companies still make decisions by consensus. This is a time-consuming process, another reason to bring patience to the negotiating table.

Role of the Contract. The final written agreement is less important than the strength of the relationship with your counterpart. But do put everything in writing anyway. The Japanese side may expect to renegotiate the contract if circumstances change. For them, the contract is an expression of intent.

Some Westerners like to hand the other side a draft contract to be used as the outline for the negotiation and then discuss each item point by point. With the Japanese it is better to keep the draft to yourself. Look for areas of agreement before discussing the difficult items. And keep your lawyers in the background during the negotiating process.

The Chinese Negotiator

Though many Chinese negotiators speak foreign languages, especially English, you may need to employ an interpreter.

Concern with "Face". Face has to do with self-respect, dignity, reputation. You can *lose face* by appearing childish or lacking in self-control – for example by losing your temper. You can cause your counterparts to lose face by expressing sharp disagreement, embarrassing them, criticizing them in public or by showing disrespect. Causing serious loss of face can completely disrupt a promising business negotiation.

You can *give* your counterpart face by using polite forms of address and observing local customs and traditions. Giving face is an effective way build a solid relationship. If you make a mistake you may be able to *save your face* with a humble apology. And you can save the other party's face for example by allowing him a graceful exit from a difficult negotiating position.

Business Protocol

Dress Code. Suit, white shirt, conservative tie for men. Conservative suit or dress for women.

Meeting and Greeting. Expect a soft handshake and moderate eye contact. Avoid a bone-crushing handshake or an overly direct gaze.

Names and Titles. Use the person's family name or organizational title. Thus, Lee Er Peng is Mr. Lee, not Mr. Peng. Avoid calling a Chinese person by his or her given name unless specifically asked to do so.

On business cards printed in Chinese the family name comes first, followed by two given names. But on cards printed in Western languages some Chinese reverse the order. When in doubt, ask which is the family name.

Exchanging Business Cards. The exchange of name cards is done using both hands. When you receive your counterpart's card, read it and then put the card away in a leather card case or place it on the table in front of you. Do not write on someone's name card in the presence of the giver.

Exchanging Gifts. Exchanging gifts is an important part of the business culture, contributing to relationship building and the development of *guanxi.* Be prepared with appropriate gifts for your counterparts. A good choice would be an expensive cognac. Other ideas are items typical of your own country or tasteful logo gifts. Present the gift with both hands. The recipient will probably put it aside and open it after the meeting. You should also receive a gift with both hands and open it later.

Wining and Dining. Entertaining and being entertained is an essential part of building a close relationship with your counterpart. In China you may be invited to one or more formal banquets, depending on the length of your stay. Have your local contact or your hotel help you reciprocate with an appropriate banquet.

In your homeland or in a third country, a restaurant offering local specialties is usually a good choice. However, business visitors from China often appreciate a good Chinese meal as well. To show your commitment to Chinese customs, master the fine arts of eating with chopsticks and toasting your counterparts appropriately.

Women are not expected to keep up with the rounds of banquet toasts, and they are definitely not expected to get drunk. Males who prefer not to drink alcohol can legitimately excuse themselves on the grounds of religious objection or ill health.

Negotiating Behavior

Adapting Your Sales Presentation. Avoid opening with a joke or humorous anecdote. This would show inappropriate informality. Take care not to over-praise your product or company. Instead offer testimonials or articles written about your firm. Let others praise your product and your firm. Likewise, avoid making negative comments about your competitors. Rather, you may want to pass along critical comments about your competitors made by respected third parties. Let others criticize your competitors and their products.

Bargaining Range. Chinese negotiators often bargain vigorously and expect their counterparts to grant major concessions on price and terms during the course of the negotiation. They may measure their success at the bargaining table by how far they are able to move you away from your opening offer. Wise negotiators build some margin into their opening offer so as to leave themselves room for bargaining.

Concession Behavior. Take care to make any concession with great reluctance, and only on a strict "if...then," conditional basis, demanding something equivalent in return. Expect pressure tactics. For example, at a critical point in the negotiation you may spot your chief competitor seated in the reception area, waiting to meet your Chinese counterpart after your session.

Ploys and Counter-Ploys. Although Chinese negotiators generally mask negative emotions, they may on occasion display anger as a pressure tactic. Government negotiators sometimes plead the poverty of their country to obtain a lower price. They may also flatter you as an "old friend." Be aware that "friends" are expected to help China by offering better terms.

Decision-Making Behavior. Negotiating in China tends to be a long, time-consuming process requiring patience and a calm disposition. This is especially true when doing business with a government entity or a public sector company. Decisions take time.

Role of the Contract. Chinese may regard the final written agreement as less important than the strength of the relationship with you and your company. This is fine, but do be sure to get everything in writing anyway. The Chinese may expect to renegotiate the contract if circumstances change. For them, a contract is more an expression of intent. Remember, renegotiation of terms can work for both sides.

Role of Legal Advisors. While you will of course dialog with your lawyers throughout the bargaining process, keep them in the background until towards the end of negotiations, when agreement is near. The presence of lawyers at the bargaining table may be perceived as a sign of mistrust.

The South Korean Negotiator

When meeting your Korean counterparts for the first time, ask them whether an interpreter will be needed. Some Korean negotiators may have difficulty expressing themselves and understanding what you say in English.

Hierarchy, Status and Gender. Korean society is a steeply vertical one, with a strict hierarchy. Remember to show proper respect to people of high status, including the elderly and high-ranking company executives. Younger, subordinate individuals are expected to defer to older, higher-ranking persons.

Since very few women have reached positions of authority in Korean companies, most Korean men are not used to dealing with females on the basis of equality in a business context. In general, young foreigners – especially women – are likely to face significant cultural obstacles when trying to sell to Korean customers.

Verbal Communication. Reserved and formal, somewhat introverted. Less reliance on written and telephone communication, more emphasis on meeting face-to-face. South Korean negotiators tend to employ a more direct, explicit verbal style than the Japanese. Nevertheless, to reduce the chance of giving offense Koreans also resort to circumlocution and evasive language. They are skilled at controlling their emotions and hiding their true feelings.

Paraverbal Communication. Koreans are more comfortable with silence than many foreign visitors. Expect significant pauses between conversational exchanges. Korean negotiators try to avoid interrupting the other party since this would be considered rude. Foreign negotiators should likewise wait until their Korean counterpart has finished speaking before saying their piece.

Nonverbal Communication

Space Bubble. Expect an interpersonal distance of about an arm's length.

Gaze Behavior. Expect moderate eye contact. Most Koreans look into your eyes about half the time during a conversation. Avoid using a very direct, intense gaze: This would signal anger or hostility.

Touch Behavior. Korea is a relatively low-contact culture as regards foreigners: Expect little touching beyond the handshake.

Gestures and Facial Expressions. In Korea a smile may mask disapproval or anger. Body language is restrained, formal, with small gestures. Avoid arm-waving and other large, vigorous gestures.

Taboo Behavior. Visitors should avoid sneezing or blowing their nose at the dinner table. It is better to sniffle during the meal or better yet, leave the room and blow your nose out of earshot.

Business Protocol

Introductions. In Korea introductions are not made casually. Arrange for a formal introduction to your business contact.

Dress Code. Dark suit, white shirt, conservative tie.

Forms of Address. Korean names normally consist of the family name first followed by two (occasionally one) given names. Refer to your counterpart by his family name, as in "Mr. Kim." To show respect to senior people, substitute his title for the "Mr". For example, "President Kim" or "Director Park." You may never need to use your local counterpart's given names.

Meeting and Greeting. Expect a bow and moderate eye contact, often followed by a handshake. Respond with a bow before exchanging name cards. You normally use your right hand only when passing something to a Korean. *Exception:* Use both hands when presenting an object to a person of very high status. Or use the right hand with the left supporting your right elbow.

Exchange of Business Cards. Exchanging name cards is very important. Receive your counterpart's card with both hands. Present your own card with the right hand, or with the right hand supported at the elbow by your left hand. Study the other party's card, then put the card away in a leather card holder or place it on the table in front of you.

Gift Giving and Receiving. If you are meeting your counterpart at his office, consider bringing a gift if you have just arrived from abroad. If invited to a Korean's home, always bring a present. Appropriate gifts include items typical of your own country or region as well as an expensive cognac or whiskey. Present the gift with both hands. The recipient will probably put it aside and open it later. You should also receive a gift with both hands and open it later.

Wining and Dining. Entertaining and being entertained are essential parts of building a close relationship with your Korean counterpart. For males, ritual drinking is a traditional way to get to know your counterpart. It is appropriate to drink heavily, even to get drunk. Alcohol often seems to dissolve the stiffness and formality often encountered during business meetings. Drinking can be a good lubricant to a sticky negotiation.

Women are not expected to drink, and certainly not expected to get drunk. Not joining in the male drinking ritual could represent somewhat of a handicap for women doing business in Korea.

Males who prefer not to drink alcohol can excuse themselves on grounds of illness or religious rules. They may however miss out on some opportunities to deepen the relationship and to learn more about their Korean partners.

Negotiating Behavior

Making a Presentation. Avoid opening with a joke or humorous anecdote. This would show lack of respect for the topic and for the audience. Speak clearly and simply.

Bargaining Range. South Koreans are known as tough negotiators. When calculating your initial offer, do allow some room for bargaining. That way you can give in gracefully if need be – while of course demanding an equivalent concession in exchange.

Decision-Making. Bring a large supply of patience with you to the bargaining table. Big decisions are made at the top of Korean companies, and chief executives are busy people.

Role of the Contract. To Koreans, the final contract is less important then the strength of the relationship between the two parties. The legal agreement is akin to an expression of intent. Hence your local counterpart may well try to renegotiate if circumstances should change. Just remember, renegotiation of terms can work both ways.

Negotiating in Singapore

The Republic of Singapore is unique in the world marketplace. Flourishing on a lush tropical island just a stone's throw from the equator, this modern city-state stands out as the world's only industrialized economy outside of the temperate zone. The Republic's economic success is due to many factors including hard work, frugality, effective government...and air conditioning.

Those who have worked under conditions of tropical heat and maximum humidity can fully appreciate the impact of climate on productivity and the work ethic. So the advent of cooled air certainly played a supporting role in Singapore's rapid rise to wealth.

A more important factor in Singapore's success as an entrepot is its multilingual and multi-ethnic blend of Chinese (78%), Malays (15%) and Indians (6%). Most of the ethnic Chinese business people speak both Mandarin and English, the world's number one and two languages respectively.

Fluency in Mandarin provides Singaporeans special access to the booming China market, while competence in English makes doing business easy for exporters, importers and investors around the world. In addition, the Malay connection is useful in the neighboring markets of Malaysia and Indonesia while Singapore's diverse Indian community eases entry to the India market.

In brief, Singapore is a case study in how ethnic and linguistic diversity can contribute directly to a nation's economic success.

The Business Culture. English language facility is not the only reason visiting negotiators find it easy to do business in the Island Republic. Growing convergence in business customs and practices is another. While the national culture continues to emphasize traditional Asian values such as the importance of family, concern for "face" and respect for authority, Singapore's *business* culture is quickly evolving towards an international style with which globe-trotting executives are familiar.

Hundreds of European, U.S. and Asian companies have found that Singapore's geographic position plus the familarity of language and business customs make it the ideal site for their Asia/Pacific headquarters.

High costs in Hong Kong and Tokyo are driving more and more regional head offices to the Lion City.

Making Contact. The rapidity of change in business customs and practices has opened something of a generation gap within the Singapore business community. Local entrepreneurs and managers who are in their 50s and 60s tend to do business in a more traditional, relationship-focused mode, while younger business people are usually more deal-focused.

With companies managed by younger executives, although an introduction never hurts, you can usually save time by making direct contact. With more traditional companies however the indirect approach via a third party is the route to go.

Visitors sometimes perceive Singaporean Chinese as overly aggressive because of the way they ask questions. For instance, "You want this sample now or not?" may sound rude, but it simply means, "Would you like to have a sample now?"

Paraverbal and Nonverbal Behavior

Most Singaporeans speak relatively softly. Loud talk is a sign of poor manners.

- Expect a rather gentle handshake. Avoid responding with a bone-crushing grip. Men usually wait for a woman to offer her hand first.
- Singaporeans sometimes smile to cover anxiety or embarrassment rather than to express amusement.
- When seated, be careful not to cross your legs in such a way that the sole of your shoe is pointed at someone. Do not ouch or move objects with your foot.
- As in other parts of Southeast Asia, avoid beckoning someone with a crooked forefinger. The polite way is to extend your right arm palm down and make a scooping motion.

Business Protocol

You can generally get down to business without elaborate rituals and hours of small talk, and you can expect your Lion City counterpart to be fairly punctual for meetings as well. That said, visiting negotiators will do well to heed these tips:

- Avoid using first names until your Singapore counterpart suggests it. This is especially important when dealing with older people.
- Take care not to interrupt the other party in mid-sentence. Conversational overlap is considered rude here.
- When dealing with government officials, remember that gift-giving is taboo and that if they go to lunch with you they will insist on paying their share. Singapore officials have earned an enviable reputation for honesty and efficiency around the world.
- Introductions: When introducing two people, state the name of the more important or more senior person first, e.g., Chairman Lee, meet Mr. Jones.
- Exchanging business cards (called "name cards" in Southeast Asia): After the introductions the visitor presents his or her card first, preferably with both hands but never with the left. The card should be handled with respect as it represents the person who gave it to you. Do not toss it casually onto the conference table, put in your back pocket, or write on it.
- Good topics for conversation: Food, travel, sightseeing, history, business. Avoid discussing local politics, religion or sex.
- Wining and Dining: Spouses are usually invited for dinner but not for lunch. Meals are a very important part of life in Singapore.

Negotiating Behavior

To conclude an important deal, expect to make a number of trips to Singapore over the course of several months. The pace of negotiations is slower than in more deal-focused business cultures. Visiting business people find Singaporeans polite but tough and persistent negotiators.

Singaporeans are extremely hospitable, and the island's famous cuisine is as delicious as it is varied. Two of the most famous local specialties are pepper crab and durian – the latter an "aromatic" delicacy regarded by Southeast Asians as the King of Fruits. Some Singaporeans tease visitors by pushing them to sniff the powerful odor of the durian. While the taste is quite bland, to most outsiders the scent is reminiscent of a clogged sewer.

My favorite food in Singapore remains fish-head curry. South China contributed the fish head, India the basic curry sauce and Southeast Asia some of the spices. It is a fitting symbol of the unique Chinese/Malay/-Indian potpourri that is Singapore.

Group 3

Relationship-Focused, Formal, Polychronic and Expressive

Saudi Arabia – Egypt – Greece – Brazil – Mexico

The Arab Negotiator

Many Arabs speak English fluently, but be prepared to employ an interpreter in case of need.

Exchanging Favors. The exchange of mutual favors is the cornerstone of any relationship with an Arab. If asked for a favor, agree to do it even if you think you may not be able or willing to do it. Your Arab friend will understand if circumstances later make it impossible to fulfill his request and will appreciate the fact that you agreed to try to help.

Hierarchy, Status and Gender. An Arab's status is determined primarily by his or her social class and family background. Saudis and many other Arabs are not used to seeing women in business. For this reason they may have difficulty relating to female executives. Tips for women wishing to do business in the Arab World:

- Be introduced by an older, high-ranking male. His gender and status can rub off on you.
- Gradually establish your professional or technical credentials, without appearing cocky or boastful. Expertise confers status.
- With luck you may be regarded as a foreigner who happens to be female.

The Role of Islam. The Arab world is a conservative, traditional society strongly influenced by Islam, which pervades every aspect of life. Visitors are advised to learn as much as possible about Arab customs, practices and taboos before arriving.

Honor and the Family. An Arab's honor, dignity and reputation are precious to him and must be protected at all cost. Loyalty to the family is a paramount value. Family needs often come before individual needs.

Expressive, Indirect Communication Style. Arabs readily express emotion and use elaborate verbal language marked by frequent exaggeration for effect. Because Arab negotiators try to avoid confrontation, they usually avoid saying "no" to your face. You will do well to avoid overly blunt language.

Business Protocol

Meeting and Greeting. Expect a gentle handshake and strong, direct eye contact. Arabs of the same sex like to stand or sit very close to each other, closer than many foreigners are accustomed to. Try not to move away, since this would signal coldness to your Arab counterpart.

Touch Behavior. As representatives of an expressive culture, Arabs engage in frequent touching among friends. The amount of physical contact between business acquaintances varies within the Arab world. Observe those around you and take your cue from your local counterparts.

Taboos. Always use your right hand only when eating or when passing something to an Arab. The left hand is considered unclean. If you are left-handed, train yourself to use your right hand as much as possible. When seated, avoid showing the soles of your shoes to an Arab. The feet and shoes are considered unclean.

Dress Code. Conservative suit and tie. Accessories such as watch, pens and briefcase should be of high quality. Some Arab business people judge foreign counterparts by how they dress.

Forms of Address. Address your Arab counterpart by the first of his three names, preceded by "Mr." Example: Mr. Aziz. Expect to be addressed in the same way, as in "Mr. Bob." Titles are important, more widely used in Arabic than in English. "Sheikh" is a title of respect for a wealthy, influential or elderly man. Address government ministers as "Excellency." It is a good idea to find out any titles a person may have and use them.

Exchanging Business Cards. Present your business card with your right (clean) hand only. Receive your counterpart's card in the same way.

Refreshments. You will frequently be offered tea or coffee. This is an important feature of Arab hospitality; it is impolite not to accept.

Gift Giving. Gifts are always welcome but not expected. Choose something for which your own country is well-known, but avoid giving alcohol or any other item forbidden to Muslims. Be careful about admiring any of your counterpart's possessions. He might present you with the object of your admiration and feel insulted if you decline.

Entertaining. Entertaining and being entertained is an essential part of building a close relationship with your counterpart. If invited to dinner at an Arab businessman's home expect to eat a great deal as a way of showing your appreciation. Your host will press you to eat more you than really want to. Eat as much as you can. When you have reached your limit, you may have to decline further helpings three times, emphatically, in order to make the point.

Similarly, when hosting Arabs you must keep pushing them to eat and drink. But remember that alcoholic beverages and pork products are forbidden to Muslims.

Negotiating Style

Bargaining Range. Arab negotiators tend to be enthusiastic bargainers and may expect their counterparts to grant major concessions on price and terms during the course of the negotiation. Some Arab businessmen measure their success at the bargaining table by how far they are able to move you away from your opening offer. They think of negotiating as a challenging contest, a competitive sport. For this reason it is wise to build plenty of margin into your initial offer, leaving room for maneuver during the lengthy negotiating process.

Concession Behavior. Be prepared for "bazaar haggling" – hard bargaining. Take care to make each concession with great reluctance and only on a strict "if...then," conditional basis. Always demand something equivalent in return for each concession in price, terms or other issues.

Decision-Making. Negotiating in the Arab world tends to proceed at a leisurely pace. It would be a tactical error to press hard for a quick decision. Go with the flow. Decisions take time, so adjust your expectations accordingly.

The Contract. Get everything in writing to avoid future misunderstandings.

The Egyptian Negotiator

Time and Scheduling. One of the most important cultural characteristics relates to time and scheduling, where visitors may find a non-level playing field. Egyptian businessmen and government officials are often late for meetings, but foreign visitors are expected to be on time.

However, business visitors should not take offense at this apparent lack of concern about punctuality. If you are kept waiting in Cairo it's probably because your counterpart was held up in traffic. Like Bangkok, Cairo is in the grip of quasi-permanent gridlock – that's why Cairenes hold so many meetings in their cars these days.

On the other hand, perhaps his previous meeting simply ran longer than expected. Most Egyptians find it impolite to abruptly end a meeting just because they have another one scheduled soon. Or maybe your counterpart was called upon to help a friend or relative out of a jam. In this culture people are far more important than clocks, schedules and agendas. Whatever the reason may be for being kept cooling your heels, it is important to avoid displaying open irritation and impatience.

For example, I have seen northern Europeans and Americans in waiting rooms glancing repeatedly at their watches, drumming their fingers on their briefcase and making snide comments to their associates. You may get by with such behavior if you are in Egypt as a buyer. But if your mission is to sell something, to promote a project or to negotiate a joint-venture agreement, the appropriate response to tardiness is to grin and bear it. In this culture it is inexcusably rude for a seller to become visibly upset at having to wait for someone – especially if that someone is a customer.

Verbal and Nonverbal Communication

Expressiveness. Egyptians readily express emotion and tend to use emphatic, elaborate verbal language marked by exaggeration for effect. When they have something important to say they may say it loudly and repeatedly, reinforced with intense eye contact and frequent gestures for emphasis.

Conversational Overlap. Some foreign visitors are confused by the Egyptian tendency to engage in conversational overlap – starting to talk before another speaker has finished. If you experience this kind of behavior, just remember that no offense is intended: conversational overlap is quite normal in expressive cultures.

Touch Behavior. As demonstrative people Egyptians engage in frequent touching among friends, but until they know someone well they usually confine physical touching to the handshake. Back-slapping and elbow-grabbing are definitely out of place.

Interpersonal Space. In hotel lobbies in Alexandria and Cairo I have seen visiting businessmen step back involuntarily when their local counterparts walk up to greet them. While this is perhaps an understandable reaction, to back away from someone in Egypt is nevertheless a serious gaffe – it signals you dislike or mistrust that person. While Egyptian men are most comfortable at about half an arm's-length distance or less in a business situation – say about 10 inches or so – North Americans and northern Europeans usually prefer a full arm's length. If visitors are not prepared for this degree of closeness they might feel uncomfortable and move back, giving local counterparts the feeling they are disliked.

Eye Contact. During a business or social discussion, Egyptian men expect you to look them in the eye all the while you are conversing with them. If you frequently glance away it indicates lack of interest in the discussion. Or worse, lack of respect for them. On the other hand, a woman visitor should avoid making direct eye contact with an Egyptian male on the street: It could be interpreted as an invitation to a sexual approach.

Taboos. As in other Islamic societies, the left hand is considered unclean. Always use only your right hand when eating or when passing something to an Egyptian. If you happen to be left-handed, train yourself to offer your business card with your right hand, for example. When seated, avoid showing the soles of your shoes – they are also unclean.

Business Protocol

Dress Code. The appropriate business dress for men is a conservative suit and tie during the winter and a shirt and neat pants in the summer. Women visitors should wear a simple, elegant Western suit or dress and carry a scarf to cover their hair when called for, such as on a visit to a mosque. For casual wear neither sex should wear shorts and women should take care not to appear in revealing apparel such as halter tops, sleeveless blouses and short skirts.

Forms of Address. Visitors from informal cultures may need to be reminded that although Egyptians tend to be friendly and outgoing they do not like being addressed with excessive informality at the first few meetings. Yes, you may use a person's first name, but remember to precede it with Mr., Mrs. etc. or with the appropriate professional or academic title. So it would be Madam Leila or Dr. Hisham until they ask you to drop the formality.

Meeting and Greeting. When introduced, men shake hands with both men and women and women shake hands with other women. But avoid a bone-crushing grip: Egyptians are accustomed to a gentle handshake.

Topics of Conversation. Good topics of conversation are Egyptian history, food and monuments. On the other hand, stay away from Middle Eastern politics. In fact, it's a good idea to avoid politics in general unless your local counterpart raises the issue. While it is permissible to talk about families, avoid asking about the counterpart's wife or daughters.

Interrupted Meetings. It is rare to have a private tête-a-tête in this market. The more senior is the person you are trying to talk to, the more distractions you are likely to encounter. Do not expect your counterpart to hold incoming phone calls. In Egypt it is rude to turn away drop-in visitors or to refuse to take a phone call.

Meeting Refreshments. Egyptians are warm, friendly and hospitable people. Return their friendliness by always accepting their offer of tea or coffee. Take at least a sip even if you are not thirsty. The drink is really a symbol of Egyptian hospitality – to refuse a cup is to spurn that hospitality. Likewise, if your local counterpart comes to your office or hotel meeting room be sure to offer him something to drink. Failure to do so indicates coldness or lack of interest.

Gift Giving. Gifts are always welcome but not expected. Choose something for which your own country is well-known, but avoid giving alcohol or any other item forbidden to a Muslim person. Good ideas are quality "coffee table" books or illustrated calendars showing scenes from your home country or region. Present the gift with both hands or with the right hand only, never with the left (unclean) hand.

Guest Behavior. If invited to someone's home for a meal, bring a cake or high quality chocolates. Flowers are for weddings and to cheer up sick people. Expect to eat a great deal as a way of showing your appreciation. Your host will press you to eat more you than really want to. Eat as much as you can. When you have reached your limit, you may have to decline a further helping two or three times, emphatically, in order to make the point.

It is appropriate to show appreciation for the fine food when dining in someone's home, but avoid overdoing the compliments. To Egyptians, the food is less important than the opportunity to relax and interact with friends. Furthermore, in middle- and upper-class homes most of the food is prepared by servants. So thank your hostess enthusiastically for a lovely evening...of which the good food was a part.

Host Behavior. Similarly, when hosting Egyptians you should keep urging them to eat and drink. But remember that over 90% of Egyptians are Muslims, so avoid offering alcoholic beverages and pork products.

Negotiating Behavior

Egyptian negotiators tend to be enthusiastic bargainers, often expecting their counterparts to grant major concessions on price and terms during the course of the negotiation. Be prepared for bazaar haggling. Negotiating proceeds at a leisurely pace. It would be a tactical error to press hard for a quick decision. Decisions take time, so adjust your expectations accordingly.

The Greek Negotiator

Expressive Communication. Style Like other Mediterraneans most Greeks are masters of what academics call "conversational overlap". By the time you are halfway through your statement a Greek has already figured out what you are going to say next, so he exuberantly breaks in to agree, disagree or change the subject. While many North Americans and northern Europeans find this behavior rude, it is simply an example of the outgoing, expressive Hellenic communication style.

Nonverbal Communication

Interpersonal Space. Greeks display their friendliness and warmth by standing or sitting close to other people. If visitors unconsciously step back, Greeks may read this retreat as a sign of unfriendliness.

Eye Contact. When negotiating with Greeks, be sure to maintain strong eye contact whenever you are speaking or being spoken to. Letting your gaze wander during a discussion is rude, indicating lack of interest on your part.

Gestures and Facial Expressions. Greeks tend to speak loudly and communicate with lots of facial expression and gestures – other signs of expressiveness. Unfortunately, business visitors sometimes misunderstand the local body language. For example, to signify "no" many Greeks tip their head back without saying a word, a movement which foreigners may misinterpret as a nod of the head meaning "yes".

And for Greeks, lifting one's eyebrows is another nonverbal way of saying no. To make things even more interesting, should you hear a word which sounds like "nay", be aware that it could be the Greek word for yes.

Hellenes also sometimes misinterpret foreigners' body language. As an example, the familiar "thumbs up" sign is an obscene sexual gesture in northern Greece. And a friendly wave with palm showing and fingers extended is a serious nonverbal insult to a Greek.

Business Protocol

Dress Code. Men should wear a suit and tie, women a dress or suit, even if your local counterpart is dressed more casually. During the hot summer months men will be invited to doff jackets and loosen ties and women can wear lighter weight business attire.

Meeting and Greeting. As in most of Europe, do address Greeks by their family name until they suggest moving to a first-name basis. However, in contrast with many other European cultures you can normally dispense with formal academic and professional titles. Male visitors being introduced to a Greek male should give a firm handshake and look the other party in the eye. Women tend to use a lighter handshake. Shake hands whenever you meet and again when you take leave.

Wining and Dining. Sharing a meal is a great way to learn about each other, to develop a relationship. Greeks are generous hosts. Forget about power breakfasts, though – think lunch instead. In Athens most business people get to the office early, say between 7:00 and 7:30, and except for a mid-morning break work straight through until around 3:00 or 3:30. An invitation to lunch means you are making good progress in getting to know your local counterpart.

Dinnertime is usually around 9 pm or later. Greeks normally entertain business visitors in restaurants, so if you are honored with an invitation to dinner at home be sure to accept. In such cases suitable hostess gifts are chocolates, pastries or fine cognac. A potted plant also makes an excellent gift, but remember that it should be wrapped when you present it to your hostess.

During the meal expect your host to insist that you sample everything and take second helpings. Be sure to keep both wrists on the table – Greeks would wonder what you're doing with that hand in your lap. To signal that you have really had enough to eat, place your napkin on the table. It is polite to stay until at least 11 pm.

When it is your turn to host a lunch or dinner it is a good idea to ask your Greek partners to select the restaurant. And be sure to urge them repeatedly to eat and drink. Whereas North Americans may feel uncomfortable with such pushing, in the Near East this comes across as the ultimate in good manners.

Negotiating Tips

Budget plenty of time and patience. The negotiating process may take longer than you expect, and decision-making also takes time. Avoid showing irritation or impatience.

Greeks enjoy vigorous bargaining, sometimes to the point of bazaar haggling. They are usually reluctant to accept an initial quotation as final. Therefore it is wise to build some bargaining room into your opening offer so as to leave room for concessions.

Any concession you make should be granted with a show of great reluctance, even pain. And be sure to make any concession conditional. That is, demand a quid pro quo each time.

Keep smiling, even in the face of occasional confrontational tactics.

The Brazilian Negotiator

The Language of Business. The national language is Portuguese. Only a minority of Brazilian business people speak fluent English. Visitors who speak Spanish should know that using that language implies to some Brazilians that Spanish is a more important language than Portuguese. Inquire about the possible need for an interpreter before your visit.

Initial Contact. In Brazil local contacts are essential. Potential buyers do not react well to the direct, "cold" approach. Plan to attend a trade show or join a trade mission to meet interested parties. You can also arrange for a chamber of commerce, trade association, government agency, bank or business associate to introduce you to Brazilian companies.

Your first written correspondence should be in Portuguese, stating that if possible you would prefer to correspond in English from then on. Request an appointment about two weeks in advance. Expect to meet in a office rather than in a restaurant or bar. Schedule only two meetings per day, one between 10 and 11:30 am and the second starting at 3 pm.

Don't expect to get down to business quickly. Brazilians need time to get to know you.

Importance of Relationships. Expect to invest a considerable amount of time developing good rapport and a pleasant, relaxed relationship before discussing business. Establishing an atmosphere of trust is a precondition to a successful business relationship. Good topics for small talk are football (soccer), Brazilian history, literature and places to visit as well as information about your home town and region. You will probably need two or three visits to the country before you can expect to do serious business. Like other Latins, Brazilians value deep, long-lasting relationships.

Orientation to Time. In the southern part of Brazil business people increasingly value firm schedules and punctuality – particularly in Sao Paulo, the commercial capital of the country. This is in marked contrast to tropical Brazil, for example Rio de Janeiro. The clock ticks at a different speed for the fun-loving Cariocas of Rio. There you might find yourself waiting an hour or more for your local ounterpart. However, business visitors are expected to be punctual.

Hierarchy, Status and Respect. In Brazil one's status depends more on social class, education and family background than on personal achievement. Business visitors can enhance their status by displaying a lively interest in intellectual pursuits, dressing elegantly and staying in top hotels.

Expressive Communication Style. A warm and friendly people, Brazilians tend to be talkative, nonverbally expressive and open about showing emotion in public. Don't be offended if you are sometimes interrupted in mid-sentence – conversational overlap is not rude in Brazil. Do however avoid direct confrontation during negotiations.

Nonverbal Behavior. Men and women shake hands warmly when introduced and again when departing. Visiting men should expect to shake hands with another male for a considerable length of time – take care not to withdraw your hand prematurely.

Brazil is definitely a high-contact culture. After they get to know each other two men will shake hands and touch each other on the elbow or forearm, perhaps slap each other on the back or shoulder. Male friends will exchange the *abraço* or embrace while women friends brush cheeks with a kissing motion of the lips.

In another sign of friendliness, Brazilians stand very close to each other when talking and maintain strong eye contact with the person they are conversing with. Both sexes use frequent gestures. Avoid using the "A-OK" sign, a very rude gesture in Brazil. On the other hand the "fig" sign, considered vulgar in some other Latin American countries, signifies good luck. This gesture involves clenching the fist with the thumb pointing upwards between the index and middle fingers.

Business Customs and Protocol

Dress Code. Male executives tend to wear fashionable three-piece suits. Office workers wear the two-piece version. Male visitors should note that proper business attire always includes long-sleeved shirts, even in hot weather. Brazilian men make fun of male visitors wearing short-sleeved dress shirts. Women in business wear elegant suits or dresses as well as blouses and skirts. Blouses and jackets may have short sleeves. Both sexes should avoid wearing green and yellow – the colors of the Brazilian flag.

Meeting and Greeting. Address your male counterpart as *Senhor* plus the family name. For women it is *Senhora* and her family name. Medical doctors, lawyers and all university graduates are addressed as *Doutor* (Doctor). Expect to move to a first-name basis fairly soon, but wait until the Brazilian party starts using your given name.

Convesational Overlap. Expect frequent interruptions during business meetings, especially in government offices. This is not regarded as rude or improper behavior.

Wining and Dining Women drink wine, spirits and liqueurs – beer is considered a man's drink. Brazilians normally eat a light breakfast between 7 and 9 am and a substantial lunch between noon and 2 pm. Dinner usually starts after 7 pm but dinner parties don't normally get underway until after 10:00 pm.

Table Manners. Avoid using the side of your fork to cut anything and do not pick up food of any kind with your hands. Although they are a very expressive people, Brazilians do not like a lot of conversation during meals. Wait until coffee is served before talking business.

Gift Giving. Good gifts to bring from abroad for men are music tapes and small electronic gadgets such as quality calculators. For women, perfume. If invited to dinner at home bring chocolates, champagne or or a container of fresh strawberries. Avoid purple flowers, which are associated with funerals.

Women in Business. Female business visitors who dress and act professionally encounter no great barriers to getting things done in Brazil. Unwanted male attention should be politely but firmly ignored.

Exchanging Favors. Brazilians frequently ask friends and business acquaintances for small and large favors and expect these requests to be granted. Be careful of asking favors of Brazilians, however. They might very well agree to do what you ask even if they would much rather not, since refusing you would be rude.

Negotiating Style. Brazilians are widely known as tough bargainers, not afraid to turn down offers rather bluntly. Such frankness is however not intended to be rude or confrontational. They simply want you to know where they stand. Budget enough time for a lengthy negotiating process and include a substantial margin in your opening offer so as to leave room for concessions. Expect very few silences during these bargaining sessions: Brazilians seem to talk constantly.

Wise negotiators include plenty of time for socializing during these drawn-out discussions. If you wish to entertain a high-level executive, ask his secretary to recommend a restaurant. It is important to host your counterpart only at elegant, prestigious establishments. Similarly, business visitors should only stay in top hotels while in Brazil.

The Mexican Negotiator

The Language of Business. Fluency in Spanish is a great asset to doing business, though today more Mexican businessmen speak English. This is especially the case in Monterrey, along the northern border and to a lesser extent in Mexico City and Guadalajara. Inquire about the need for an interpreter before your visit. Remember to have your company and product literature translated into Spanish before arriving in Mexico.

Making Contact. A local connection is very important. Avoid a "cold" approach to a prospective business partner. Start at the top: Approach the most senior person in the company. Your first letter or fax should be in Spanish, but specify that if possible you would prefer to correspond in English from then on. Request an appointment about two weeks in advance; let the Mexican party decide the time and place to meet.

Build a Relationship before Talking Business. Get to know your counterpart before starting to talk business. Good topics for small talk are Mexican art and literature as well as your home country. You will need two or three meetings to establish trust, after which serious business discussions can begin.

Mexicans value deep, long-lasting relationships. Personal contacts and relationships are major factors in business success. You need *palanca* – pull or clout – to get things done quickly. It's very often who you know that counts.

Orientation to Time. Although things are changing in the northern part of the country, do not expect absolute punctuality in Mexico. Local business people may be half an hour to an hour late without causing offense. Visitors however should always be punctual.

Avoid scheduling multiple meetings in any one day. One meeting at 10 am and another in the late afternoon is about right. If someone gives you a meeting time and adds *a la gringa,* expect them to be roughly on time. On the other hand, *a la mexicana* would indicate a more relaxed approach to scheduling.

Expressive Communication Style. Mexicans are expressive, both verbally and nonverbally. During a lively discussion they may start talking before you have quite finished. This is not considered rude behavior.

Indirect Language. Verbal communication is often indirect. For example, during a negotiation your counterparts may avoid a direct answer to a question. You may need to rephrase the question or ask it in a different way.

Paraverbal and Nonverbal Communication

Interpersonal Distance. Like other Latins, Mexicans tend to stand and sit closer to others than northern Europeans, North Americans and Asians are accustomed to.

Touch Behavior. Among themselves, Mexicans tend to engage in a good deal of physical contact. Wait for your local counterparts to initiate hugging, kissing and the like.

Gaze Behavior. Maintain steady eye contact with the person you are conversing with.

Gestures. Expect large and frequent hand and arm gestures.

Taboos. It is impolite to appear in public with your hands in your pockets. Putting hands on hips signifies a challenge or threat to others. If someone shakes their hand from side to side with forefinger extended, they are saying "no." In contrast, the thumbs up sign indicates "yes" or approval of what has just been referred to.

Business Protocol

Dress Code. Men should wear a dark suit and black shoes, women a good dress or suit with heels, makeup and jewelry. Staying at a top hotel gives you status – as do age, level of education, position in your company and a basic knowledge of Mexican history, geography and culture.

Meeting and Greeting. Shake hands with men both when meeting and departing, using a moderate grip. Avoid further physical contact until you know the person well. Give women a slight bow and wait for them to extend their hand.

Even if you don't speak Spanish, learning the principal greetings will be appreciated. *Buenos dias, buenas tardes* and *buenas noches* mean good morning, good afternoon and good evening or good night respectively.

Forms of Address. Mexicans value formality. Until you get to know your local counterpart use his title and family name, e.g. *Doctor* Morales, *Director* Reyes, *Profesor* Santana. Later you can switch to just the title without the family name. For example, use *Licenciado* to refer to someone with a college degree. Do not use first names until the Mexcian party suggests it. And remember that the person's "middle" name is part of his or her family name.

Meeting Behavior. Expect frequent interruptions: Phone calls as well as visitors dropping in without an appointment. These interruptions are not considered impolite; Mexicans would consider it rude to turn away drop-in visitors or to refuse to take phone calls.

Interacting with Secretaries. Refer to an office secretary as Señorita whether she is young or not and whether she is single or married. On your second trip to Mexico, bring small gifts such as perfume for the secretaries of important people. Tell her your wife bought it for her.

Gift Giving. Good business gifts are premium cognacs and Scotches, cocktail table books, desk clocks and gold pens or lighters. Remember that silver objects are only for tourists. Give gold items to your business contacts.

Women in Business. Women business visitors may not be treated with the same respect they are used to at home, since Mexican men are not used to dealing with female executives. Women are advised to dress conservatively and to behave professionally at all times.

Wining and Dining It is important to entertain your local counterparts only at top restaurants. Suggest several and let your guests choose the one they prefer.

Breakfast and lunch are good opportunities to talk business, while dinner should be reserved strictly for socializing. Breakfast can be as early as 8 am, lunch normally starts around 2 pm and dinner begins after 9 pm. Be careful to reciprocate all meal invitations.

If accompanied by your spouse it is OK to invite your counterpart's spouse. Foreign business women should always include the wives of their Mexican male customers or contacts in any dinner invitation. When entertaining male guests women should also make prior arrangements with the headwaiter for payment; otherwise Mexican men will absolutely insist on picking up the check.

Negotiating Behavior

Consider putting some extra padding into your opening offer. The negotiating process can be long and vigorous, and Mexicans tend to be hard bargainers. They may also be optimistic with deadlines and schedules, so it's wise to mentally add a few days or weeks to any target date you are given.

Always take time to think over any proposal your Mexican counterparts make. Quick acceptance makes the other party think they may have conceded too much. Tell them you need time to consider the idea. Similarly, Mexicans take their time coming to a decision on your proposal.

Group 4

Relationship-Focused, Formal, Polychronic and Variably Expressive

---

Russia – Poland – Romania

The Russian Negotiator

Despite the many challenges of this huge market, many foreign companies are doing good business in Russia today. One is F. Uhrenholt Meat A/S, a Danish firm exporting food products worth some $100,000 per year. Speaking with the experience of 35 visits to the market, Managing Director Jann Jensen emphasizes that 90% of business in Russia is done face-to-face. You build your business on personal relationships.

For Uhrenholt, a key step was establishing their own representative office in Moscow staffed by English-speaking local people. They also regularly check the references of new customers through the Danish embassy. In general, Jensen finds there is really little or no difference today between doing business in Sweden, Germany and Russia.

As one might expect, not all foreign companies report such positive experience. Chaos, crime and corruption – along with capricious regulations and bureaucratic red tape – continue to present real barriers to trade. But as the world's largest (11 time zones) and fifth most populous (150 million people) country, Russia is a tempting market for those who know how to overcome those barriers.

Obviously, one step in surmounting the obstacles is to develop an understanding of Russian business behavior.

Personal Relationships. In underlining the key role played by connections, Jann Jensen provides good advice. As is the case in other relationship-focused markets around the world, you need personal relationships to get things done. It's who you know that counts. The Chinese and other East Asians call these vital relationships *guanxi*, the Latin Americans *palanca*, the Egyptians *wastah*. In the Russian language the corresponding word is *blat*.

As Jensen also points out, most business there is done face-to-face. Frequent visits to the market and frequent phone calls are essential. This again is true of the RF business cultures of Asia, the Middle East, Africa, Latin America and much of eastern Europe.

And while written contracts are as important as anywhere else in today's global marketplace, be prepared for your Russian counterparts to renegotiate the agreement not long after it was signed.

Direct, Low-Context Communication. Russia's version of relationship-focus does however differ from most other RF cultures in an important respect: verbal communication. Unlike East and Southeast Asians for example, Russian negotiators tend to be direct, even blunt, saying pretty much what they mean and meaning what they say.

This is in contrast to the majority of relationship-focused cultures where people commonly use indirect, high-context communication. The Russian combination of an RF approach to business with fairly direct, low-context communication behavior is somewhat of a rarity. Among the handful of other business cultures exhibiting this feature are France, the Catalan region of Spain, parts of Chile, Venezuela and northern Mexico and parts of east/central Europe.

Formality, Status and Hierarchies. Here again we have a special case. Russians belong to the more formal wing of Europeans, closer to the Germans and French than to the informal Danes. And we know that formal cultures are usually also hierarchical – see Japan and France, – just as informal cultures are normally also egalitarian, as in Australia and Denmark.

But while Russian culture is formal and hierarchical, at the same time a key value is *uravnilovka*, egalitarianism. Russians deeply resent it when others have more than they do. In the old joke, God gives Ivan the peasant a wish: He can ask for anything he wants. Well God, says Ivan, You know my neighbor owns a cow.

So I suppose you want two cows then? God replies. Oh no God, says Ivan, What I want is for my neighbor's cow to die.

In this sense Russian "uravnilovka" is close to the Scandinavian version of egalitarianism, which looks askance at people who seem to rise above the rest. A similar value is expressed in the Australian saying, The tall poppy gets cut down. So we have an apparent contradiction: egalitarian values coexisting with formal, hierarchical behavior. But such cultural contradictions are common in the real world. Look at the USA, where egalitarian ideals have coexisted with hierarchical attitudes for generations.

Russian formality shows up in the way people dress and in their meeting and greeting rituals, while hierarchies are evident in the top-down approach to management as well as the scarcity of women in positions of authority. Visitors are expected to observe a certain degree of formality in dress and in public behavior. The latter is especially important at the first meeting with Russian counterparts.

Hierarchical attitudes affect business visitors in two ways. First, while visiting female executives will be treated with delightful Old World gallantry, they can also expect to be patronized. Few women have reached positions of authority in Russian business organizations, so the men are not used to interacting with women on anything approaching a basis of equality.

Second, both male and female visitors will note that all important decisions are reserved for the top man in the organization. Typical of strongly hierarchical societies, this characteristic slows progress and can bring about long delays in negotiations. In Russia it is even more important than in most other business cultures to make sure one is negotiating with the real decision-maker.

Polychronic Time Behavior. Most Russian managers admit that while they are usually unconcerned with punctuality, they try hard to be on time when meeting with foreigners. Most visitors from time-conscious, monochronic cultures report little evidence of these efforts to be on time. Expect meetings to start late (often an hour or more), to run on well beyond the anticipated ending time and to be frequently interrupted. Russian top executives seem to find it normal to conduct three or four different conversations simultaneously, some face-to-face and others on one or more telephones.

Variable Expressiveness. While it is generally possible to classify cultures as either Reserved (Finns, Japanese, Thais) or Expressive (southern Europeans, Latin Americans, Mediterranean people), Russian negotiators frequently display both types of behavior during the same meeting.

At the first meeting, expect a quiet, restrained manner; at subsequent sessions be prepared for more demonstrative behavior. Be ready for emotional outbursts and displays of temper at critical points in the discussions.

Paraverbal and Nonverbal Behavior

- Voice Volume: Moderate. Visitors should avoid loud, boisterous conversation in public.
- Interpersonal Distance: From close to medium – 12 to 18 inches (20 to 30 cm).
- Touch Behavior: Among friends, frequent touching, bear hugs and cheek-kissing.
- Eye Contact: Direct gaze across the negotiating table.

– Taboo Gestures: The "A-OK" thumb-and-forefinger sign is obscene. Standing with hands in one's pockets is rude.

Business Protocol

Dress Code. Conservative. In winter, adopt the layered look. Expect to check your overcoat in most public buildings.

Meeting and Greeting. Shake hands and state your name. Formulas such as "how are you?" are unnecessary.

Forms of Address. When introduced, use title plus last name, not first names. Later you might move to using the first name plus patronymic, but wait until your counterpart suggests it.

Exchanging Cards. Bring plenty of cards which show your organizational title and any advanced degrees. Do not be surprised if your Russian counterpart does not have a card.

Topics of Conversation. Avoid discussions of war, politics and religion. And remember, Russians tend to be sensitive about their country's recent loss of superpower status.

Business Gifts. Quality pens, books, music CDs, solar-powered calculators, liquor, card wallets, gift soaps, T-shirts.

Business Entertaining. It is a signal honor to be invited to a Russian home: Be sure to accept. Most business entertaining is done at restaurants.

Drinking. Russians seem to have a high tolerance for alcohol. Few foreigners succeed in staying with the locals drink for drink. To limit your intake, drink only when someone proposes a toast. If there are many toasts, switch to sipping. Be prepared to drink at least one or two small vodkas.

Russian Negotiating Behavior

Making a Presentation. Especially at the first meeting, avoid starting off with a joke. Show that you are taking business seriously. Pack your presentation with facts and technical details.

Local Sensitivities. Avoid statements such as, "We are planning a really "aggressive" marketing campaign." The word "aggressive" has a negative connotation in Russian. Also avoid proposing a "compromise" during the negotiation – most Russians regard a "compromise" as morally wrong. Instead, suggest meeting each other halfway, or make your proposal conditional on an equivalent concession from your counterparts.

Bargaining Style. Be ready for hardball tactics – a tough, sometimes confrontational approach, possibly punctuated with table-pounding, temper tantrums, emotional outbursts, brinkmanship, loud threats and walkouts. With some Russian negotiators these components of the "Soviet" style of bargaining have survived into the post-Soviet era. Counter these tactics by staying calm. More often, your counterparts will simply try to out-wait you, exploiting your presumed impatience. Counter this with patience, patience and more patience.

Resolving Disputes. Insist on a clause calling for arbitration in a third country. Sweden is currently a popular choice.

The Polish Negotiator

Polish business people often exhibit features of both the relationship-focused and deal-focused approaches to business. For example, while it is important to have the right contacts and to build strong relationships, at the same time Polish negotiators tend to be verbally direct.

Most Polish business people are formal and moderately polychronic. Their communication behavior is likely to be reserved at the first meeting, more expressive as they get to know you.

Geography and history provide important clues to this country's business culture. Positioned as it is between Germany and Russia, Poland has for centuries been influenced by both East and West.

Poles were less influenced by decades of communist rule than some of their neighbors. There are two main reasons for this difference. First, the strength and popularity of the Roman Catholic church ("Is the Pope Polish?"). Second, the prevalence of private agriculture: Collective farms played a smaller role in Poland than in most other countries on the eastern side of the old Iron Curtain.

Personal Relationships. As with most markets outside northwestern Europe, North America and Australia/New Zealand, it is vital to have the right connections in Poland. Who you know counts for a great deal. That said, visitors will observe a trend: Younger Polish business people are becoming more deal-focused – i.e., more like the Germans and Scandinavians – while still retaining elements of the RF approach. In other words, like the French and Russians, Poles can be classed as either moderately relationship-focused or moderately deal-focused.

Verbal Directness. At the bargaining table in Poland you will experience verbal directness rather than polite circumlocutions most of the time. The Polish combination of a relationship-oriented approach to business along with low-context communication is relatively uncommon in the global marketplace. Other examples are the Russians, the French and the Spaniards from Catalonia.

Formality, Status and Hierarchies. Poles are more formal than Danes, Australians or North Americans – something like the Germans and French, for instance. This formality is evident in the way people dress and in their meeting and greeting rituals. Hierarchies are evident in the top-down approach to management and in the relative scarcity of women business managers.

Women in Business Women can expect to be treated by their older male counterparts with Continental gallantry. Among men of the older generation, hand-kissing is as prevalent as it used to be in Vienna. But on the other hand, women negotiators may find they are being patronized. Few women have reached positions of authority in business, so many men are not used to interacting with women on a basis of equality.

Polychronic Time Behavior. Younger Polish business people are aware of the importance of punctuality, schedules and deadlines. They admit with some embarrassment that visitors are often kept waiting. Expect meetings to start 15 to 20 minutes late, to run on beyond the anticipated ending time, and to be interrupted from to time.

Variable Expressiveness. At the first meeting, expect a reserved manner; thereafter be prepared for more demonstrative behavior. Poles do not always hide the fact that they are irritated, frustrated or angry.

Paraverbal and Nonverbal Behavior

- Voice Volume: Moderate. Avoid raising your voice during negotiations as well as in public.
- Interpersonal Distance: Medium – 15 to 25 inches (25 to 40 cm).
- Touch Behavior: This a low-contact culture in a business setting. Except for the handshake, expect little or no touching in a business situation: Closer to the German style than the French.
- Eye Contact: Direct gaze across the negotiating table, less intense perhaps than in the Middle East and southern Europe but more direct than is common in East and Southeast Asia.

Business Protocol and Etiquette

Dress Code. Conservative suits and ties for men, dresses for women.

Meeting and Greeting. Shake hands, make eye contact and state your name. Formulas such as "how are you?" are unnecessary. Shake hands again when leaving the meeting. It is polite for men to wait for a Polish woman to extend her hand. Male visitors are not expected to kiss a woman's hand; instead, a slight bow may accompany the handshake.

Forms of Address. When introduced, address your counterparts by their professional or academic title plus family name. Only relatives and close friends address each other by first names.

Exchanging Cards. Your cards should show your organizational title and any advanced degrees.

Topics of Conversation. Most Poles regard their country as part of Central Europe rather than of Eastern Europe. Referring to Poland as part of East-Central Europe is acceptable.

Business Gifts. At the first meeting, a bottle of imported spirits such as scotch or cognac is appropriate, but not vodka: Good vodka is readily available locally.

Social Gifts. Bring flowers when invited to someone's home for a meal. While the florist will usually give you good advice, remember to bring an uneven number and avoid both red roses and chrysanthemums – the former imply romantic intentions, the latter are for funerals. Other good gifts are imported wine, chocolates, coffee, perfume and cigarettes.

Business Entertaining. It is an honor to be invited to a Polish home: Be sure to accept. However, most business entertaining is done at restaurants.

Wining and Dining. As in many other East-Central European countries, Poles tend to take breakfast between 7:00 and 8:00, then work straight through the day without a lunch break. So they eat lunch ("obiad") around 3:00 or 4:00. This is the main meal of the day. If invited to a business lunch, expect to eat between 4:00 and 5:00. The evening meal is usually a light repast around 8:30 or so.

Negotiating Behavior

Making a Presentation. To show you are serious, avoid starting off with a joke at the first meeting. As you would in Germany, load your presentation with background information, facts and technical details.

Bargaining style. Wise negotiators keep some bargaining chips in reserve until the endgame. Your opening bid should be realistic but at the same time should include room for maneuver.

Decision Making. The negotiating process usually takes longer when dealing with the government or public sector than when doing business with the private sector.

The Romanian Negotiator

Next to Albania, Romania experienced the most oppressive post-war Communist rule of any Eastern European country. The infamous Ceausescu dictatorship alone lasted 24 bitter years. Business visitors will encounter the residual effects of a failed centralized economy for years to come, as the society slowly recovers. Patience is advised.

Romania falls into the southeast quadrant of the north/south and east/west fault lines which divide European business cultures. The country's business behavior reflects Romania's geographic location in eastern European, while its communication style reflects the influence of Latin Europe to the south.

The Language of Business. Like their Hungarian neighbors, Romanians speak a non-Slavic language. Romanian is a romance language distantly related to French, Italian, Spanish and Portuguese as well as the Romansch or Ladino of eastern Swtizerland. Partly for that reason French remains an important language of business, although younger people are increasingly choosing English as their second language. German is also used for business.

Relationship-Oriented Market. As in the rest of East-Central Europe, cold calls do not work well in Romania. It is vital to have the right connections. Especially at the beginning of a business relationship, expect to discuss important business issuees face-to-face or on the telephone rather than via fax or e-mail. Budget plenty of time for getting to your counterparts before getting down to business.

Verbal Indirectness. Romanians often prefer a roundabout way of saying things, rejecting northern European and North American directness. Negotiators will get better results if they avoid asking too many direct questions, instead probing gently for the information they need while gradually building a pleasant relationship with their Romanian counterparts.

Formality, Status and Hierarchies. Romanians interact more formallly than Danes, Australians or North Americans. Formality is evident in the way they dress as well as in local meeting and greeting rituals. Hierarchies are evident in the top-down approach to management and in the scarcity of women business managers.

Visiting female executives are likely to be treated by senior male counterparts with traditional Continental gallantry. Among men of the older generation, hand-kissing is as prevalent as it used to be in Vienna. On the other hand, women negotiators may feel they are being patronized. Few women have reached positions of authority in business, so men are not used to relating to women on the basis of equality.

Polychronic Time Behavior. Meetings often start 30 to 60 minutes late and last beyond the anticipated ending time, but visitors are expected to be punctual.

Expressive Paraverbal and Nonverbal Behavior

Interpersonal Distance. Romanians stand and sit closer together than northerners, so be ready for the same interpersonal distance you find in Greece – about half an arm's length.

Touch Behavior. Be prepared for much more touching than in the other countries of East-Central Europe. This is a high-contact culture, with (among friends) lots of hugging and kissing.

Eye Contact. Steady, considerably more focused than the gaze behavior negotiators encounter in East and Southeast Asia.

Gestures. The broad and frequent Italian-style hand and arm gestures may startle some visitors from the reserved cultures of East and Southeast Asia.

Business Protocol and Etiquette

Making an Appointment. Your letter will be given more attention if written in English rather than Romanian. Write two to three weeks before the desired meeting date and then follow up by fax, telephone or e-mail.

Dress Code. Conservative suits and ties for men, dresses or suits and heels for women.

Meeting and Greeting. Shake hands, make eye contact and state your name. If you meet the same person again later that day, shake hands again. In fact, expect to shake hands every time you meet. Shake hands again when leaving a meeting. Wait for a Romanian woman to extend her hand. Male visitors are not expected to kiss a woman's hand; instead, bow slightly when shaking her hand.

Forms of Address. When introduced, address your counterparts by their professional or academic title plus surname. Only relatives and close friends address each other by given name.

Exchanging Cards. Your cards should show your organizational title and any advanced degrees.

Topics of Conversation. Sports, travel, films, books, fashion and food. Avoid personal questions about someone's family or job.

Business Gifts. Inexpensive gifts are given to celebrate the signing of an agreement or perhaps for the Christmas holidays. Tasteful logo gifts such as pens or lighters are acceptable.

Social Gifts. Bring wrapped bouquets of flowers when invited to a private home for a meal.

Wining and Dining. People usually take breakfast around 7:00, lunch about noon and dinner at 7:00 or 7:30. Lunch is generally the main meal of the day.

Toasting. This is the custom at both formal and informal meals. Touch glasses, nod and say, "To your health" or "Good luck".

Negotiating Behavior

Making a Presentation. Avoid starting off with a joke at the first meeting. Use plenty of visuals and clearly-written handouts. Include background information, facts and technical details.

Facilitation Payments. Some low-level officials expect a "tip" for handling routine applications and other paperwork. A pack or carton of Kent cigarettes used to be the preferred currency for such transactions. Consult with your local contacts on this delicate issue.

Bargaining Style. Romanians are tough negotiators. Keep some bargaining chips in reserve until the endgame. Your opening bid should be realistic but should also include some room for maneuver.

Dishonest Practices. Take precautions to avoid being cheated. Romania is the second-poorest country in Europe after Albania and has just started on the long road to developing a free market economy.

Decision Making. Count on the negotiating process taking longer than it would in Western Europe or North America.

Group 5

Moderately Deal-Focused, Formal, Variably Monochronic and Expressive

---

France – Belgium – Italy – Spain – Hungary

The French Negotiator

French negotiators belong to a class by themselves. A product of Teutonic influences from the north of Europe combined with Latin infusions from the south, France's business culture is unique.

For example, while the French are relationship-focused they are at the same time a nation of individualists. Moreover though they dislike getting straight to the point and often employ indirect, high-context communication, they are quick to argue and bluntly disagree with you across the bargaining table. And despite the fact that the word "egalitarian" is derived from *egalité*, France remains one of Europe's most hierarchical societies today.

In other words, French business executives tend to be relationship-focused, high-context, highly status-conscious individualists – an unusual combination of cultural traits.

While of course no two Gallic negotiators operate exactly alike, the following profile should help prepare you for your next business meeting in France.

The Language of Business. Despite the fact that so many French business people speak English well, French is the language of business. Foreign buyers can get by with English or German, but export marketers are usually expected to speak French. Parisians especially seem to find it physically painful to hear their language spoken poorly. Written correspondence should be in French and the key parts of your product literature should be translated as well.

Good interpreters are easy to find in Paris or Lyon, but marketers who do not speak the language are likely to find themselves at a disadvantage. Despite the local sensitivity to the language, do try to use your French even if you make mistakes or have a foreign accent. You will be given credit for trying.

Making the Initial Contact. Connections count heavily in this market. Trade shows and official trade promotion missions are good ways to make initial contact. The alternative is to arrange for a formal introduction to potential customers, distributors or partners. Ask your country's embassy to introduce you.

Other useful intermediaries are chambers of commerce, trade associations and international banks, law and accounting firms. But don't overlook that golf buddy or neighbor of yours whose company has a big office in Paris!

Your letter requesting a meeting should be in flawless business French. As in other hierarchical cultures, it is wise to start at the top. Address the letter to the President/Directeur General and if you are a senior person in your company request a meeting with him.

Importance of Relationships. France is definitely a country of personal networks. You get things done more quickly by working through inside contacts than by "going through channels."

The French want to know a good deal about you before discussing business, but building rapport involves less small talk than in some other cultures. Showing a knowledge of French history, literature, art and philosophy is a good way to build rapport. Discussing French cuisine and wine over a meal is another good way.

Orientation to Time. Business behavior tends toward the polychronic, though visitors are expected to be roughly on time for business meetings, particularly if they are selling. Outside of Paris and Lyons it is not unusual for your local counterpart to appear a few minutes late. Nor do meetings always follow a fixed agenda as they commonly do across the border in Germany. Instead you may experience free-form discussions with everyone present having his say.

Hierarchy and Status. Level of education along with family background and wealth determine status in France. Graduates of the select Grandes Ecoles hold high positions in government and industry. Three out of four top managers of the 200 largest French companies come from wealthy families, whereas in Germany the figure is one out of four and in the U.S. one out of ten.

French bosses tend to run their companies in an authoritarian style. Managers are expected to be highly competent and to know the answer to virtually every question that arises. They are often reluctant to delegate authority. Fraternization with the rank and file is not common.

Communication Style. The French are verbally and nonverbally expressive. They love to argue, often engaging in spirited debate during business meetings. Negotiators from less confrontational cultures such as East Asia should not mistake this love of debate for hostility.

Verbal Communication. While they relish verbal conflict the French dislike getting straight to the point. They tend to favor subtle, indirect language and like to present their point of view with Cartesian logic, elegant phrasing and verbal flourishes. This is one reason Gallic business people prefer to negotiate in French: Their verbal pyrotechnics are lost when expressed in another language.

Nonverbal Communication. Among friends and relatives the French display high-contact behavior, including in public. A study of comparative touch behavior at cafés in Paris and London showed that within the space of an hour French couples touched each other over one hundred times while the British couples did not touch each other at all.

Always shake hands both when meeting and when leaving someone. The French use many more hand and arm gestures than Asians and Anglo-Saxons. The thumb-and-forefinger circle signifies "zero" in France. To indicate "A-OK" they flash the thumbs-up sign instead. Taboos include standing or speaking with hands in one's pockets and slapping the palm of one hand over a closed fist.

Business Protocol

Dress Code. As might be expected in a hierarchical, status-conscious society the French dress and behave formally in a business setting. And of course being French they dress with style, panache and elegance. Male business visitors should wear a dark suit; women should choose tasteful, somewhat conservative clothing and accessories.

Meeting and Greeting. Handshake with moderate pressure and steady eye contact. Among males the older or higher status person should initiate the handshake. Women of any rank can decide whether or not to offer their hand.

Forms of Address. Greet your local counterparts with *monsieur, madame* or *mademoiselle* without the person's name, as in *"Bonjour, monsieur!"* Always use the *vous* (formal) pronoun rather than the informal *tu*.

Because you are a foreigner, once you have built a relationship it is possible that your French opposite number may suggest using first names. Do wait for the local person to take this step however. And remember that you will continue to use *vous* even when on a first-name basis.

Women in Business. Because relatively few women have reached high positions in French companies, female business visitors may occasionally feel somewhat out of place. Businesswomen should dress and act professionally at all times and should avoid negotiating behavior that could be interpreted as overly aggressive.

Wining and Dining. Entertaining and being entertained is an important way to build rapport. According to a recent study two out of three French business people regularly lunch in restaurants while more than eight out of ten of their Dutch and British colleagues wolf a sandwich at their desks. And while almost half of the Brits and Germans surveyed felt business lunches were a waste of time, 70% of the French think they are an important part of doing business.

There is a certain ceremonial aspect to dining in France. Many Western ideas of proper table manners orginated in France, so visitors are advised to observe some key rules of etiquette.

Breakfast usually consists of coffee and a roll, but the American custom of the "power breakfast" is being adopted by an increasing number of Frenchmen.

Business lunches often last two to three hours over at least that many glasses of wine. In some cultures it is a sign of generosity to fill a wine glass to the brim. In France – as elsewhere in Europe and North America – when pouring wine for your neighbor at table remember to fill the glass only two-thirds full. Avoid discussing business at least until dessert is served unless your host broaches the subject earlier.

Dinner at Home. Such invitations are more common in the provinces than in Paris. Always accept and plan to arrive about 15 minutes after the appointed time.

Hostess Gifts. Flowers may not be your best choice: Your hostess may not appreciate having to search for the right size vase in the midst of all her other duties. And then you would have to remember to bring an uneven number (but never 13), to avoid chrysanthemums (funerals only), red roses (they signify you are having an affair with your hostess) and yellow flowers (they imply your host is having an affair with someone else).

Nor is wine a better choice. A bottle of undistinguished plonk brands you as ignorant or cheap while with the good stuff you run the risk of insulting your host by insinuating that his cellar is inadequate. The best solution therefore is usually a box of the very best chocolates you can find.

Wait at the door until the host or hostess invites you in. Men should not take off their jacket unless encouraged to do so by the host. Wait for your host or hostess to start eating. If you are accustomed to keeping one hand in your lap, leave this custom behind. Your table companions are liable to roll their eyes and ask each other what you are doing under the table.

Table Manners. When the salad arrives, do not cut your lettuce with a knife. Instead fold it into small pieces with your fork. Peel the fruit with a knife and eat it with a fork. It is impolite to take two servings of cheese, and extremely gauche to slice the tip from a wedge of cheese.

Negotiating Behavior

Sales Presentation. Avoid hard-sell tactics, hyperbole and flippant humor. Prepare a sober presentation with a logical sequence of arguments. If you encounter forceful disagreement on some points, be prepared to respond with factual counter-arguments. Vigorous disagreement with specific issues does not necessarily signal lack of interest in your overall proposal.

Bargaining Style. Be prepared for long, relatively unstructured negotiating sessions punctuated frequently with verbal confrontation. Your counterpart may also attack the thought process behind your bargaining position. The French pride themselves on their logical thinking and often seem to relish faulting the logic of others.

Although the senior member of the French team is likely to make most of the decisions, that does not mean those decisions will be made quickly. Expect decision-making to take longer than in Anglo-Saxon countries.

The Belgian Negotiator

Business visitors from outside of Europe find that learning Belgian business customs and practices will help them conduct successful negotiations in many other markets of Western Europe.

The Language of Business. The Flemish/French linguistic division has helped promote English as the neutral medium of international business communication in Belgium. While English-speaking negotiators are unlikely to need an interpreter these days, it is still courteous to offer to bring one to the first meeting. Visiting negotiators who speak French should preferably speak English when doing business in the northern part of the country to avoid irritating Flemish speakers.

Verbal Communication. Flemish negotiators tend to use direct, straightforward language. If they disagree with you can count on them to say so clearly rather than couching their disagreement in elaborate diplomatic verbiage. While perhaps less abrupt than the Dutch they do value frankness.

Paraverbal Communication. Most Belgians speak more softly than Americans and Latins. They also avoid conversational overlap, so negotiators from expressive cultures should take care to wait for their local counterparts to finish talking before speaking their piece.

Nonverbal Behavior

Visitors coming north from business meetings in Italy or the Mediterranean region will notice that Belgians generally stand and sit somewhat further apart from each other while talking than southern Europeans. The common interpersonal distance in Belgium is an arm's length – about the same distance most northern Europeans are accustomed to.

Slouching, talking with hands in one's pockets or chewing gum in public are all considered impolite. Men rise when women enter the room and step aside for women to enter a room first.

One important taboo concerning body language: Belgians find it rude to point with one's forefinger.

The Use of Time. Belgian negotiators tend to be monochronic in their use of time: They value punctuality and avoid interrupting business meetings.

You are expected to be on time for meetings and you can normally expect your negotiation to proceed on schedule, much as it would in Germany or Switzerland.

Expressiveness. Within Europe the peoples of the Latin south are typically less reserved and more demonstrative than their northern cousins. This distinction holds true within Belgium where the Flemish-speaking northerners are more taciturn and less expressive than the French-speaking Walloons.

Business Protocol

Dress Code. Businessmen should wear a dark suit and tie with well-polished shoes. The tie should not be removed even in hot weather. Stylish dresses or skirts and blouses are the appropriate attire for businesswomen.

Meeting and Greeting. When introduced, shake hands with a quick motion and light pressure while speaking your name clearly and repeating the other person's name. Shake hands again when it is time to leave. It is polite for men to wait for a woman to offer her hand when being introduced to her. At business meetings it is common courtesy to shake hands with everyone, both when arriving and when departing. It is customary to include secretaries in this ritual.

As in the rest of Europe, handshaking is a very important ritual. Remember to shake hands both when greeting people and when saying goodbye, meanwhile maintaining good eye contact. Physical contact beyond the handshake should be avoided.

Forms of Address. In contrast to the practice in many other European cultures, in Belgium it is usually unnecessary to use professional titles. However, do address Belgians by Mr., Mrs. or Miss plus the surname. It would be highly inappropriate to call a business acquaintance by his or her first name. If you are from an informal culture, your counterpart may suggest a shift to first names after you have known each other for a few months.

Topics of Conversation. Good topics for conversation are the history, art and special attractions of the city or region you are visiting. It is a good idea to do some relevant background reading before you arrive. Belgians like to talk about European sports, especially bicycle racing and football. They appreciate questions and comments about Belgian cuisine and beer – both of which rank among the very best in Europe. Topics to avoid include the French/Flemish linguistic division and local politics.

Business Gifts. An excellent choice would be the latest book related to the branch of business you and your counterpart are engaged in.

Business Entertainment. Because most Belgians prefer to spend evenings with their families, you are more likely to meet your local customer or partner for lunch rather than dinner. But expect little conversation about business since in this part of the world mealtimes are really for relaxing and getting to know your local counterpart.

Visiting business women may meet resistance when trying to pay for lunch. To avoid argument, make payment arrangements with the head-waiter in advance or make it clear that the meal is a company expense.

Social Etiquette. It would be somewhat unusual to be invited to a Belgian home for dinner, though somewhat more common in the Flemish-speaking region. If you are invited for dinner, bring flowers or candy. Stand until the hostess is seated and also wait for her to start eating. Avoid talking about business unless your hosts raise the issue first.

Belgian cuisine ranks among the world's very best. Local specialties include "French" fries and waffles as well as fine chocolates. Food and drink make good topics for dinnertime conversation.

Negotiating Behavior

You can expect your Belgian counterparts to move things along a bit slow-er than would be the case in the U.S. but much faster than for example in the Middle East, Latin America or South Asia. Avoid giving the impres-sion of impatience.

The Italian Negotiator

When in Rome, Do as the Romans Do? As a veteran business visitor to Italy, a variation on the old chestnut works makes more sense to me: When in Rome, observe how the Romans are doing things...and then act appropriately. Let's say your Roman counterpart shows up half an hour late for a major meeting, offering a big smile but no excuse. Should you match his casual attitude towards punctuality at your next get-together?

Orientation to Time. Certainly not, especially if you are the seller. All over the world today the customer is king. Turning up late would show disrespect for your prospective buyer. Italians tend to be very sensitive to issues of *rispetto* and *honore.*

Instead, the appropriate reaction to tardiness is to open your briefcase and tackle some of that paperwork that's been piling up on you. Convert waiting time to working time. Your Roman business associate almost certainly meant no offense by showing up a little late. Time seems to take on a different meaning as you move south in Europe.

Building a Relationship. While Americans and many northern Europeans expect to get right down to business, Italians want to get to know you first. They prefer to build a personal relationship before getting down to the nitty gritty.

We are not talking about just a few minutes of small talk here. In Italy it takes much longer to get to know your counterpart...though a plate of good pasta and a couple of glasses of wine can accelerate the process. Wining and dining is a key part of the business scene in this part of the world. So take your time, don't rush things. It's fun to do as the locals do.

Business Protocol

Dress Code. The way we dress for business meetings should also be influenced by the way Italians do things. Italian business men and women dress with style and elegance, setting great store by the concept of *la bella figura.*

Milan and Florence are among the fashion capitals of Europe. One's outward appearance reflects one's inner values. So we show proper respect for our business counterparts by dressing appropriately.

Forms of Address. Another occasion to defer to the local custom is in forms of address. Some informal Scandinavians and North Americans for instance are mislead by the warmth and friendliness of Italians into moving too quickly to a first-name basis. But in a business setting it is customary to start off using any applicable academic title or honorific, followed by the person's last name.

If Giorgio Bianchi has a university degree, address him as *Dottor* Bianchi. An engineer would be *Ingeniere,* your lawyer *Avvocato* and a respected local bigwig might be called *Commendatore.*

When should you start calling Italian business acquaintances by their first names? Right after they invite you to do so.

Paraberbal and Nonverbal Communication

Conversational Overlap. There are other instances where it is safer to just take note of the local customs while sticking to your own rules of behavior. One good example is what scholars call "conversational overlap". A business discussion in Rome or Naples frequently evolves into what appears to be a verbal free-for-all. Italians are exuberant, enthusiastic talkers. They are quick thinkers who can figure out what you are going to say long before you have finished saying it, so they jump in with their response while you are still talking.

In Italy, when chairing a meeting between locals and northern Europeans or North Americans I sometimes had to restrain my Italian colleagues, because northerners find it rude to be interrupted in mid-sentence. If you respond by trying to outshout the locals, things quickly get out of hand. So in this case we should stay with the behavior we have been taught is polite, namely conversational turn-taking.

Interpersonal Distance. When there were only two passengers in an Italian elevator they stand close to each other. In fact in both social and business situations Italians like to stand relatively close to others, which can be disconcerting for visitors with big space bubbles. As friendly, expressive people they do not feel comfortable at arm's length.

Touch Behavior. Italians are a tactile people. While visiting negotiators observe that Italians engage in frequent physical contact, outsiders should not initiate the hugging and kissing. Wait for your local counterpart and then respond in a way that seems comfortable.

Visiting business people from more reserved cultures such as northern Europe and East Asia should realize that frequent touching reflects Latin expressiveness and warmth, and prepare themselves accordingly. A person who shrinks from physical contact is liable to be labeled as cold, unfriendly or arrogant.

Gaze Behavior. Another example of contrasting behavior is the use of eye contact. In Italy, direct eye contact shows we are interested in what the other person is saying while lack of steady eye contact indicates lack of interest. It is polite to maintain steady eye contact across the conference table when negotiating with Italians.

Gestures. A whole book could be written on Italian body language. Fortunately, Italian negotiators usually tend to restrain themselves when conducting business with foreign counterparts. It is not really true that an Italian with his hands tied behind his back is mute.

"Campanilismo". Local Patriotism. One complication of trying to decide which local customs to adopt is that you will encounter major cultural variations within the peninsula. You will hear people say, There are 57 million people in this country – but not a single Italian. That exaggeration points up the fact that many inhabitants think of themselves first of as Florentines, Milanese, Venetians, Romans, Calabresi, Sicilians et cetera and secondarily as Italians.

The Spanish Negotiator

The largest European country in terms of area, Spain is also a land of sharp regional contrasts. That means that while the national business culture of Spain is relationship-focused, formal, polychronic and moderately expressive, visitors can expect significant regional variations.

For foreigners the most important of these variations are usually those between Castile and Catalonia, represented by Madrid and Barcelona respectively.

Regional Differences. Madrileños refer to the people of Catalonia as the Germans of Spain. The businessmen of Barcelona – the largest European city which is not a capital city – are often described by other Spaniards as hard-working, aloof, frugal, lacking a sense of humor and dressing so as to appear less wealthy than they are. They are regarded as "more European" than their Castilian counterparts.

In response Catalonians often stereotype Madrileños as work-shy, bureaucratic, phony, arrogant people who dress to look wealthier than they are. For foreigners however the key difference between the two regions is the language difference: Castilian Spanish versus Catalan.

The Language of Business. Business visitors who do not speak Spanish will find that many younger Spaniards can communicate effectively in English while older people are more likely to speak French.

Relationship-Focus. Having the right personal contact – *enchufe* – is more important than in the more deal-focused markets of northern Europe. This is especially true of Castilians, whereas such connections are somewhat less important in Catalonia. Face-to-face personal contact in business is extremely important in Spain, as it is in the other Latin countries of Europe.

Indirect Verbal Communication. Compared to northern Europeans the Spaniards often prefer high-context, roundabout language and tend to avoid responding with a blunt "no". Here again the Catalonians depart somewhat from the mainstream culture: They are considered quite direct, even gruff by other Spaniards.

Formality, Status and Respect. Honor and respect are very important for Spanish people. Age confers status. Few women reach top positions in local companies. Formality in forms of address is a way of showing appropriate respect. Visitors should address older people and professionals by their family name plus title, e.g. *Señor* Garcia. With others, *Don* or *Doña* plus the first name would be appropriate, e.g. Don Antonio.

A Fluid-Time Culture. Although the word *mañana* literally means "tomorrow," in practice it refers to some time in the indefinite future. Latin Europe in general and Spain in particular are "mañana" cultures – polychronic, to use the technical term. Punctuality is not a key concern, especially in the southern part of the country.

Moderately Expressive. Although less demonstrative than most French or Italians, the Spanish tend to be more expressive than the more reserved British, Dutch, Germans or Scandinavians. This is true of both paraverbal and nonverbal communication. But again, Catalonians are usually considered less expressive than Castilians and other Spaniards.

Paraverbal Communication. The expressive Spanish tend to speak loudly in comparison to more reserved northern Europeans. Spirited communicators, they also frequently engage in conversational overlap – interrupting each other as well as their foreign counterparts in mid-sentence during business meetings.

For example, when Swedish researchers taped a series of negotations between Swedish and Spanish companies they found that the Spaniards interrupted the Swedes five times for each time the Swedes interrupted the Spanish. Conversational overlap is normal in Latin cultures, but is considered rude behavior in northern Europe.

Nonverbal Communication. While northerners tend to maintain an arm's length distance between each other in a business context, Spaniards value a smaller space bubble. They also value strong eye contact: The Spanish like to "read" each other's eyes.

Business Protocol. The dress code is formal: Dark suits and conservative ties for the men. In terms of business entertaining, power breakfasts are more common in Barcelona than Madrid. Business lunches often run over two hours in Barcelona, three or more in Madrid.

While many Castilians prefer not to talk business at dinner, Catalonians regard it as quite acceptable. Madrileños begin thinking about dinner around 10:30 or 11:00 pm whereas in Barcelona you will probably meet for drinks around 8:30 and go to dinner about 9:30.

Gift-giving is not as important a part of the Spanish business culture as it is in many other relationship-focused markets.

Negotiating Behavior. Like the Italians, Spanish negotiators often rely more on quick thinking and spontaneity during a bargaining session than on the painstaking preparation and planning typically favored by Germans and Swiss. Because they rely on thorough discussion of the issues at the conference table, negotiating sessions are often lengthy affairs. Visitors should come prepared for vigorous give-and-take and a certain amount of bazaar haggling.

The Hungarian Negotiator

If you have done business in other major European markets, you will find many Hungarian business customs and practices similar to those of Western and Central Europe. However, you will also find that in its particular mix of traits, Hungary's business culture is one of a kind.

To wit, the Hungarians blend is one of relationship-focus, indirectness in communication and negotiations, formality and hierarchical relations in business interaction as well as a high degree of expressiveness, verbally and nonverbally. These characteristics are common enough in southern Europe – though not among Hungary's immediate neighbors.

What makes Hungarians so special is they are also monochronic: Valuing punctuality and adherence to schedules and deadlines. We normally associate such time-consciousness more with northerners (e.g., the Germans and Swiss) than with southern Europeans. In this sense Hungarians are more akin to the Milanese or Catalans than to say the Romans or Neapolitans.

From Central Asia to Central Europe. Geography and history are two keys to understanding Hungarians today. On the map Hungary appears as a non-Slavic wedge separating the southern Slavs (Bulgarians and the peoples of the former Yugoslavia) from those of the north – the Czechs, Slovaks and Poles. As a non-Slavic people surrounded mostly by Slavs, Hungarians sometimes feel like outsiders.

Ethnically most Hungarians are descendants of the warlike Magyars who pushed into Europe a thousand years ago from their original homeland in Central Asia. Thus their language is not an Indo-European tongue but rather part of the Finno-Ugric group. It is distantly related to the languages spoken by other ancient settlers from Central Asia: The Finns, Estonians and Lapps.

Industrialization came very late to Hungary, as was the case with the rest of East-Central Europe except for the Czech lands. That's why values derived from the landowning nobility and gentry persisted well into the 20th Century, rather than being displaced by a middle-class mindset. In this, Hungarian cultural values resemble those of the Poles rather than those of the Czechs.

As with the Polish "szlachta", the Hungarian nobility and gentry accounted for between 5 and 10 percent of the total population – an unusually large proportion. The persistence of distinctly rural, aristocratic values may account for the formality and hierarchical behavior still found Hungary today.

This contrasts with the Czechs, for example, whose values reflect a more urbanized, middle-class, industrial society. There, industry and commerce were eclipsing agriculture as early as the 1930s, when Hungary was still in a pre-industrial phase of development.

While Poles and Hungarians share a number of cultural features, they do differ somewhat in terms of religious affiliation. Almost all Poles are Roman Catholics, whereas some 20 percent of Hungarians are Protestants – Calvinists and Lutherans. So when it comes to religion, Hungary forms a sort of bridge between Catholic Poland and the more Protestant Czech Republic.

Language of Business. Well aware that Magyar is hardly a world language, most Hungarian business people today speak either English or German, often both. You can write them for an appointment in either of those languages. But before arriving for a meeting it's a good idea to ask whether you should arrange for an interpreter. Whereas most Hungarian firms employ translators, they don't always have skilled interpreters on board.

Despite the fact that Magyar is a non-European tongue, the language issue is not as big a problem as one might expect. While conducting a seminar on cross-cultural business behavior recently in Pécs, in southern Hungary, I found that each of the participants was fluent in four languages and several could speak five.

Personal Relationships. Critical business issues need to be discussed face-to-face in Hungary; frequent visits and phone calls are required. Expect lengthy, rapport-building preliminary small talk before getting down to business.

Verbal Indirectness. As in most other relationship-focused cultures, when negotiating business in Hungary you will often experience verbal indirectness and polite evasions. Hungarians prefer to avoid rude words such as "no".

Formality, Status and Hierarchies. Hungarians are more formal than Danes, Australians or North Americans – more like the French and Germans, for instance. Formality is expressed in the way people dress and in their meeting and greeting rituals. Hierarchies are evident in the top-down approach to management and in the relative scarcity of women business managers.

Monochronic Time. Most Hungarians place a high value on punctuality, schedules and deadlines. They are usually on time for meetings – sometimes even five minutes early – and seldom keep visitors waiting. Visitors are expected to match this behavior.

Expressiveness. At the first meeting you can expect a relatively reserved manner, but once the ice is broken Hungarians become more demonstrative. Germans and Austrians for example used to describe them as fiery, explosive, unpredictable. Expect your counterparts to speak for effect, indulging in exaggeration, overstatement, even bombast. Unlike their Central European neighbors, the verbal behavior of Hungarians is sometimes reminiscent of the Middle East and Latin Europe.

Paraverbal and Nonverbal Behavior

- Voice volume: Moderate. Avoid raising your voice and pounding the table during negotiations.
- Interpersonal distance: Medium – 15 to 25 inches (25 to 40 cm).
- Touch behavior: A moderately high-contact culture socially, when it comes to business touching it is more restrained. Good male friends make cheek-to-cheek contact (first left, then right) while shaking hands when they haven't seen each other for a while. But in a business situation, expect little or no touching except for the handshake.
- Eye contact: Direct gaze across the negotiating table: less intense than in the Middle East and southern Europe but much more direct than in East and Southeast Asia.

Business Protocol

Dress Code. Men wear conservative suits and ties; women wear dresses or suits.

Meeting and greeting. Shake hands, make eye contact and state your name. Shake hands again when leaving the meeting. Wait for a Hungarian woman to extend her hand. Male visitors are not expected to kiss a woman's hand; instead, a slight bow may accompany the handshake.

Forms of address. When introduced, address your counterparts by their professional or academic title plus family name. Only relatives and close friends address each other by first names.

Exchanging cards. Your cards should show your organizational title and any advanced degrees. Expect to exchange cards with each business person you meet.

Topics of conversation. Hungarians regard their country as part of Central Europe rather than of Eastern Europe. The term East-Central Europe is also acceptable. Sports and music as well as Hungarian food and wine are safer topics than politics and religion.

Gift giving. Business gifts are not expected. Bring imported liquor (not wine), chocolates or a bouquet of flowers when invited to someone's home for a meal. Present the bouquet in its wrapping, remembering to bring an uneven number and avoiding both red roses and chrysanthemums (the former imply romantic intentions, the latter are for funerals).

Business entertaining. It is a rare honor to be invited to a Hungarian home; be sure to accept. Most business entertaining is done at restaurants.

Wining and dining. Breakfast is served between 8:00 and 9:00, lunch from 1:00 to 2:00 and the evening meal around 7:00 or 8:00. Power breakfasts are not common.

Business is also not usually discussed at dinner, which is reserved for relaxing and getting to know one another. You may discuss business over lunch if your local counterparts agree.

Table manners. Wish everyone at the table good appetite before the meal begins. Wait for your host or hostess to start eating. Like all Europeans, Hungarians keep the fork in their left hand rather than switching from left hand to right as Americans do.

Social etiquette. A man is expected to walk to the left of a woman or of an honored guest of either gender.

Negotiating Behavior

- Making your presentation: To show you are serious, avoid starting off with a joke at the first meeting. As you would in Germany, load your presentation with background information, facts and technical details.
- Bargaining style: Most Hungarian business people seem to enjoy bargaining. Wise negotiators keep a few bargaining chips in reserve until the endgame. Your opening bid should be realistic but at the same time should include enough room for maneuver.
- Decision-making: As in many other cultures, the negotiating process usually takes longer when dealing with the government than when doing business with the private sector.

Group 6

Moderately Deal-Focused, Formal, Variably Monochronic and Reserved

The Baltic States

Bargaining in the Baltics

The business behavior of Estonians, Latvians and Lithuanians corresponds generally to that of their northern European neighbors – the Scandinavians, Germans, Poles and Russians.

However, first-time visitors may be to learn that the Baltic business cultures also reflect the north-south divide of the European continent. Estonians, northernmost of the three, are relatively individualistic, deal-focused, direct in the way they communicate across the bargaining table and also the most reticent and reserved of the Baltic peoples.

The Estonians' reserve and verbal directness as well as their task-focused approach to the business at hand remind many visitors of Swedish negotiators – perhaps even more so of the Finns, to whom the Estonians are in fact ethnically and linguistically related.

At the other extreme, Lithuania is the southernmost of three Baltic lands. Sometimes called "the Latins of the Baltic region," the Catholic Lithuanians are more group-oriented and relationship-focused than the Estonians. They also tend to be indirect in their communication behavior as well as expressive and outgoing.

The Lutheran Latvians, as befits their geographical location between the other two and the long history of German cultural influence, are in an intermediate position in terms of their business behavior. They are moderately deal-focused, indirect and demonstrative compared to Estonians but comparatively more direct and more reserved than their Lithuanian cousins to the south.

In other words, expect northern European-type negotiating behavior in the Baltic states, but at the same time be prepared for intra-regional differences.

Languages of Business. The Latvian and Lithuanian languages belong to the Baltic branch of the Indo-European language family while Estonian is part of the Finno-Ugric language group, related to Finnish. English-speaking business visitors to Riga and Vilnius will find more of their counterparts speaking English than was the case just a few years ago. In general, visitors are more likely to find fluent English-speakers in Latvia than in Lithuania.

German, Russian and Polish are other languages commonly under-stood in the two countries. Despite the strong Scandinavian influence in Latvia, few Latvians speak a Nordic language. When making appointments visitors should inquire about the need for an interpreter. Your Baltic counterpart will normally be quite willing to arrange for linguistic support should it be necessary.

Moderately Deal Focused. Compared to Asians, Arabs and Latin Americans, most Latvians and Lithuanians are deal-focused. In Vilnius and especially in Riga you can expect to get down to business fairly quickly; preliminaries are not as drawn-out as in southern Europe or the Mediterranean region. Business discussions tend to move along point by point in a linear fashion as in Germany rather than take off in unexpected directions as often happens in France.

On the other hand, making direct contact with prospective customers and business partners is less effective than in the deal-focused cultures of North America and northern Europe. Marketers from abroad will have better luck if they have a good referral or introduction – even better luck if they meet prospects at a trade show or on an organized trade mission. In this sense Latvia and Lithuania can perhaps be best described as moderately or variably RF business cultures while Estonia is definitely more deal-focused.

Formality, Status and Hierarchies. Danish visitors remark that their Baltic counter-parts dress and act more formally than most Scandinavians. Reflective of their hierarchical cultures, Latvians and Lithuanians conduct business in a more formal manner than Americans and the egalitarian Canadians, Australians and Scandinavians. It is important to show a certain degree of respect to older and senior persons.

Moderately Monochronic. Time Business meetings generally start on time; visitors are expected to be punctual. As opposed to more polychronic societies, meetings in Lithuania and Latvia tend not to be interrupted. This is another facet of business behavior which is more Germanic than Latin. Schedules and deadlines are generally adhered to – of course, always within the limitations imposed by the poor infrastructure of both countries. As in Scandinavia, if you are invited to someone's home for dinner be sure to arrive on time: no more than five or ten minutes late.

Paraverbal and Nonverbal Communication

- Voice volume: Like Scandinavians, most Balts speak relatively softly in business situations.
- Silence: Expect long pauses during discussions in Estonia, less often in Latvia.
- Conversational overlap: Interrupting another speaker in mid-sentence is considered rude behavior, especially in Estonia and Latvia. Wait until your counterpart has finished talking before speaking up.
- Interpersonal space: Expect the typical northern European-sized space bubble – about an arm's length between people in a business situation, whether standing or seated.
- Touch behavior: Little physical touching in a business situation. Expect somewhat more expressiveness after a relationship has been established.
- Eye contact: It is polite to maintain a steady (but not intense, in-your-face) gaze across the conference table, much as one would in Germany or Scandinavia.
- Gestures: Especially in Latvia and Estonia, expect controlled facial expressions and few gestures. Avoid hands in pockets while conversing. Chewing gum in public is considered impolite.

Business Protocol

Dress Code. Neat and conservative. For men, business suit, white or pastel solid-color shirt with a subdued tie. For women, an elegant suit or dress.

Meeting and Greeting. When meeting male counterparts, men should state their name clearly and shake hands firmly, then exchange business cards. Shake hands again when leaving. Men should wait for women to offer their hand. Female business visitors who feel comfortable shaking hands should feel free to do so. For both sexes: Bring plenty of business cards; give one to each person attending the meeting.

Forms of Address. Expect to use your counterpart's family name and professional title, if any. Avoid use of first names until your Baltic counterpart clearly invites you to do so.

Gift Giving. Business gifts are welcome but not expected. If invited to someone's home, bring flowers in an odd number, and remember to unwrap the bouquet before offering it to your hostess. Other good choices are imported wine, cognac or good chocolates.

Wining and Dining. Business entertainment normally takes place outside the home, at lunch or dinner. A few younger Balts may feel comfortable talking business over breakfast.

Women in Business. Women business visitors normally encounter few problems in the Baltic markets. To avoid possible misunderstandings, women should not act in a way which could be construed as flirtatious. Some older Latvian and Lithuanian men may not be accustomed to negotiating with business women on the basis of equality. To ensure being treated with the appropriate level of respect:

- Inform your Baltic counterparts of your title and level of responsibility before you arrive for the first meeting.
- When you are introduced, make sure your business card clearly states your position.
- Find an opportunity during the preliminary conversation to further explain your status.

Negotiating Behavior

- Negotiating an agreement is likely to take longer than it would in Western Europe or North America. It takes time to build a climate of trust.
- Finding the right local representative or distributor is the main key to achieving satisfactory results. Having patience is another important key.
- Expect older Latvians and Lithuanians to show the influence of decades of Soviet influence. Many younger Balts are less bureaucratic, more open and more deal-focused.
- Visitors should stay cool, avoid table-pounding and open displays of temper.
- Be prepared for occasional hardball tactics, e.g. brinksmanship. Perhaps due to Soviet tutelage, Balts sometimes try to use an artificial deadline to put pressure on foreign counterparts. The most effective counter is to this tactic is to insist on a *quid pro quo* of equal value for whatever concession your counterparts are pressing for.

– When you do reach agreement, expect it to be formalized in a detailed contract. Take the time to review the document carefully before signing, and insist that the English-language version be the binding one.

Group 7

Deal-Focused, Moderately Formal, Monochronic and Reserved

Britain – Denmark – Finland – Germany –
The Netherlands – Czech Republic

The British Negotiator

In view of the significant regional differences within Great Britain, it is important to note that this profile focuses on the negotiating behavior of business people in England. For the sake of variety we will use "Britain" and "England" as well as "British" and "English" interchangeably.

Visiting negotiators from Asia, the Mediterranean region, Africa and Latin America can expect to do business with deal-focused, individualistic, direct, reserved, monochronic counterparts. But German, Swiss and Scandinavian visitors instead find the English moderately relationship-focused, indirect, hierarchical and mildly polychronic.

Meanwhile, from across the Atlantic, U.S. negotiators see the Brits as reserved, formal, class-conscious and relaxed about time and scheduling.

In fact, all of these conflicting descriptions are correct. British negotiators do tend to be direct, deal-focused and time-obsessed compared to most Latins, Arabs and Asians. At the same time however, they are also more indirect, relationship-oriented and relaxed about time than northern Europeans as well as more formal and reserved than Americans.

The Language of Business. Few Britishers today speak another language well enough to handle a serious business negotiation. Visitors whose English is not fluent should consider arranging for an interpreter.

Making Contact. Famously a land of old school ties and the old boys' network, Britain is a market where referrals, recommendations and testimonials are extremely useful. Write in English with basic information about your company and your product, adding that you will contact them soon to set up an appointment. Follow this with a phone call requesting a meeting two or three weeks hence. Your British counterpart will suggest the time and place.

Orientation to Time. The pace of business life in London is somewhat leisurely relative to that of Hong Kong or New York. And while visitors are expected to be on time, locals are often a few minutes late for meetings. Still, the British are definitely clock-obsessed compared with most Latins, Arabs and Africans as well as the majority of South and Southeast Asians.

Formality, Hierarchies and Status Differences. Status in England is largely determined by one's regional origin, social class, family background and accent. This contrasts with the situation in the U.S. for example, where personal achievement is regarded as more important than one's class or family tree. And with Australia and the Nordic countries, where people are uncomfortable with obvious status differences.

The existence of relatively large status distinctions explains the formality in social interaction noted by Australian, American and Scandinavian visitors. While Americans for example like to switch almost immediately to the use of given names in business meetings, the English usually prefer to stay with Mr or Mrs until at least the second or third meeting.

That said, visitors find that younger English business people are becoming less formal. Today it is increasingly common to hear a Brit introduce himself as Bob or herself as Mary in a telephone conversation. And, as elsewhere, the rapidly growing use of electronic mail acts to "informalize" the communication process.

Communication Style. In common with their German, Dutch and Scandinavian neighbors, the English are reserved rather than expressive or demonstrative in the way they communicate. This is evident in their use of understatement, large space bubble, low-contact body language, restrained gestures and in their preference for always keeping a "stiff upper lip."

While the British may appear somewhat more expressive and extroverted than the Japanese, they come across as reserved and introverted compared with the Latins of Europe and the Americas.

Verbal Communication. The British also occupy an in-between position among the world's cultures when it comes to verbal directness. Upperclass Brits favor vague, oblique language while others speak more directly. Visiting negotiators should be mentally prepared to encounter either verbal style.

Paraverbal Communication. British negotiators rarely interrupt their counterparts across the bargaining table. They are also less likely to raise their voice than are negotiators from more expressive societies such as those in southern Europe and Latin America.

Nonverbal Communication

The Handshake. When meeting and greeting, a light handshake is common. The British normally do not shake hands with colleagues upon meeting in the morning and again when leaving the office, as is common practice in some Continental cultures.

Interpersonal Distance. The normal interpersonal distance in a business context is about an arm's length. The British tend to stand and sit further apart than the Arabs and Latins.

Moreover, two Englishmen in conversation will often stand at a 90-degree angle to each other rather than facing each other directly as two Italians or two Arabs usually do. Face-to-face conversation seems to make some Brits uncomfortable.

Gaze Behavior. Eye contact tends to be less direct than in expressive cultures such as the Italians, the Greeks and the Brazilians. A very direct gaze may be interpreted as rude and intrusive.

Touch Behavior. This is a low-contact culture. Except for the handshake, most English people avoid touching others in public. For example, the American custom of back-slapping, elbow-grabbing and arm-around-the-shoulder is considered slightly vulgar.

Gestures. As is the case with other reserved cultures, the British use relatively few hand and arm gestures. When flashing the two-finger "peace" sign, make sure your palm is facing outward. With palm inward this is an obscene gesture. Avoid pointing with your index finger; instead indicate direction with a nod of your head.

Business Protocol

Dress Code. Men wear a dark suit, plain shirt, conservative tie and polished black shoes. Avoid striped ties – they can be seen as imitating prestigious British regimental ties. The black shoes should be of the laced type rather than loafers, which are considered too casual. Natural fibers are considered much more acceptable than synthetics. Women should likewise dress conservatively, avoiding garish colors and too much jewelry.

Meeting and Greeting. While men exchange light to moderate handshakes, some women chose not to offer their hand. Men should always wait for the woman to extend her hand.

Forms of Address. Use Mr, Mrs., Miss or Ms. until your counterpart suggests switching to given names. Medical doctors, dentists and clergy expect to be addressed with their titles, but a male surgeon is plain Mister. Visitors accustomed to saying "Yes sir" and "No sir" as a sign of respect to older or senior people should avoid this practice in Britain.

Business Gifts. This is not a gift-giving culture. A better idea is to invite your counterparts to dinner.

Social Etiquette

Hostess Gifts. If invited to an English home, bring chocolates, liquor, champagne or flowers. Avoid white lilies (only for funerals) and red roses (unless you wish to signal a romantic interest). Be sure to send along a handwritten thank-you note the next day. During the meal keep both hands on the table but both elbows off the table.

Wining and Dining. Pub lunches are customary for business entertainment; dinners tend to be more of a social event. Avoid talking business unless your British counterpart clearly initiates such a discussion.

Pub Etiquette. Patrons take turn ordering drinks. When ordering drinks at the bar, catch the publican's eye and say, "Another pint, please!" rather than shouting or silently holding up your glass for a refill. In fact, "please" and "thank you" are very important words throughout Britain.

Negotiating Behavior

Making a Presentation. Accustomed to understatement, British buyers are turned off by hype and exaggerated claims. Presentations should be straight-forward and factual. Humor is acceptable, but visitors from abroad should remember that it rarely translates well. The safest humor in England is of the self-deprecatory variety.

Bargaining Range. English negotiators have been doing business all over the world for hundreds of years. They may put a wide safety margin in their opening position so as to leave room for substantial concessions during the bargaining process. This practice may put off negotiators from Germany and Sweden, where the "high-low" tactic is frowned upon.

Decision-Making Behavior. Time-is-money Americans may find the British process too time-consuming, but for the rest of the world's business cultures it is quite normal.

Role of the Contract. Expect emphasis on the legal aspects and the fine points of the written agreement. Should a dispute or disagreement arise later the British tend to rely on the terms of the contract and could become suspicious if their counterpart invokes non-contract issues such as the importance of the long-term relationship.

The Danish Negotiator

The Danish business culture is deal-focused – more so than the British, though a bit less than the Germans and distinctly less than Americans. Danish negotiators also tend to be moderately informal, relatively monochronic and quite reserved.

Language of Business. Most Danish people speak and read English fluently. Many are also competent German speakers. Visiting negotiators who do not command English will have no problem arranging for a competent interpreter.

Openness to Dealing with Strangers. One can contact a Danish company directly to make an appointment rather than going through an intermediary. Having the right contacts and personal connections can be helpful, but is much less important in Denmark than in most business cultures of Asia, Latin America and the Middle East.

Making Contact. As with other deal-oriented cultures, an introduction can be helpful but is not necessary. Danes are relatively open to dealing with foreigners. For example, one U.S. exporter of telecommunications equipment contacted five potential Danish distributors directly by fax and met with one of them the next week near Copenhagen. The two companies reached agreement a few weeks later, whereupon the Danes placed their inital order.

In contrast, the same U.S. company required two years of correspondence and meetings to make its first sale with the relationship-focused Japanese.

Deal-First. At the first meeting Danes usually get down to business after only a few minutes of small talk. They get to know their counterparts while talking business whereas in relationship-focused cultures the visitor must build rapport *before* discussing business.

Direct Language. Danes normally say what they mean and mean what they say, while in much of Asia, Latin America and the Middle East people often favor vague, indirect, oblique language so as to avoid offending one's counterparts.

Importance of the Contract. Danish negotiators regard the written agreement as definitive and refer to it whenever subsequent disagreements arise.

An Informal Business Culture

Egalitarian. The Danes are very egalitarian and hence relatively informal in contrast to more formal, hierarchical cultures. Knowing this, visitors can anticipate certain behaviors with a reasonable degree of probability.

Showing Respect. In Denmark it is not necessary to show special deference or overt respect to people of high status. Danes tend to address each other informally and often dress relatively informally even for business meetings. In Copenhagen it is common for male taxi passengers to sit in the front seat next to the driver – an interesting example of the egalitarian spirit of Denmark.

Visitors encounter relatively few etiquette rituals in Denmark whereas more formal, hierarchical societies value rituals as ways to ease interaction between strangers and to show appropriate respect to high-status persons.

A Rigid-Time Business Culture

Business cultures differ markedly in the way they use time. Denmark is a rigid-time culture as opposed to the fluid-time cultures of the Mediterranean region, the Middle East, South and Southeast Asia and most of Latin America.

Meetings usually begin on time, business visitors are expected to be punctual and are rarely kept waiting. Schedules and deadlines are firm. Meetings are rarely interrupted – most Danes consider it rude when meetings are frequently interrupted by phone calls or other intrusions.

A Reserved Communication Style

Danes tend to be relatively restrained in their style of paraverbal and nonverbal communication compared with the more expressive Latin Europeans and Latin Americans as well as many North Americans. This cultural characteristic can lead to confusion during international negotiations with more expressive counterparts.

First let's take a look at *paraverbal* communication:

Vocal Behavior. Danes are relatively soft-spoken compared with people from more expressive cultures, though not so soft-spoken as for example the Japanese. Latins and Arabs sometimes misinterpret the Scandinavian's restrained speech as lack of interest in the discussion.

Conversational Turntaking. While in Denmark it is considered rude to interrupt another speaker in mid-sentence, in southern Europe and South America such "conversational overlap" is accepted practice. Negotiators from more expressive cultures sometimes cause offense by interrupting their Danish counterparts in mid-sentence. While conversational overlap is common in Athens, Rio de Janeiro and New York, in Copenhagen interrupting people is considered rude.

Silence. Visiting negotiators are unlikely to experience the long gaps in conversation that are often encountered in more reserved cultures such as Finland and Japan.

These are the main elements of Danish *Nonverbal* communication:

Interpersonal Space. Most Danes stand at an arm's length distance from conversational partners in business gatherings. In contrast, expressive Latins and Arabs step in much closer, causing discomfort and stress to Danes who are unaware of this difference.

Touch Behavior. Again, Latins and Mediterranean peoples engage in more physical contact than the reserved, low-contact Danes. Visitors from high-contact cultures may interpret Danish reserve as coldness or arrogance. Negotiators from expressive cultures may be accustomed to more physical contact than Danes are comfortable with.

Eye Contact. Danes normally engage in moderate gaze behavior while Arabs and Latins favor strong eye contact across the bargaining table. The Japanese and most Southeast Asians on the other hand avoid a direct gaze, which they perceive as rude, hostile – perhaps even threatening.

Gestures. Whereas the expressive Latins employ numerous vigorous hand and arm gestures and facial expressions during negotiations, most Danes employ a more restrained body language.

Business Protocol

Dress Code. Young Danish business people tend to dress less formally than their elders. Male business visitors can perhaps be a bit more relaxed than when are meeting their German, French or British counterparts, but should still wear suit or jacket and tie to the first meeting. Women negotiators should wear a suit or dress.

Meeting and Greeting. Expect a firm handshake and steady, moderate eye contact. Business cards are normally exchanged with one hand. Address your counterparts with their surname until they suggest moving to first names – which often happens fairly early in the business relationship.

Wining and Dining. Most Danes are friendly, generous hosts. Business entertaining is done at lunch or dinner, rarely over breakfast. Among other things, Denmark is famous for *smørrebrød* – a selection of delicious open-faced sandwiches – often washed down with good local beer.

Invitations to a private home are not common. Evening meals are taken relatively early, often at 6:30 pm or so. Visitors are expected to be punctual: No more than ten or 15 minutes after the time stated in the invitation. Guests from some East Asian cultures should remember that in Denmark is considered impolite to leave soon after dinner. Expect to stay and chat for an hour and a half or two hours.

Gift Giving. Business gifts are less common here than in relationship-focused cultures. Bring a quality logo gift, an item your country is famous for, or a good book about your home country. If invited for dinner at home, bring liquor or flowers. Flowers should be presented wrapped.

Negotiating Behavior

Sales Presentation. As for the verbal part of your presentation, many Danish managers are irritated by "hard sell" tactics. They react better to a well-documented, straightforward approach with no exaggerated claims.

Bargaining Style. Many Danes dislike that common international negotiating tactic, the "high-low" gambit – starting off with a highly inflated initial offer. Business visitors fresh from negotiating in the Middle East, China or Brazil where negotiators expect this tactic will do better opening with a more realistic offer in Denmark.

Equally irritating to Danes is the use of artificial deadlines as a pressure tactic. "You've got to make your decision this week! Next Monday we are putting through an across-the-board price increase. Sorry about that..."

Management Style: The "Scandinavian Model"

Today more and more foreign companies are forming joint ventures in Denmark to help them access emerging markets in the Baltic states, Poland and Russia.

Although expatriate managers generally enjoy their stint in Copenhagen, those from more hierarchical corporate cultures may encounter unexpected problems in dealing with the Scandinavian model of management. For instance, some Danish managing directors will ignore the chain of command to talk directly with a junior executive on a project. This is normal behavior in many Danish companies but it can be unsettling to a middle manager from a less egalitarian culture. Many executives are used to a more formal leadership style.

Expatriate managers newly arrived from more expressive cultures also often tend to come on too strong. U.S. executives in particular are often criticized for being too aggressive, being boastful of past accomplishments and "blowing their own horn."

Egalitarianism. What provokes this particular criticism? The answer is simple: Danes tend to be governed to some extent by the Nordic egalitarian code of conduct called *jantelov*. This "Law of Jante" ordains that no one should set himself or herself up as better, smarter or richer than anyone else.

Modesty. Danes are so self-effacing and modest that they often mumble their name when introducing themselves. Moreover they typically understate their achievements and make a lot of self-deprecating remarks.

Indeed, it would be fair to say that modesty is a national characteristic of Danes – who may in turn be put off by the breezy self-confidence and self-promotion they see in people from certain other cultures. Foreign visitors will make a far more favorable first impression by letting the Danes find out for themselves how smart they are.

The Finnish Negotiator

The Language of Business. Some executives are concerned about dealing with Finland because they anticipate communication problems, knowing that the Finnish language is unrelated to the Western European languages. However, while Finnish belongs to the Finno-Ugric rather than the Indo-European language family, today Finns learn Swedish, German and English in school and many speak French or Spanish and other languages as well. Their linguistic skills have largely erased the communication barrier. And in case an interpreter is needed your local counterpart will have no difficulty providing one.

Business Protocol

At first acquaintance Finns tend to be somewhat reserved and formal by U.S., Danish or Australian standards. However, they lose some of this reserve after you get to know them.

The dress code for men is suit and tie, for women a suit or dress. Use last names plus any academic title until your local counterpart suggests moving to a first-name basis.

Punctuality is very important for social encounters as well as for business meetings. As for small talk, conversational topics to avoid include politics, jobs and money – and be wary of too many negative comments about the weather.

Shake hands with both men, women and older children when meeting and departing, but avoid further physical contact. Finns do not really appreciate arm-grabbing and back-slapping. They also tend to be relatively taciturn, soft-spoken and avoid showing emotion in public. Interrupting another person during a conversation is considered rude.

It is polite to maintain eye contact with the person you are speaking to. When seated, men should avoid crossing their legs in such a way that an ankle rests on the other leg. When standing it is impolite to talk with hands in one's pockets or with arms akimbo: the former posture is too casual and the latter indicates arrogance.

Social Etiquette

Power breakfasts have not yet caught on in this northern outpost. For lunch and dinner, Finnish formality extends to table manners. Be as prompt as you are for a business meeting. Men keep their jackets on throughout the meal unless the host removes his.

Do not start eating until your host or hostess has begun, and remember not to touch your wine glass until the host offers a toast. Speaking of which, in contrast to some other European cultures you do not propose a toast to the host or hostess.

Be sure to avoid picking up food with your fingers. This taboo extends even to fresh fruit. For example, spear an apple with a fork and peel it elegantly with your knife.

Among the special local dishes worth trying are reindeer steak and fresh wild berries. Don't miss the cloudberries, for example.

Be prepared for plenty of liquid accompaniment to the food. Finns especially enjoy vodka and beer, but wine is becoming more popular as import duties have been reduced.

You will find that just because Finns tend to be somewhat formal at table does not mean they are stiff or unfriendly. They are gracious and generous hosts. Spouses (and children) are usually included in meal invitations. You are encouraged to take seconds, but do finish whatever is on your plate. And when the check arrives, remember there are no "Dutch treats" in Finland: The inviter pays the whole check.

If you are invited to a smorgasbord or buffet meal it may be a good idea to let your host or hostess lead the way. In any case, here is the correct way to attack the buffet table:

- Start with the potatoes and cold fish – often herring. This may be washed down with a small glass or two of "snaps", the local firewater.
- Then you take a fresh plate and dig into the salads and the cold roasted and smoked meats.
- Next, another clean plate for whatever hot dish may be on offer.
- After that come the cheese and fruit courses. Coffee is served after the meal, and only after the coffee do you start talking business!

The rules for tipping are simple. Restaurant checks normally include the tip in a 15% service charge, but you may wish to leave the small change. In taxis it is enough to let the driver keep the small change. However, do tip porters, doormen and coat checkers.

Imported liquor is very expensive in Finland so consider bringing a bottle or two in with you to give as gifts. If invited home for dinner, cut flowers in an uneven number make a fine hostess gift. Avoid white and yellow flowers as too funereal and a huge bouquet as too ostentatious.

Negotiating Behavior

Sales Presentations. Since Finns avoid displays of emotion in public, don't expect them to wax enthusiastic when you present your product or project. Prepare a methodical, well-organized presentation with plenty of facts, figures and documentation. Be careful of hype and exaggerated claims. Use handouts and slides or overheads for numbers and the most important points.

Bargaining Range. It is usually unwise to build a wide bargaining margin into your initial offer. Finns do not appreciate bazaar haggling. Open with a realisitic bid and be prepared to adjust price or terms in response to proposals from your counterpart.

Decision Making. A methodical, deliberate process. Expect your local partners to take more time than you would expect for example in North America.

The German Negotiator

There are important north/south and east/west differences in German business customs, not to mention significant individual variations. Keeping this in mind, the following profile describes the important general tendencies in business behavior you are likely to encounter whether your meeting takes place in Hamburg or Munich, Leipzig or Cologne.

Language of Business. Many German managers are comfortable conducting business in foreign languages, especially English. Larger companies usually have competent English speakers on staff. However, since the language of business is the language of the customer, a professional export sales team should include a fluent speaker of German. If the purpose of your meeting is to negotiate a purchase, a joint venture or strategic alliance, check with your counterparts about the possible need for an interpreter.

Initial Contact. Banks play a powerful role in the German business world. Since it is always useful to have a referral you may want to ask your international bank to arrange an introduction. However, in contrast with more relationship-focused business cultures such as Japan, Korea, Brazil or Saudi Arabia, making direct contact is also a viable option in Germany.

Send a letter in good business German along with basic information about your company and the purpose of the meeting. Request an appointment with two to three weeks' advance notice. If making a "cold" approach, address correspondence to the department concerned rather than to a specific individual. Once you have been introduced or have a referral you may address your letter to the appropriate person.

Verbal Communication. Germans generally pride themselves on speaking their mind. Clarity of understanding is the prime goal of communication. Even negotiators from other northern European cultures may not be fully prepared for Germanic abruptness and readiness to get to the point. Expect Germans answer the telephone by giving their last name rather than saying hello. Germans tend to be uncomfortable with the effusive compliments that are common in some other cultures. Similarly, foreigners are unlikely to be overwhelmed with flattery – with one exception: Germans are quick to show appreciation for a visitor's efforts to speak their language.

Orientation to Time. Germany is a strongly monochronic culture. That is, *Pünktlichkeit* is very important: Tardiness signals unreliability. If you are half an hour late for a meeting you may be half a month late with your delivery! Therefore, should you be unavoidably detained be sure to phone your counterpart as soon as possible to reschedule the meeting.

Business Protocol

Forms of Address. Formal behavior shows appropriate respect to people with high rank, professional titles and higher academic qualifications, especially in southern Germany. This can be very important since more German managers have doctorates than anywhere else in the world. Some 40% of the board members of the 100 largest corporations have a doctor's degree.

Address Dr. Wilhelm Schmidt as Dr. Schmidt or Herr Doktor. His female colleague with a Ph.D would be Frau Doktor. It is polite to address less exalted business contacts with "Herr", "Frau" or "Fräulein" followed by their last name. This includes secretaries. Whereas in the U.S. for example female secretaries are usually addressed by their first name, in Germany it is "Frau Braun," not "Waltraudt." Also remember that women about 20 or older should be addressed as *Frau* whether married or single.

As the case with most other European tongues, the German language employs two different personal pronouns for "you." *Sie* is the formal pronoun appropriate for business relationships while the informal *Du* is reserved for close personal friends, small children and pets. Stay with titles, family names and *Sie* unless and until your counterpart suggests moving to a less formal mode of address. You can expect to work with a German business counterpart for many years without shifting to first names.

Reserved Communication Style. Your counterparts are likely to be reserved, not given to enthusiastic public displays of emotion – although southern Germans are somewhat more expressive. As opposed to Latin Europeans and Latin Americans, most Germans eschew wide gestures, animated facial expressions and conversational overlap. Interrupting another speaker is regarded as very rude.

Nonverbal Communication

The normal interpersonal distance in a business context is about an arm's length. Germans tend to stand and sit further apart than Arabs and Latins and may feel ill at ease when their "space bubble" is invaded.

A low-contact culture: Expect little physical contact beyond the obligatory handshake.

Hand and arm gestures are restrained. It is rude (as well as against the law) to tap one's forehead while looking at another person.

Business Protocol

Dress Code. A dark suit and conservative tie for men, suit or dress for women. The exchange of business cards is less formal than in East and Southeast Asia but less casual than in North America. Present your card after greeting your counterpart and shaking hands.

Meeting and Greeting. Handshakes (one or two vigorous pumps) are expected whenever you meet or leave someone. Many Germans believe that a soft handshake reflects weakness and that lack of eye contact indicates shiftiness, unreliability or even dishonesty. The handshake may not be accompanied with a broad smile: Many Germans save their smiles for friends and family, regarding smiling at strangers as a silly, even false mannerism.

Business Gifts. This is not a gift-giving culture. German negotiators are likely to feel uncomfortable if presented with an expensive gift. If you do wish to bring something small, choose a tasteful logo gift or an item your country or region is famous for. Asians should not be surprised if their German counterpart unwraps the gift in their presence.

Wining and Dining. Many Germans prefer to maintain a clear separation between their professional and private lives. Although they are excellent hosts, Germans may place less emphasis on business entertainment than visitors from many relationship-focused cultures.

Do not expect to talk business over *Frühstück:* the power breakfast has yet to make an impact in the Federal Republic. When you go out to lunch or dinner, expect to talk business before or after rather than during the meal unless your local counterpart takes the initiative.

Social Etiquette

Manners. A man precedes a woman when entering a bar, restaurant or other public place and walks to the lady's left when outdoors. It is polite to stand when a woman, older person or an individual of high rank enters the room.

Dinner at Home. If invited to a German home for dinner, be sure to accept. Avoid arriving early but do show up within ten or 15 minutes of the time given.

Hostess Gifts. Avoid bringing wine unless it is a good vintage from a top wine-producing area. Flowers make a good *Mitbringsel* but avoid red roses (for lovers only) and canna lilies or chrysanthemums (for funerals only). Bring an uneven number (except for 6 or 12) but never 13 and remember to unwrap the bouquet before presenting it to your hostess. If all those floral taboos have you confused, a box of high quality chocolates is an excellent alternative.

Negotiating Behavior

Making a Presentation. Germans respond best to thorough, detailed presentations supported by copious facts. They look for plenty of history and background information rather than fancy visuals. Use references and testimonials whenever possible. Be wary of including jokes in your presentation. Humor rarely translates well and sales presentations are a serious business in Germany.

Bargaining Range. Most Germans respond better to realistic initial quotations than to the classic "high-low" tactic. They may react negatively to what they perceive as bazaar haggling. Consider building a small margin into your opening bid to cover unexpected developments, but take care to avoid over-inflating your initial offer.

Preparation. Like the Japanese, German negotiators are known for very thorough preparation. They are also well known for sticking steadfastly to their negotiating positions in the face of pressure tactics.

Decision-Making. Germans take their time to deliberate and to confer with responsible colleagues before making an important decision. Expect them to take more time than Americans but perhaps less than the Japanese and most other Asians.

The Contract. Look for heavy emphasis on the legal aspects and the fine points of the written agreement. Germans tend to depend more on the wording of the contract than on the relationship with their counterpart to solve any problems and disagreements that may develop. Contract terms are considered "cast in concrete," so attempts to renegotiate the contract soon after it has been signed may not be welcomed.

The Dutch Negotiator

The Dutch have been world traders for centuries – they really know how to do business.

Language of Business. Even though most Dutch business people speak English fluently, it is polite to offer to bring an interpreter to the first meeting, just in case. Nine times out of ten you will be told no interpreter will be needed.

Making the Initial Contact. You may phone for an appointment and then confirm the arrangements in writing. Address the letter to the person you wish to see and include all the information your counterpart will need to prepare for the meeting. The letter should be formal, using the addressee's correct title. Give your counterpart several weeks notice – impromptu meetings are not popular with the well-organized Dutch.

Verbal Communication. The Dutch value direct, straightforward language. They like to get right to the point, avoiding polite circumlocution. This trait is normally not a problem for negotiators from low-context cultures such as northern Europe and North America. However, when the Netherlanders mix directness with assertiveness it can be misunderstood. I have attended meetings in Europe at which their legendary bluntness actually did manage to offend one or two of the Yanks present.

The Dutch distrust flowery language and empty rhetoric. They want you to say what you mean and mean what you say. In contrast with some other cultures, a Dutch "yes" can be taken as a commitment. And when they mean "no" they will say it quite plainly rather than mincing words to spare your feelings.

Reserved Communication. Style Expect a sober, somewhat reserved approach until you get to know them. The Dutch sometimes accuse Americans for example of superficial friendliness. They are less likely to smile at people they have just met – maintaining a certain polite reserve while they size you up.

Nonverbal Communication

Body language in the Low Countries is less casual than it is in more informal cultures. Keep your hands out of your pockets when talking to people, even in a fairly relaxed situation.

If you have done business in France or Italy you have probably learned that tapping your head while looking at someone means you think they are crazy or stupid. (In Germany in fact this rude gesture is actually illegal – if the police catch you doing it you will be socked with a heavy fine.) So it's important to understand that if your Dutch counterpart taps the right side of his head while looking your way it actually has the opposite meaning: he is complimenting you on your intelligence. Had your contact wanted to impugn your sanity he would have pointed his forefinger at the middle of his forehead. Or perhaps grabbed at an imaginary fly in front of his face.

Business Protocol

Dress Code. Men should wear a suit or blazer and slacks, women neat business attire.

Punctuality. Perhaps the most important rule of Dutch business protocol is to be on time for meetings. If you find that you are going arrive late, phone the person you are scheduled to meet and explain the problem.

Meeting and Greeting. When introduced, repeat your name while shaking hands. Your handshake should be firm and accompanied with strong eye contact. At gatherings where you introduce yourself, just give your last name – it's not necessary to say Hello or How are you? Be very sure to shake hands again when you leave.

Men wait for women to offer their hand. At a social gathering also shake hands with the children you meet. Visitors from informal cutures should remember to avoid using first names until their counterpart suggests it. This is a low-contact culture. Until you become good friends, avoid any physical contact beyond the handshake.

Remember that "Holland" refers to only a part of the country; the correct name is The Netherlands.

Women in Business. Although very few local women have reached senior positions in Dutch companies, American business women should encounter no particular problems doing business in the Low Countries.

Business Gifts. The Netherlands is not a gift-giving business culture. If you do wish to bring something small, choose a tasteful logo gift or an inexpensive item your country or region is famous for and present it at the end of the meeting.

Wining and Dining. Remember that the expression going Dutch reflects an important local custom. Unless you have been unambiguously invited as a guest, be prepared to pay for your share of the meal. If your counterpart has treated you to lunch or dinner be sure to reciprocate as soon as it is practical. A female business visitor entertaining her local male counterparts normally encounters little serious resistance when she insists on picking up the check, especially if she pays with a credit card. The Dutch normally drink wine with lunch or dinner unless eating Chinese, Indian or Indonesian food, when beer is usually the beverage of choice.

Social Etiquette

Good Manners. When outdoors it is polite for men to walk on the street side. This custom arose as a way of protecting the lady from the mud splashed up by passing carriages. In today's Amsterdam it is a good way of preventing a thief on a motorbike from grabbing the woman's handbag.

Dinner Guest in a Dutch Home. Since business entertainment in the Netherlands normally takes place at restaurants, an invitation to dinner at home is a very friendly gesture. Do send or bring flowers for the hostess, remembering that red roses are for lovers and white lilies are for funerals. Men stand until the ladies are seated, and everyone waits for the hostess to start eating. Keep both hands above the table. Plan to stay for an hour and a half or so after dinner.

Hostess Gifts. If your host picks you up at your hotel it is acceptable to ask him to stop at a florist shop on the way. Unwrap the bouquet before handing it to your hostess. Avoid bringing a bottle of wine for the host: Some men would take it as a comment on the inadeqacy of their cellar.

Negotiating Behavior

Making a Presentation. Like many other European business people, the Dutch are put off by "hard-sell" tactics and hype. Prepare a straightforward presentation, making sure that every claim you make is fully supported by the facts. On the other hand, there is no need to understate or to downplay the benefits of your proposal. Just be as factual as possible, even at the risk of being slightly boring. To your Dutch counterpart, business is inherently interesting. There is no need to put on a "dog and pony show" to hold your audience's attention.

Bargaining Range. You can expect your counterparts to be tough, shrewd negotiators. Do not insult their intelligence by heavily padding your opening offer in the expectation of granting generous concessions later. Just as most Dutch negotiators want to get down to business quickly and avoid lengthy preliminaries, they also value a realistic bargaining range.

Bargaining Style. Within Europe the Dutch are know to be tenacious and persistent, at times perhaps even a wee bit stubborn. When things get tense at the negotiating table take care not to raise your voice – this would definitely be counter-productive.

Decision-Making. Dutch negotiators rarely make snap judgments but neither do they agonize unnecessarily over business decisions.

The Czech Negotiator

The Czech Republic is the western-most Slavic country, bordering both Germany and Austria.

So it's hardly a surprise that the Czechs are the most westernized of the Slavic peoples, often dubbed the Germans of East-Central Europe. The latter comparison however is one the Czechs do not find flattering: The Nazi occupation left enduring wounds in this country.

Czech values, attitudes and beliefs have been influenced by German culture in various ways. First of all there were the centuries of Austro-German Habsburg rule. Second, the presence of German people living in Bohemia ("Böhmen"), the western-most province of the Czech lands. And then, between the wars and especially again after 1989, came the enormous flood of German trade, tourism and investment.

Geography and history have combined to make the Czechs the most deal-oriented business people among East-Central Europeans. They are relatively willing to talk business with strangers and usually quick to get down to business. Their communication style tends to be more reserved than that of their more outgoing, expressive Polish and Hungarian neighbors.

Today the Czechs, along with the Poles and Hungarians, are leading East-Central Europe back into the modern world. Investment and know-how from Western Europe and other sources is a key factor in stimulating the recovery.

Language of Business. While the national language is Czech, the younger business people are likely to speak English or German, frequently both. Still, wise visitors ask their local counterparts whether an interpreter will be needed because senior Czech managers may not speak foreign languages. French is not as popular as it was between the wars, and Russian is definitely passé.

Deal-Focused Business Behavior. Most Czech companies today are relatively open to contact from foreigners. As noted above, they tend to get down to business without the elaborate preliminaries expected in relationship-oriented cultures. In fact, Czechs note that even Americans – so famous for their "Let's get down to business!" approach – at times engage in too much small talk.

Verbal Directness. Visiting negotiators can usually expect to encounter the same frank verbal communication characteristic of northern Europe. Urban Czechs are almost as direct as the Germans, Dutch and Swiss-Germans.

Formality, Status and Hierarchies. Czechs are likely to be more formal than North Americans or Australians. Business behavior is more akin to that of the French, Germans and British than that of the informal Danes, for instance. Formality is expressed in meeting-and-greeting rituals as well as in the way business people dress. Hierarchical values are evident in the top-down approach to management and in the relative scarcity of women business managers.

Visiting female executives will encounter rather traditional attitudes towards gender roles. But once a business woman has established her professional credentials, she will be taken as seriously as she would be in most of Europe.

Monochronic Time Behavior. Visitors are expected to be on time for meetings and can expect the same of their local counterparts. Business meetings usually run without serious interruptions. On the other hand, negotiations often last longer than they would in markets such as the U.S. or Germany. Wary after decades of semi-isolation from the global marketplace, many Czechs take their time in sizing up potential foreign business partners before coming to a decision.

Reserved Communication. Visitors from expressive cultures must be prepared for a more restrained manner than they may be used to. Czechs tend to avoid open displays of emotion. Negotiators accustomed to dealing with northern Europeans will find few surprises in this regard.

Paraverbal and Nonverbal Behavior

If your local counterparts suddenly become very quiet or avoid eye contact at the negotiating table, you know you have stepped on their toes. To get back on track, make a light-hearted remark – perhaps a self-deprecatory one. Other tips:

– Keep your voice down. Czechs are put off by loud voices; avoid histrionics and table-pounding.
– Maintain an interpersonal distance of between 15 to 25 inches (25 to 40 cm).
– Use little touch behavior. Czechs avoid physical touching except for the handshake.
– Expect moderate eye contact. You will encounter a direct gaze across the negotiating table, less intense than in the Middle East and southern Europe but more direct than is considered polite in East and Southeast Asia.

Business Protocol and Etiquette

Making Contact. Make appointments by telephone, fax or e-mail about two weeks in advance. Corresponding in English is quite acceptable, although taking the trouble to have your letter translated into Czech will really impress your prospective customer or business partner. Best times for business meetings: between 9:00 am and noon and from 1:00 to 3:00 pm.

Dress Code. Dark suits and ties for men, conservative dresses or suits for women.

Meeting and Greeting. In a business situation, say "dobry den" ("hello"), shake hands, make direct eye contact and state your full name. Formulas such as "how are you?" are unnecessary. Shake hands again when leaving the meeting. In social settings the verbal greeting often suffices; handshakes are unnecessary. Whereas in many cultures men wait for women to extend their hand, in the Czech Republic the man often offers his hand to a woman first.

Forms of Address. When introduced, address your counterparts by their professional or academic title plus family name. Only relatives and close friends address each other by first names.

Exchanging Cards. Your cards should show your organizational title and any advanced degrees.

Topics of Conversation. Remember that Czechs consider their country part of Central Europe rather than of Eastern Europe. Referring to the Czech Republic as part of East-Central Europe is acceptable. Avoid references to politics in general and to the Communist era in particular. Good topics are soccer, ice hockey, hiking, biking and all kinds of music.

Gift Giving. While not expected, gifts of moderate value are welcome. Bring a bottle of good Scotch or cognac or small items such a quality pen or cigarette lighter. A bottle of imported wine or liquor is the best choice when invited to someone's home for a meal. In some circles, a bouquet of flowers may be considered inappropriate – flowers tend to carry a romantic connotation.

Negotiating Behavior

Expect slow, methodical progress. Your opening offer should be realistic: the "high-low" tactic common in many business cultures will backfire with the Czechs. Patience and a soft-sell approach will get you the best results.

Group 8

Deal-Focused, Informal, Monochronic and Variably Expressive

Australia – Canada – USA

The Australian Negotiator

Although Australia is a large and diverse country, visiting negotiators can expect to encounter a mainstream business culture which is deal-focused, extremely egalitarian and informal, moderately time-conscious and variably expressive. Expect Australian negotiators whose ethnic background is southern European or Mediterranean to be expressive while those of northern European or British heritage are likely to be more reserved.

The Language of Business. English-speaking visitors will have no language problems doing business in Australia.

Making the First Contact. Make direct contact by sending a letter, fax or e-mail with relevant information about your company and product, then follow up with a phone call requesting a meeting. Like people from other Anglo-Saxon cultures, Australians are usually ready to get down to business shortly after meeting a prospective business partner for the first time. The elaborate preliminaries and extensive small talk expected throughout most of the Pacific Rim are out of place in Sydney or Perth. A few beers at a pub smooths the way to getting to know each other.

Communication Style. Australian men tend to be less talkative and less demonstrative than their counterparts from the expressive cultures of Southern Europe, the Mediterranean area and Latin America. Whereas export salesmen from these regions may be proud of their silver tongues, the Australians think that silence is golden. Aussies tend to employ understatement, and their dry humor often features irony and sardonic wit.

Verbal Directness. Aussies can at times be even more direct than the Germans and the Dutch, not to mention Americans. Valuing frank and straightforward speech, they may be unaware that East and Southeast Asians visitors might find their directness offensive.

One cultural characteristic which causes major problems for many East and Southeast Asians (as well as for some Americans) is the Australian penchant for vigorous argument. Negotiators who instinctively seek to downplay areas of disagreement and differences of opinion should prepare themselves for spirited verbal confrontation. Some first-time Asian visitors misinterpret this style of communication as provocative, even hostile. Those who have negotiated with the French are less likely to misunderstand this confrontational behavior.

Furthermore, some Australians negotiating with high-context business visitors from East and Southeast Asia as well as the Arab world even suspect that the latters' indirect, ambiguous, "polite", language is meant to mislead or confuse them. Verbal directness is a virtue in this deal-focused business culture.

Informality and Egalitarianism. This may be the only culture in the world where business people interact even more informally than in Denmark, the midwestern United States or western Canada. For example, Australians perceive Americans to be overly concerned with status distinctions based on academic degrees, wealth and position in the corporate hierarchy.

Visiting negotiators should avoid trying to impress Aussies with their titles and accomplishments. Anything smacking of boastfulness or showing off gives a negative impression.

While Americans are taught, "Blow your own horn" and "Don't hide your light under a bushel" Australians learn that the tall poppy gets cut down. People who boast or flaunt their success are considered obnoxious. Some visitors from highly competitive societies such as the USA and Hong Kong look upon this attitude as simple envy, and equate it with the egalitarian Scandinavian concept of "Janteloven".

A good example of Australian egalitarianism is provided by seating etiquette in taxis. As is the case in Denmark, male passengers travelling alone are expected to sit next to the (male) driver as a sign that they do not regard themselves as above the taxi driver in social status. Women are exempt from the front-seat rule unless the driver is also female.

Speaking of gender: In contrast to Scandinavia, Australian egalitarianism does not necessarily extend to women in business. Female visitors should be prepared for behavior which they may perceive as chauvinistic or patronizing.

Orientation to Time. While definitely more monochronic than South and Southeast Asians, most Australians are a bit less obsessed with time and schedules than the Germans, Swiss, Americans and Japanese. This somewhat relaxed attitude towards time is especially noticeable outside of Sydney. Visitors are expected to be roughly on time for meetings, but few Aussies will get upset if you are a few minutes late.

The work pace in this part of the world is slower than that of New York, Hong Kong, Tokyo or Singapore. Local business people are likely to resent foreigners who try to hurry things along.

Paraverbal and Nonverbal Communication

As noted above, Australians vary from very expressive to quite reserved, depending partly on their particular ethnic background. For example, an Aussie of Greek or Italian ancestry is likely to use more and larger gestures, speak louder and interrupt others more often than their fellow countrymen whose forefathers came from Britain, Ireland or northern Europe.

Interpersonal Distance. As with northern Europeans, North Americans and East Asians, Aussies generally stand or sit about an arm's apart in a business situation. Normal interpersonal distance tends to be larger than it is with Arabs, southern Europeans and Latin Americans.

Touch Behavior. Expect less physical contact than is the case with Latin and Mediterranean cultures but more than those of East and Southeast Asia.

Eye Contact. Use steady eye contact when conversing with your counterparts across the bargaining table. Good eye contact indicates interest and sincerity.

Taboos. The "thumbs-up" sign is considered obscene by many Aussies. Also rude is extending one's first and middle fingers with the palm facing in. It is impolite to point at someone with the index finger – use the whole hand instead. When you have a cold, avoid blowing your nose loudly. It is also impolite to sniffle repeatedly. The solution is to leave the room and blow your nose in privacy.

Queue Behavior. The Australians have inherited the British custom of forming lines and politely waiting one's turn.

Business Protocol

As one might expect in an informal culture, Australian protocol rituals are not elaborate.

Dress Code. For business, men wear a dark suit and tie, often removing the jacket in the summer. Businesswomen wear a dress or skirt and blouse.

Meeting and Greeting. Expect a firm handshake and direct eye contact. Note that some Australians believe a soft handshake reflects weakness, and that lack of a direct gaze indicates unreliability or even dishonesty. A man should wait for a woman to offer her hand rather than holding out his hand.

Forms of Address. Use full names when you first meet but expect to move quickly to first names. To be polite, wait for your local counterpart to suggest switching to given names.

Business Cards. While it is customary to exchange cards, do not expect the two-handed ritual of the *meishi* commonly encountered in Japan and the rest of East Asia.

Topics of Conversation. The best choice is sports – especially water sports, Australian football, golf and tennis. Positive comments on local food, beer and wine are always welcome. Visitors should avoid invidious comparisons with elements of their own cultures. Also to be avoided are comments about hard one works; workaholics are pitied in this delightfully laid-back society.

Gift Giving. Australia is not a gift-giving business culture. If invited to dinner at home consider bringing either an item for which your city or region is famous or wine, flowers or chocolates.

Wining and Dining. Tea is the evening meal and supper a late-night snack. Don't expect to be invited to someone's home until you know them fairly well. After a big meal, avoid saying you are "stuffed"; this word has a vulgar connotation in Australia.

Pub Etiquette. You are expected to pay for a round for the group you are drinking with when it's your turn. However, avoid paying for a round out of turn. People who do this are regarded as pretentious show-offs.

Negotiating Behavior

Sales Presentations. The general advice that modesty is the best policy applies especially to making sales presentations. Marketers find that the soft sell works better. Veterans of the Australian market have also learned not to over-praise their company's product. Here it's better to show the benefits and superiority of your product or service to the customer rather than talking about them. Whenever possible, let your documentation, testimonials and third-party reports speak for you.

Bargaining Style. Since Australians tend to dislike bazaar haggling, visiting negotiators will get better results by opening discussions with a realistic bid. The negotiating process may take more time than it would in some other deal-focused business cultures, though less than in strongly relationship-focused markets such as Japan.

The Canadian Negotiator

The multicultural mosaic that is Canada complicates things a bit for visiting negotiators. You need to be aware of the cultural background of the business people you will be dealing with, be it anglophone, francophone, New Canadian or other. New Canadians are recent immigrants from Hong Kong, Eastern Europe and many other parts of the world. Due to space limitations this profile focuses on the negotiating behavior of the two major business cultures, those of English and French Canada.

Anglophone Canadian negotiators tend to be deal-focused, direct, moderately informal, very egalitarian, reserved and relatively time-conscious. In contrast, French Canadians tend to be more formal, relationship-focused, hierarchical, expressive and moderately polychronic.

Mainstream U.S. negotiators are likely to find the business culture of English Canada somewhat similar to their own. The most obvious differences are that anglophone Canadians are usually less expressive, less assertive and a bit more formal and conservative than for example U.S. Americans.

On the other hand, Yankees may encounter more serious cultural differences when doing business with French Canadians. The latter often come across as reluctant to deal with people they don't know and likely to take a more polychronic approach to time and scheduling.

The Language of Business. English-speaking visitors from overseas find it easy to communicate with Anglophone Canadians. Fluency in French is an asset for those doing business in Quebec. However, good interpreters are easy to find in major business centers such as Montreal, Toronto and Vancouver.

Making Contact. In French Canada it is important to have connections, to be properly introduced. Cold calls are unlikely to get good results in Quebec. In English Canada business people are more open to a direct approach, although of course a referral is always useful. So when contacting anglophones, send a letter, fax or e-mail in English with basic information about your company and your product, indicating you will be in touch soon regarding a meeting. Then follow up with a phone call suggesting possible dates and ask your counterpart to suggest a time and place.

First Meeting. Whereas the deal-focused English Canadians are usually ready to get down to business quickly with a potential new business partner, francophones normally prefer lengthier preliminaries. They want to know more about a prospective supplier or partner before talking specifics.

Orientation to Time. In both of Canada's mainstream business cultures visitors are expected to be on time for appointments. However, in most other respects French Canadians are less monochronic than their anglo neighbors.

Formality and Informality. Egalitarianism is a key value for English Canadians, many of whom are uncomfortable in the face of status distinctions and class differences. In this respect they differ noticeably from their British cousins.

Francophones in contrast tend to be somewhat more hierarchical – in tune with the values of their mother country. Nevertheless, one's social class and family background are usually less important than in France. Visiting women executives are unlikely to face insuperable obstacles to doing business anywhere in Canada.

Anglophones usually want to get on a first-name basis fairly quickly, even with people they have just met. This informality is a sign of friendliness and warmth. Visitors to French Canada will encounter a slightly greater degree of formality.

Verbal Directness. Low-context English Canadians tend to be more direct than high-context francophones. Valuing a frank, straightforward exchange of information, anglophones may be unaware that East and Southeast Asians for example can be offended by such directness.

French Canadians also often speak less directly than anglophones. Quebecois are also more expressive and extroverted than English Canadians, their expressiveness showing up in both paraverbal and nonverbal behavior. For example, francophones tend to interrupt each other frequently, stand closer together, touch each other more often during conversations and use many more gestures and facial expressions than their anglophone neighbors.

Variable Expressiveness. English Canadians are more reserved. In the Western and Atlantic provinces the normal interpersonal distance in a business context is about an arm's length. People tend to stand and sit further apart than Arabs, southern Europeans and Latin Americans. Touch behaviour tends to be moderate. That is, less physical contact than in Latin and Mediterranean cultures but much more than East and Southeast Asians. Gestures and facial expression are more restrained than in Quebec, and people try to avoid interrupting each other in mid-sentence.

Business Protocol

Dress Code. Male visitors should wear a suit or blazer with tie. Women may wear a suit, dress or skirt and blouse.

Forms of Address. In English Canada start out with Dr, Mr, Mrs, Miss or Ms. but be prepared for your counterpart to suggest switching to a first name basis very soon after meeting you. Most anglos are uncomfortable using honorifics and titles. Expect more formality in Quebec but still a bit less than in France.

Meeting and Greeting. Visitors should expect a firm handshake and direct eye contact. Some Canadians believe that a soft handshake reflects weakness and that lack of direct eye contact signifies shiftiness or dishonesty.

- English Canadians shake hands less often than most Europeans. Their handshakes are quite brief compared to those of Latin Americans but firmer than East and Southeast Asians.
- French Canadians shake hands more often than anglophones: when being introduced, when saying hello and when saying goodbye.

Gift Giving. Business gifts are given after a deal has been closed. But remember that expensive, ostentatious gifts are out of place in Canada. Better choices are tasteful logo gifts or an item your city, country or region is famous for. Asians should not be surprised if your counterpart unwraps the gift in your presence – that is the North American custom. Good hostess gifts are flowers, candy, wine and special items from your country.

Wining and Dining. According to North American custom it is considered rude and aggressive to repeatedly insist that a guest eat and drink. This can be a problem for visitors from the Middle East and other parts of the world where the custom is to say no thank you two or three times before "-reluctantly' accepting the proffered food or drink. You should respond in the affirmative if you wish to have something that is offered – do not assume you will be asked twice.

Negotiating Behavior

Making a Presentation. Export salespeople used to the U.S. market should note that Canadians of both major business cultures prefer the soft-sell approach. They are likely to resent an overly-aggressive, pushy sales presentation. Avoid hype and overblown product claims.

Bargaining Range. Take care not to over-inflate your initial offer: Many Canadian buyers are turned off by the classic "high-low" tactic. Instead, build a certain safety margin into your opening bid to cover unexpected developments, but avoid overdoing it.

The U.S. Negotiator

Properly speaking of course, all citizens of North and South American countries are Americans. However, there is no other convenient way of referring to U.S. citizens, so for the purposes of this profile we will use "American" to refer to people from the United States.

The USA is a complex multi-ethnic, mulitiracial, multicultural society. Because of this diversity it is not possible to predict in detail the negotiating behavior of any individual American. That said, there still is such a thing as a mainstream U.S. business culture.

For example, you can expect most American negotiators to be very time-conscious ("Time is money"), deal-focused ("Let's get down to business") and informal ("What's your first name?"). On the other hand, an American negotiator's degree of expressiveness in communication is likely to be strongly influenced by his or her particular ethnic background.

The Language of Business: American English. Very few Americans speak a foreign language well enough to handle a complex business negotiation. If your English is not adequate, consider hiring an interpreter or asking your U.S. counterpart to do so.

Making Contact. Perhaps because the USA is an immigrant society with a high degree of geographical mobility, most Americans are used to doing business with strangers. That means that while a referral or introduction is always helpful, in most cases you can approach your prospective counterpart directly, without going through an intermediary.

Deal-Focused. Americans are usually ready to get down to brass tacks shortly after meeting a potential business partner for the first time. It is not that U.S. negotiators are unaware of the importance of getting to know their counterpart, of building a relationship. It is simply that the deal-focused Yank prefers to build trust and rapport while the business discussions are proceeding. They tend to regard extended small talk and preliminaries as a waste of precious time.

Orientation to Time. Americans are as obsessed with time as many other cultures are with relationship-building. Famously monochronic, they treat time as a tangible asset which can be saved, spent, lost, found, invested and wasted.

If U.S. business people have an appointment in someone's office at 9:00, they expect their counterpart to see them right on the dot. They regard a person who keeps them waiting for longer than ten minutes as either hopelessly undisciplined, intolerably rude, or both. Similarly, once the meeting starts Americans expect discussions to proceed to conclusion without interruption. When doing business in polychronic cultures they become easily upset when discussions are interrupted by phone calls, drop-in visitors or secretaries bringing in papers to be signed.

Informality. A key American value is egalitarianism. Yanks tend to feel uncomfortable in the face of overt status distinctions, except those based on inidividual achievement. Women and young men face relatively few obstacles to doing business in the U.S., where personal achievement is generally regarded as more important than one's social class, family background or gender.

The relative lack of status distinctions is reflected in the breezy informality for which Americans are famous. They want to get on a first-name basis quickly, even with people they have just met. Informality is meant to show friendliness and warmth. Business visitors from more formal cultures should realize that easy familiarity is not intended to show disrespect to high-status persons.

Communication Style. Depending on their ethnic background as well as their individual personality, U.S. negotiators show great variation in the way they communicate. Compared with northern Europeans and East Asians, Americans may appear more expressive, more extroverted. But when compared with southern Europeans and Latin Americans those same Yanks seem bland and introverted.

Verbal Directness. The low-context Americans tend to "say it like it is." They value a frank, straightforward exchange of information and are usually unaware that East and Southeast Asians for example might be offended by their directness. They may even be suspicious of negotiators who prefer indirect, oblique, ambiguous communication.

Paraverbal and Nonverbal Communication

Vocal Volume and Conversational Overlap. Many U.S. negotiators speak louder at the bargaining table than people from more reserved cultures. Uncomfortable with silence, they may also feel compelled to quickly fill in any gaps in the conversation – a behavior which Japanese for example find offensive. Americans also know it is rude to interrupt others in mid-sentence; if they do this anyway in the course of a lively discussion no offense is intended.

Interpersonal Distance. The normal spacing in a business context is about an arm's length. Americans generally stand and sit further apart than Arabs, southern Europeans and Latin Americans.

Touch Behavior. Varies from moderate to relatively high-contact: Less physical contact than is the case with Latins and Mediterranean cultures but much more than East and Southeast Asians. Some Americans slap each other on the back and grab one another by the elbow or upper arm to express friendliness.

Business Protocol

Dress Code. Varies somewhat according to location and type of business; visitors are well advised to wear a suit and tie to the first meeting with a new contact.

Meeting and Greeting. Expect a firm handshake and direct eye contact. Some Americans believe that a soft handshake reflects weakness and that lack of a direct gaze indicates unreliability or dishonesty. Yankees shake hands less often than most Europeans. Their handshakes are quite brief compared to those of most South and Central Americans but firmer than most East and Southeast Asians.

Exchanging Business Cards. Americans may not initiate the exchange of business cards; they sometimes offer their card at the end of the meeting rather than at the beginning. The casual way Americans greet people and exchange business cards is another reflection of egalitarian values. The East Asian who politely offers his business card with both hands should not be offended if his U.S. counterpart stuffs the card in his pocket without reading it.

Forms of Address. Start out with Mr, Mrs., Miss or Ms. but do not be surprised if your counterpart suggests switching to a first name basis soon after meeting you. If such informality offends you, make it quite clear how you wish to be addressed. Titles are likely to be ignored except in formal meetings – unless you are a medical doctor or high government official. Most Americans are uncomfortable using honorifics and titles.

Gift Giving. The U.S. business world is not a gift-giving culture. Many American negotiators feel uncomfortable if presented with an expensive gift. If you do wish to bring something small, choose a tasteful logo gift or an item your country or region is famous for. Do not be surprised if your counterpart unwraps the gift in your presence – that is the American custom.

Wining and Dining. Many American negotiators prefer to maintain a separation between their professional and private lives as well as between business and pleasure. If invited to that quintessentially American invention, the cocktail party, expect to mix informally with a large number of complete strangers.

Negotiating Behavior

Making a Presentation. Americans respond best to brisk, factual presentations delivered by a competent speaker of English and enlivened by visual aids where appropriate. They may interrupt with questions rather than hold their questions until the end.

Bargaining Range. U.S. negotiators experienced in international business are used to a wide variation in bargaining ranges. Expect them to test your opening offer for flexibility. They may respond better to realistic quotations than to the overused high-low tactic. Build a safety margin into your opening bid to cover unexpected developments but avoid over-inflating your offer.

Concession Behavior. Be prepared for some hard bargaining. Take care to make each concession with great reluctance, and then only on a strict "if...then," conditional basis. Always demand something of equivalent value in return.

Ploys and Counterploys. A favorite American bargaining tactic is time pressure: "Next week our prices are going up seven percent..." The best way to counter this ploy is to simply ignore it.

Another favorite ploy is to ask for quotations on a sliding scale by quantity. For example, say you quote prices based on 1000, 10,000 and 50,000 units. Your U.S. counterpart is then likely to ask for 12,500 units – but at the low price you quoted for 50,000. Counter this ploy by smiling and repeating that the lower price is valid only for orders of the indicated quantity.

You may also encounter the Trial Order gambit in which your potential customer demands your lowest price even for a small "test" order. If you are tempted to buy this customer's business with a low "introductory" offer, you can expect to have trouble later when you try to move him up to the normal price.

Decision-Making. American negotiators are probably the fastest decision makers in the world – sometimes to their own detriment. Some U.S. executives live by the motto, "Right or wrong, but never in doubt." Expect expressions of impatience if your decision-making process seems to be taking too much time.

Role of the Contract. Heavy emphasis on the legal aspects and the fine points of the written agreement. Many U.S. negotiators include lawyers in the discussions from the start until the signing ceremony. They often bring a draft agreement to the bargaining table and proceed to negotiate clause by clause.

Should a dispute or disagreement arise later the American side may rely strictly on the terms of the contract and could become suspicious if their counterpart invokes non-contract issues such as the importance of the long-term relationship.

Resource List

– Books –

Global

Axtell, Roger E.: *Do's and Taboos Around the World.* John Wiley & Sons, 3rd ed. 1993.

Do's and Taboos of International Trade. Wiley, 2nd edition 1994.

Do's and Taboos of Hosting International Visitors. Wiley, 1990.

GESTURES: Do's and Taboo's of Body Language. Wiley, 1991.

Brake, Walker and Walker: *Doing Business Internationally.* Irwin, New York 1995.

Foster: *Bargaining Across Borders.* McGraw-Hill, New York 1992.

Morrison, Conaway, Borden: *Kiss, Bow or Shake Hands?* Adams Media Corp. (USA) 1994.

Morrison, Conaway, Douress: Dun & Bradstreet's Guide to Doing Business Around the World. Prentice Hall, New York 1997.

Trompenaars: *Riding the Waves of Culture.* Economist Books, London 1993.

Regional: Asia

Dunung: *Doing Business in Asia.* New York, Lexington Books 1995.

Enderlyn and Dziggel: *Cracking the Pacific Rim.* Probus, Chicago 1992.

Engholm: *When Business East Meets Business West.* John Wiley & Sons 1991.

Japan

Kenna and Lacy: *Business Japan.* Passport Books, USA 1994.

Rowland: *Japanese Business Etiquette.* Warner Books, New York 1985.

Zimmerman: *How to Do Business in Japan.* Random House, New York 1985.

China

Hu and Grove: *Encountering the Chinese.* Intercultural Press, USA 1991.

Kenna and Lacy: *Business China.* Passport Books, USA 1994.

Schneiter: *Getting Along with the Chinese.* Asia 2000 Ltd, Hong Kong 1992.

Seligman: *Dealing with the Chinese.* Mercury Books, London.

Sinclair and Wong: *Culture Shock! China.* Times Books International, Singapore 1990.

South Korea

Current and Choi: *Looking At Each Other.* Seoul International Tourist Publishing, 1983.

Hur and Hur: *Culture Shock! Korea.* Times Books International, Singapore 1993.

Taiwan

Kenna and Lacy: *Business Taiwan.* Passport Books, USA 1994.

The Philippines

Andres: *Understanding Filipino Values.* New Day Publishers, Quezon City 1981.

Gochenour: *Considering Filipinos.* Intercultural Press, USA 1990.

Roces and Roces: *Culture Shock! Philippines.* Times Books International, Singapore 1985.

Indonesia

Draine and Hall: *Culture Shock! Indonesia.* Times Books International, Singapore 1986.

Malaysia

Datin Noor Aini Syed Amir: *Malaysian Customs and Etiquette.* Times Books, Singapore 1991.

Munan: *Culture Shock! Malaysia.* Times Books International, Singapore 1991.

Thailand

Cooper and Cooper: *Culture Shock! Thailand.* Times Books International, Singapore 1982.

Fieg and Morelock: *A Common Core.* Intercultural Press, USA 1989.

Hollinger: *"Mai Pen Rai" Means Never Mind.* Asia Book Company Ltd, Bangkok 1977.

Holmes and Tangtontavy: *Working With The Thais.* White Lotus, Bangkok 1995.

Vietnam

Ellis: *Culture Shock! Vietnam.* Times Books International, Singapore 1995.

Jamieson: *Understanding Vietnam.* University of California Press 1993.

India

Kolanad: *Culture Shock! India.* Times Books International, Singapore 1994.

Nepal

Burbank: *Culture Shock! Nepal.* Times Books International, Singapore 1992.

Sri Lanka

Barlas and Wanasundera: *Culture Shock! Sri Lanka.* Times Books International, Singapore 1992.

Pakistan

Mittman and Ihsan: *Culture Shock! Pakistan.* Times Books International, Singapore 1991.

Regional: Middle East and Africa

Devine and Braganti: *Traveler's Guide to Customs and Manners.* St. Martin's Press, NY 1991.

McGregor and Nydell: *Update Saudi Arabia.* Intercultural Press, USA 1975.

Nydell: *Understanding Arabs.* Intercultural Press, USA 1987.

Syria

South, *Culture Shock! Syria.* Times Books International, Singapore 1995

Morocco

Hargraves: *Culture Shock! Morocco.* Graphic Arts Center Publishing Co., Portland OR 1995.

South Africa

Rissik: *Culture Shock! South Africa.* Times Books International, Singapore 1994.

Regional: Europe

Bosrock: *Put Your Best Foot Forward–EUROPE.* St. Paul MN, Internat'l Education Syst. 1995.

Braganti and Devine: *European Customs and Manners.* Meadowbrook, Inc. USA 1984.

Great Britain

Smith: *Watch Your Step.* Hoest Sprog, Copenhagen 1992.

Tan: *Culture Shock! Britain.* Times Books International, Singapore 1992.

Netherlands

Bolt: *The Xenophobe's Guide to the Dutch.* Ravette, West Sussex UK 1995.

White and Boucke: *The UnDutchables.* White/Boucke Publishing, USA 1989.

France

Hall and Hall: *Understanding Cultural Differences.* Intercultural Press, USA 1990.

Taylor: *Culture Shock! France.* Times Books International, Singapore 1990.

Germany

Hall and Hall: *Understanding Cultural Differences.* Intercultural Press, USA 1990.

Lord: *Culture Shock/! Germany.* Times Books International, Singapore 1996.

Norway

Su-Dale: *Culture Shock! Norway.* Times International Publishing, Singapore 1995.

Denmark

Strange: *Culture Shock! Denmark.* Times Books International, Singapore 1996.

Italy

Flower and Falassi: *Culture Shock! Italy.* Times Books International, Singapore 1995.

Spain
Ames: *Spain Is Different.* Intercultural Press, USA 1992.
Graff: *Culture Shock! Spain.* Times Books International, Singapore 1993.

Regional: Eastern Europe
Richmond: *Understanding the Eastern Europeans.* Intercultural Press, USA 1995.

Russia
Richmond: *From Nyet to Da.* Intercultural Press, Yarmouth ME, USA 1992.

Regional: Latin America
Devine and Braganti: *Latin American Customs and Manners.* St. Martin's Press, NY 1988.

Mexico
Condon: *Good Neighbors: Communicating with the Mexicans.* Intercultural Press, USA 1985.
Heusinkveld: *Inside Mexico.* John Wiley & Sons, New York 1994.
Kras: *Management in Two Cultures.* Intercultural Press, USA 1989.

Brazil
Harrison: *Behaving Brazilian.* Harper & Row, New York 1983.

Anglo Cultures: Australia
Sharp: *Culture Shock! Australia.* Times Books International, Singapore 1992
Renwick: *A Fair Go for All.* Intercultural Press, Yarmouth Maine 1991.

Canada
Pang and Barlas: *Culture Shock! Canada.* Times Books International, Singapore 1992.

United States of America
Althen: *American Ways.* Intercultural Press, USA 1988.
Hall and Hall: *Understanding Cultural Differences.* Intercultural Press, USA 1990.
Stewart: *American Cultural Patterns.* Intercultural Press, USA 1972.

Wanning: *Culture Shock! USA*. Times Books International, Singapore
1991.

– *Periodicals* –

Worldwide Business Practices Report. Monthly newsletter. Chicago: 847-
945-9614.

– *Culturgrams* –

David M. Kennedy Center for International Studies, Provo UT. Call 800-
528-6279 for list of 143 four-page briefings available.

– *Audio guides* –

International Cultural Enterprises, Inc. Deerfield IL. Contact Mr. Yuri
Kovalenko at 800-626-2772. Titles available:

Arabian Peninsula	Malaysia
Australia	Mexico
China	Philippines
France	Scandinavia
Germany	Singapore
Great Britain	Spain
India	Spain
Indonesia	Taiwan
Korea	Thailand
	USA

A000018385274